Alexander Balloch Grosart, Philip Sidney

Complete Poems

Alexander Balloch Grosart, Philip Sidney

Complete Poems

ISBN/EAN: 9783744691659

Printed in Europe, USA, Canada, Australia, Japan

Cover: Foto ©Thomas Meinert / pixelio.de

More available books at **www.hansebooks.com**

The Fuller Worthies' Library.

THE COMPLETE POEMS

OF

SIR PHILIP SIDNEY.

FOR THE FIRST TIME COLLECTED AND COLLATED WITH
THE ORIGINAL AND EARLY EDITIONS AND MSS.
AND IN THE QUARTO FORM
A HITHERTO UNENGRAVED PORTRAIT (FORMERLY IN POSSESSION OF
FULKE GREVILLE, LORD BROOKE) AND OTHER ILLUSTRATIONS.

Edited

WITH ESSAY ON THE LIFE AND WRITINGS, AND NOTES AND
ILLUSTRATIONS,

BY THE

REV. ALEXANDER B. GROSART,

ST. GEORGE'S, BLACKBURN, LANCASHIRE.

IN TWO VOLUMES.

VOL. I.

PRINTED FOR PRIVATE CIRCULATION.
1873.
156 *copies only.*

TO

DAVID MASSON, ESQ. M.A. LL.D.

PROFESSOR OF RHETORIC AND ENGLISH LITERATURE IN THE
UNIVERSITY OF EDINBURGH,
AUTHOR OF THE LIFE OF JOHN MILTON,
NARRATED IN CONNECTION WITH THE POLITICAL, ECCLESIASTICAL, AND
LITERARY HISTORY OF HIS TIME, ETC.

I dedicate

THIS FIRST COMPLETE EDITION OF THE POETRY OF

SIR PHILIP SIDNEY,

ASSURED THAT MY 'LABOUR OF LOVE' WILL BE

SYMPATHETICALLY REGARDED BY HIM,

AND AS A 'PEPPER-CORN' ACKNOWLEDGMENT

FOR OBLIGATIONS WHILE PURSUING RESEARCHES KINDRED

WITH HIS OWN IN 'MILTON.'

I LIKE TOO TO RE-LINK MYSELF THUS WITH MY

ALMA MATER AND AN OLD CLASS-ROOM.   ·

VERY FAITHFULLY AND GRATEFULLY,

ALEXANDER B. GROSART.

CONTENTS.

ILLUSTRATIONS IN VOL. I. 4TO.

PREFACE.

PERHAPS it will generally be admitted that it is one of the most inexplicable of the many 'Curiosities' and anomalies of our Literature, that ours should be, to all intents and purposes, the first collective edition, as it is absolutely the first critical text, of the Poems of SIR PHILIP SIDNEY. Following the trade edition of the Works (3 vols. 12mo, 1739), Gray, in his 'Miscellaneous Works' of Sidney (Oxford, 1829: Boston, 1860, 8vo), satisfied himself with 'Astrophel and Stella,' and 'Certain Sonnets' and other Poems, which he placed under the heading 'Miscellaneous Poems,'—utterly ignoring the much more numerous Poems contained in the 'Arcadia' and 'Psalms.' He added from Dr. Bliss's edition of the Athenæ Oxon. and Bibliog. Miscellanies, and elsewhere, slightly. There is no other available edition. So that it must surely be regarded as a desideratum worth supplying, to reproduce, as we herein do, the complete Poems of Sidney.

In an Essay in the present Volume we discuss such points in this remarkable poetry as in our judgment called for discussion. Thither we refer the Reader.

I have only here the pleasant duty of acknowledging my sense of obligation to the noble present owners of Penshurst and Wilton for their kind facilities in relation to their Sidney treasures. Alas that a fire within recent years swept away all the Manuscripts of Sidney preserved at Wilton, save the Lines to Elizabeth, along with a lock of her hair,—sunny as gold, and 'red' only as gold was used to be called red! Penshurst, with abundant Sidney documents, proved to hold nothing poetical except John Davies of Hereford's transcript of the Psalms,—acquired at the Bright sale for 4*l.* 16*s.*, as I learn from a priced catalogue.

To the EARL OF WARWICK AND BROOKE I am indebted for the long loan to my Engraver (Mr. W. J. Alais) of his priceless original Portrait, formerly in the possession of Fulke Greville, Lord Brooke. It seems to me a very noble Portrait, and self-authenticating in every way. The original is somewhat faded, touched with 'Decay's effacing fingers.' It has never before been engraved. As now presented, it must surely be pronounced *the* Portrait of Sir Philip Sidney, being 'sweet,' after the deep old meaning of that word, and yet mind-full, gracious in its aspect, but sheathing power; soft and tender about the mouth, nevertheless carrying mobilities of swift passion—as the tranquil sea its fierceness and strength; and above all, realising to us the many-storied steep forehead (like Scott's), telling of a sovran soul within. I cannot sufficiently acknowledge the kindness of the noble owner in permitting me the use of it,—as before of Fulke Greville, Lord Brooke's MSS. To the most noble the MARQUIS OF SALISBURY I wish to return my heartfelt thanks for the Lady Rich Letters, herein first printed,—part of very many other precious discoveries made while at Hatfield, of which more again.

By the liberality of Messrs. VIRTUE I am enabled to adorn the quarto with some exquisite illustrations of Sidney scenery.

In the Notes and Illustrations, and in the preparation of the text throughout, I have again emphatically to acknowledge infinite obligation to my unfailing friend Dr. BRINSLEY NICHOLSON : anything finer than his devoted perseverance throughout in consulting all possible authorities to aid me, I know not. I have also to thank right cordially W. ALDIS WRIGHT, Esq. M.A., Trinity College, Cambridge, for a collation of the Trinity-College MS. of the 'Psalms;' and the Authorities of the Bodleian and British Museum for their invariable helpfulness. I wish also to express my indebtedness to S. CHRISTIE-MILLER, Esq., Britwell, for his pleasant communications on books and MSS. in his incomparable Collections.

Our Essay and Notes and Illustrations give all else necessary. In conclusion here, I commend the view enunciated by me of the Astrophel and Stella Sonnets and Songs, and 'Sidera,' to the consideration of any who may have been wont to look upon them as mere literary exercises or pastimes. To my mind, such a conception of them misses the deepest, the most intense, the (in a sense) most awful chapter in Sir Philip Sidney's life-story; for it is my conviction that never was love (ultimately) more impassioned, or anguish more keen, or moral struggle more agitating, or final victory more absolute, than in Sidney and Stella, and in Stella equally with Sidney.

ALEXANDER B. GROSART.

St. George's, Blackburn, Lancashire,
    4th September 1873.

ESSAY ON THE POETRY OF SIR PHILIP SIDNEY.

Born at Penshurst, Kent, 1554: died, after Battle of Zutphen, 1586.

WHILE besides earlier and later there have been no fewer than three considerable recent Lives of Sir Philip Sidney, viz. by Bourne,[1] Lloyd,[2] and an anonymous American,[3] it must be stated that *the* Life—such as should take its place inevitably with dear old Izaak Walton's 'Lives,' or Southey's 'Nelson'—remains unwritten. This is our judgment, after a prolonged and careful study of all the Sidney - literature. We shall indulge the 'pleasures of hope' that one day such a biography of this great Englishman will appear ; for there are lights and shadows, heights and depths—ay, depths—in that Life, that have thus far been only very imperfectly sounded.

It were out of proportion for an Editor of his Poems simply, to retraverse the Facts and Teachings of the full Biography. But there are certain things in relation to

[1] A Memoir of Sir Philip Sidney. By H. R. Fox Bourne. 1 vol. 8vo, 1862 (Chapman and Hall), pp. xv. and 557.

[2] The Life of Sir Philip Sidney. By Julius Lloyd, M.A. 1862 (Longman), pp. xvi. and 244.

[3] The Life and Times of Sir Philip Sydney. Boston (Ticknor), 1859: pp. 281.

the Poems, which may be considered acceptably, as a con-
tribution to the ultimate Life, and as a fitting introduction to this first complete, critical, and adequately anno-
tated collection of these Poems. The incompleteness of
all editions hitherto lies on the surface, inasmuch as the
amount of ours is increased by more than a half compared
with Gray's (Oxford, 1829), and its American reprint (Boston, 1860), or any other so-called collective edition of
Sidney's Poetry ; while our Notes and Illustrations reveal
a literary chaos in the text. We propose to consider the
following points in this Essay :

    I. The original and after editions of the successive
sets of Poems as herein reproduced.

    II. The texts of our edition, punctuation and line-
arrangement, classification, &c.

    III. The story of Lady Rich and Sidney in the *morale*
of it, with hitherto unprinted letters.

    IV. The characteristics of Sidney's Poetry, with the
praises of it by his contemporaries and onward. These
in order.

I. *The original and after editions of the successive Poems as herein reproduced.*

    The entire Writings of Sidney, Prose and Verse, were
posthumously printed. He was known and even 're-
nowned' for his Poetry and Prose during his lifetime, but
wholly through manuscript copies put into circulation, as
was the *mode*, by himself and friends.

    His ' Arcadia'—which contains so large a portion of
his Verse—was ' designed' to be published immediately
after his death in 1586, and it was his first appearance
from the press, but this was not until 1590 : ' The Covn-
tesse of Pembrokes Arcadia, written by Sir Philippe Sid-
nei : London, Printed for William Ponsonbie, Anno
Domini 1590' (4to). A copy is in the British Museum.

A Letter preserved in the State-Paper Office from Fulke Greville, Lord Brooke, to Sidney's father-in-law Sir Francis Walsingham, is indorsed ' November 1586 ;' and as it sheds light on various points to be afterwards noticed, must be here given, as follows :

' *To the Right honorable S^r francis Walsingham.*

' S^r, this day, one ponsonby, a booke-bynder in poles church yard, came to me and told me that ther was one in hand to print Sr Philip Sydney's old arcadia, asking me yf it were done with your honors consent, or any other of his frendes ? I told him, to my knowledge, no : then he advysed me to give warninge of it, either to the archbishope or doctor Cosen, who have, as he says, a copy to peruse to that end.

' S^r, I am loth to renew his memory unto you, but yeat in this I must presume ; for I have sent my lady, your daughter, at her request, a correction of that old one, don 4 or 5 years sinse, which he left in trust with me ; wherof there is no more copies, and fitter to be printed then the first, which is so common : notwithstanding, even that to be amended by a direction sett downe undre his own hand, how and why ; so as in many respects, espetially the care of printing of it, is to be don with more deliberation.

' Besydes, he hathe most excellently translated, among divers other notable workes, monsieur du Plessis book against Atheisme, which is sinse don by an other ; so as both in respect of lov between Plessis and him, besydes other affinities in ther courses, but espetially Sr Philip's uncomparable judgement, I think fit ther be made stay of that mercenary book, so that Sr Philip might have all thos religious works which ar worthily dew to his lyfe and death.

' Many other works, as Bartas his Spanyard, 40 of the psalms translated into myter, &c. which requyre the care of his frends, not to amend, for I think it falls within the reach of no man living, but only to see to the paper, and other common errors of mercenary printing. Gayn ther wilbe, no doubt, to be disposed by you : let it be' to the poorest of his servants ; I desyre only care to be had of his honor, who, I fear, hath caried the honor of thes latter ages with him.

'S^r, pardon me, I make this the busines of my lofe [=love], and desyre God to shew that he is your God. From my Lodge, not well, this day in hast. Your honors
                                        ' FOULK GREVILL.

' S^r, I had wayted on you my selfe for answer, because I am jelous of tyme in it, but in trothe I am nothing well. Good S^r, think of it.'[1]

It is to be observed that the 'Ponsonby' named by Lord Brooke was the Publisher of the 'Arcadia' of 1590 (4to), as he was likewise of the folios of 1593, 1598, and later. In 1588, '23 Augusti,' he had entered 'Arcadia' for the press, as appears from the following entry in the Stationers' Registers:

'Wm. Ponsonby. Rd. of him for a booke of Sr Php. Sidney's makinge, intitled Arcadia : authorised under the Archb. of Cante. hand .   .   .   .   .   . vj^d'[2]

The ' Arcadia' of 1590 is defective in many ways, as an examination of a copy in the British Museum has shown us ; but it was not until 1593 that another and more accurate edition appeared. To it was prefixed a notable Epistle signed ' H. S.,'[3] pointing out the errors of the former, and claiming for the new all authority. Who

---

[1] J. Payne Collier's Life of Spenser (Works, vol. i. pp. liii.-iv.); also in his Bib. Catalogue under 'Sydney.' I have bracketed 'love' instead of 'life' of Mr. Collier's, as more probably Lord Brooke's word.

[2] Collier, as before, p. liv.

[3] See the Epistle *in extenso* at close of our Notes and Illustrations to 'Astrophel and Stella,' in this vol. p. 167.

'H. S.' was has never been discovered. The 'S.' suggests one of the family; but the 'H.' perplexes. From 1590 to 1725 the 'Arcadia' was a 'quick' book in successive (folio) editions. Of certain of these, more in the sequel.

'Astrophel and Stella' was first published in 1591. There were three editions of this year. The first, which has been designated 'surreptitious,'[1] bears this title-page:

'Syr P. S. his Astrophel and Stella. Wherein the excellence of Sweete Poesie is concluded. To the end of which are added sundry other rare Sonnets of diuers Noblemen and Gentlemen. At London, Printed for Thomas Newman, Anno Domini 1591' (4to).

A second edition of 1591 has this title-page:

'Sir P. S. his Astrophel and Stella. Wherein the excellence of Sweete Poesie is concluded. At London, Printed for Thomas Newman, 1591.'

The former contains forty-four leaves, this thirty-two leaves only; the latter omitting the 'sundry other rare Sonnets,' and the Epistles of the Publisher and Thomas Nash. A third edition, 'At London, Printed for Matthew Lownes,' corresponds with the first. A copy is in the Bodleian (Malone), and is without date; but another copy, at Britwell,[2] is dated, like the others, 1591; not 1595, the date assigned to it by Mr. Hazlitt (Bibliography of Old English Literature, s. n.). Of the relative authority of these editions I shall hereafter speak.

The 'Arcadia' of 1598 first published the set of Poems that in all the after folios appeared as 'Certaine Sonets Written by Sir Philip Sidney. Neuer before printed.' Of these onward.

The 'Apologie for Poetrie' appeared originally in 1595. 'At London, Printed for Henry Olney, and are to be sold

---

[1] By Mr. Collier, as before, p. cxv. and Bib. Catalogue, s. n.

[2] I owe special thanks to S. Christie-Miller, Esq., for his many painstaking communications to me on his Sidney and other treasures.

at his shop in Paule's Churchyard, at the signe of the
George, neere to Cheap-gate.' It was of this 'Apologie'
—later named 'Defence'—William Cowper was thinking
when he finely sang of Sidney as 'warbler of poetic prose;'
but as it does not contain any of his Verse, it falls not to
be noticed further by us.[1]

The 'Psalms' in 'myter' remained in manuscript until
so recently as 1823. Of these and our text of Sidney's
portion I speak fully in the relative introductory Note in
vol. ii.

The minor pieces, which we have arranged under the
heading of 'Pansies from Penshurst and Wilton,' appeared
in Davison's 'Poetical Rhapsody' (1602) and other collections, as pointed out in their places.[2]

The translations from Du Bartas seem to have perished.
That they existed is clear, not only from Lord Brooke's
mention of them, but also from Ponsonby's entry in
the Stationers' Register, thus, under same date with the
'Arcadia' (23d Aug. 1588):

'Wm. Ponsonby. Item, Rd. of him for a translation
of Salust de Bartas, done by the same S[r] P. into eng-
lishe . . . . vj[d]'

[1] Had not the 'Defense of Poetrie' been admirably reprinted by
Mr. Arber, we should certainly have included it in our edition of
the Poems, instinct as it is with poetry. Now it were superfluous,
seeing it is to be had for a mere trifle, as well as the related books
of Stubbes and Gosson.

[2] The reprints of Davison give full details of the different authors.
Looking beyond Davison, it may be noted that Puttenham in his
'Art of Poesie' quotes Sidney, e.g. last two lines of 'To the tune of
a Neapolitan Villanel' (p. 212, Arber's reprint); the ditty in full,
Arcadia, B iii. p. 352 (1613) (p. 233, ibid.); and the last two lines of
quatorzain in Arcadia, B iii. p. 283:

> What medcine then . . .
> Where loue . . .

(p. 225, ibid.). So too in England's Parnassus there are various passages from Arcadia and Astrophel and Stella.

Florio too, in the dedication of the Second Book of his Translation of Montaigne (fol. 1603), tells Lady Rutland and Lady Penelope Rich that he had 'seene the first septimaine of that arch-poet Du Bartas' rendered into English by Sidney, and he entreats them to honour the age by making it public.

So much for the original and after editions of the Poems. We have to notice next,

II. *The texts of our edition, punctuation and line-arrangement, classification, &c.*

The posthumousness of all the editions of Sidney's Writings, as explained, together with the semi-furtive character of the first 'printing' of nearly all, compels an Editor to sit in judgment on the entire available texts ; and this is no slight task, as the 'various readings' are very abundant throughout.

To begin with 'Astrophel and Stella,' as incomparably presenting Sidney at his best as a Poet, independent of its priceless biographic interest and heart-revelation, this set of Poems, we have seen, was first published in 1591 in such a form as led Mr. Collier to pronounce it 'surreptitious'—as already noted. We cannot go this length ; for, as will appear immediately, with all its errors, it must have been printed from authoritative though early transcript MSS. Our collations show that the alleged 'innumerable errors' of Nash's quarto (1591) were in the greater number of instances not errors, but variant readings from earlier MSS. than the second quarto (in part); and also show that the second quarto, which has been so exalted over the first, is, to a large extent, simply a reprint of the first. It is also found that the ' Arcadia,' &c. vol. of 1598 (not of 1593, as usually stated) fulfils the promise of ' H. S.,' that the Countess of Pembroke would publish Sidney's Defence of Poetrie and his Poems. In the second quarto of

1591 nothing was added to the first quarto. This was for the first time done in the 'Arcadia,' &c. of 1598, viz. Sonnet xxxvii., part of Song viii., part of x., and all Song xi. Neither were any of the scattered pieces added until 1598.

Notwithstanding all this, the Nash quarto of 1591 was certainly disapproved by some who claimed to interfere. The proof of this is found in the Stationers' Register, under the date of 18th September 1591, where we read : 'Item, paid to John Wolf, when he ryd with an answere to my L. Treasurer, beinge with her majestie on progresse, for the takinge in of bookes intituled Sir P. S. Astrophel and Stella.'[1] It is scarcely possible to pronounce as to the particular edition here indicated. For (a) it is to be remarked that the first, or so-called 'surreptitious' edition (of 1591) spells 'Syr,' not 'Sir,' as in the Register entry ; while the second edition (of 1591) spells, as in the entry, 'Sir.' (b) It seems not unlikely that Newman sought to hinder Matthew Lownes—who afterwards published Sidney complete, e.g 1613 (folio)—from issuing his edition, which, as we have stated, is in the Britwell copy also dated 1591, though without date in the Bodleian copy. (c) It does not harmonise with an absolutely 'surreptitious' publication, that the Publisher of it was also the Publisher of the alleged authorised edition (Thomas Newman). Further, when we come to examine the first edition of 1591, along with the second edition, it is discovered that the second has errors not found in the first, as well as the first errors which are corrected in the second. But above all, I must reiterate a previous fact, viz. that the alleged authorised second edition to a large extent was dependent on the first, and continues and aggravates its mispunctuation, &c. Our Notes and Illustrations place this beyond dispute. The objection was probably twofold.

---

[1] Mr. Collier, as before.

(1) A number of the added Sonnets in the first edition were by Samuel Daniel, a friend of the Countess of Pembroke, as of Sidney. He may therefore for personal reasons have urged on the family the fact that Sir Philip Sidney's fame might suffer from the Nash edition being printed from a transcript of the Sonnets in their earlier and less revised form. There is an element of doubt here, in that Daniel may have himself contributed the added Sonnets, and so aided in the Nash edition. (2) The Countess of Pembroke may have shrunk, on the one hand, from the over-laudation of her by Nash ; and on the other, we can understand that the association of the Earl of Oxford (Sidney's insulter), along with 'other diuers noblemen and gentlemen,' with her brother's Poems would be anything but agreeable to her.

Our text of ' Astrophel and Stella' is that of Arcadia edition 1598; but with a constant critical comparison with the 1591 separate editions and the 'Arcadia' texts onward. Wherever we depart from 1598 text (as above), reasons are given in relative Notes and Illustrations ; and repeatedly it will there be seen that the first edition furnishes admirable readings, and also that of 1613.

Our text of the ' Certain Sonnets,' entitled by us ' Sidera,' and of all the Poems from the ' Arcadia' itself—the latter never before collected—is fundamentally that of 1613 ; with like continuous collation of the texts of 1598 onward, as shown in the Notes and Illustrations. We attach much weight to the folio of 1613, as it is the only edition known to have been in the library of the Countess of Pembroke. Among Heber's books (from Mason's and the Duke of Grafton's collections) was a copy of this 1613 edition, in old morocco, and with the initials of the Countess of Montgomery, and the following inscription: ' This was the Countesse of Pembroke's owne book, given me by the Countesse of Montgomery her daughter, 1625. Ancram.' This has been erroneously described (by Mr. Hazlitt, *s. n.*) as 'the dedication-copy.' The edition has no special dedication, simply the original one by Sidney himself. It was *the* edition selected for her own library by the sister of Sidney ; and I have traced other gift-copies of the same edition. From 1598 (folio) there was little or no change beyond orthography ; but 1613 appears to us to give, as a whole, the best text of the whole Writings of Sidney. Nevertheless we have not hesitated to accept readings from 1598 and others—all as stated in the Notes and Illustrations in the places.[1]

Our sources for the minor Writings are specified in their several places, and do not call for further notice here.

The punctuation of all the editions is arbitrary and uncritical, over and over confusing the construction and perverting the sense. We have spent no little pains on it, and we hope not without success : and all the more that we have had the full benefit of the long experience and accurate knowledge of the head of our Printers' Firm.[2]

[1] The 1593 Arcadia does not contain the Poems. As stated elsewhere in these remarks, H. S. in 1593 refers to the intention of the Countess of Pembroke to do what was done in 1598 Arcadia, viz. reprint the 'Defense' and the 'Poems.' Hence 1598 text was throughout authorised by the Countess; and all after it (including our adopted text of 1613) adhered closely to its readings—inevitable errors excepted. Examination of the 1598 text shows that its Poems were printed from a revised copy of Q 2, the main changes being in the orthography, line-arrangement, and punctuation.

[2] The punctuation, as stated above, is constantly bad, and sometimes wholly wrong. The Arcadia of 1598 made numerous alterations in the punctuation of Q 2, but often erroneously, and in 2 qu. and it (;) and (:) are thrown in anyhow and anywhere. One thing that seems to have led to a wrong punctuation in A. (1598) and all the Arcadia editions, was the division of each Sonnet into sets of 4 and 4, 3 and 3 lines, divided by spaces, and the consequent tendency of the punctuator to make each division end with a strong stop. It is impossible to punctuate Sidney's sentences with the (.) and (,) of modern punctuation, but the excessive use of (;) and (:) can be much reduced, and I have done it. In one part only is a stronger than ordinary

Let any who may differ from us spend even half an hour in examining any text, early or modern, with ours, and we do not fear the verdict. Our Notes and Illustrations furnish reasons for many of our constructions and punctuations. In the arrangement of the lines in ' Astrophel and Stella,' and the Sonnets generally, we have returned to the solid printing, i.e. making the beginning of all the lines range. The 1591 line-arrangement in all the three editions, and even in 1613, is mechanical ; viz. (in 1613):

that is, two quatrains and two of three lines, with the 1st, 5th, 9th, and 12th projecting, although the rhymes are 1st and 3d, 5th and 7th ; 2d and 4th, 6th and 8th ; 9th and 11th, and 10th and 12th, and 13th and 14th. This is the usual structure ; and it will be observed that the line-arrangement pays no heed to it, nor to the thought as it flows on. Passionate as are these remarkable Sonnets, they are as a whole stringently modelled after Petrarch ; and those separated from 'Astrophel and Stella' (in our ' Sidera'), as ' Certain Sonnets,' owe their separation ap-

---

punctuation necessary. The Sonnets end somewhat after the manner of the Epigrams,—that, is, with a clause which is either intentionally different from the rest, or a summing-up,—and was often meant to come in the manner of a surprise, or with a previous pause. Hence (:) or (,—) are frequently required.

parently to their non-Petrarchian form, and departure
from the fórm of the rest of the series.　Be this as it
may, it is as English Sonnets we study them, and it had
been mere pedantry to have adhered to the artificial line-
arrangement of the original or other early editions.　Nor
less so, I opine, to have wasted pains in separately arrang-
ing each according to the rhyme-words or endings.　I am
glad to be supported in this by Charles Lamb in the 'Last
Essays of Elia,' in his delicious paper on ' Some Sonnets
of Sir Philip Sidney ;'[1] and in our own day by the present
Archbishop of Dublin (Trench) in his ' Household Book
of English Poetry' (1868), in his quotations from Sidney.[2]
Similarly I have placed the Eleven Songs of 'Astrophel
and Stella' at the close by themselves, as in 1591 editions.
Granted that Petrarch introduces among his Sonnets the
like, as also Lord Brooke in ' Cœlica,' and Earl of Stir-
ling in ' Aurora,' none the less does such introduction interrupt the flow of the thought and snap the links of the
marvellous story.[3]

[1] More of this paper onward.　It is in all the editions of Lamb:
ours is 4 vols. 12mo, 1855, vol. iii. pp. 332-341.

[2] See pp. 27, 28.

[3] It does not appear that the departure from the original arrangement of placing the Songs at the close proceeded on any certain
principle.　Looking at their distribution, (1) There is no apparent connection between Song i. and any Sonnet proceeding or following it.
It is placed after Sonnet lxiii.　The same may be said of Song iii.,
which is placed after Sonnet lxxxiii.　(2) The second Song (after
Sonnet lxxii.) is clearly on the same subject, and, in all probability,
of the same date with a marked point in the history of Sidney's love,
the kiss spoken of in the succeeding Sonnets lxxiii. lxxiv. lxxix.
lxxx. lxxxi. and lxxxii.　So that Song iv. fits-in after Sonnets
lxxxiv. and lxxxv., which are supposed to have been written on the
journey.　Song v. appears to agree with, and to coincide in date with
its preceding Sonnet, lxxxvi.　The 6th Song does not, and with Song
vii. may be placed with Songs i. and iii.　This last, namely vii., refers
to a meeting not spoken of in the Sonnets, and different from that
narrated in Song iv. ; for that was at night ; this, as shown by st. i. 14

In the other Poems I have adhered substantially to the line-arrangement and otherwise of 1613 (as before). Exceptions are noted in the relative places. Subsidiary points bearing on our text come up in the Notes and Illustrations.

It only remains that in this division of our Essay I give a detailed account of a supposed autograph MS. in the British Museum (15,232), which, as containing a number of the Sonnets of 'Astrophel and Stella,' together with other Verse, demands critical examination, all the more that we have been constrained to pronounce it comparatively valueless.

The MS.—which I shall immediately describe from the sale-catalogue—appears to be in its original green pasteboard cover, and the paper and water-mark (of which anon) are the same in all.

At bottom of *verso* of cover, written when the book was upside down, is ' 6 Janry. . 32'—the 3 plain, the 2 more doubtful. This seems a different handwriting from any in the MS. Before it, in another hand, is an illegible word.

There are at least six handwritings in the body of the MS. :

---

and 15, to one in the daytime. The 9th Song connects itself with viii., and with its succeeding Sonnet (lxxxvii.), on which see relative note. The 10th agrees with this time and Sonnet xcii., and Song xi. agrees with that absent presence (see relative note), which, as I think, begins as far back as Sonnet xciii., and is certainly continued in Sonnets cv. cvi. I have an idea that both in the Sonnets and Songs there was an intentional irregular intermixture, with a view to present them as Poems simply, not as the record of an actual and intense love-story. Stella was still living, it must be remembered, and saw various editions of 'Astrophel and Stella' and the Sidera poems. The latter carry the same passion with them as do the Astrophel and Stella Sonnets. The ' *Ring out, wild Bells,*' which Tennyson has caught up in his 'In Memoriam,' and related pieces (xvii. to xix.) invite commentary. They are all autobiographic in the most pathetic and truthful way.

(*a*) Scraps of Latin, which, by appearance and subject, I judge to be the hand of a youth learning philosophy.

(*b*) 'A most careless content' (p. 9 *v.*) ; 'The truth' (p. 10) ; 'Love by the beams' (p. 12 *v.*)—all apparently one hand, the last somewhat doubtful.

(*c*) A heavier, well-formed, regular, and angular hand.

(*d*) A similar hand, yet clearly different. The ink faded to red-brown.

(*e*) 'Iffe that,' &c. (p. 19)—of which onward.

(*f*) The Astrophel and Stella Sonnets.

(*g*) On one of the blank leaves between the earlier and later Sonnets is what I take to be written as a young person's ' copy' or trial of penmanship.

In making out this list I have been confirmed in my own conclusions by experts at the British Museum, and by the repeated examination of the MS. by Dr. Brinsley Nicholson.

Passing from ourselves, the MS. is thus described in the sale-catalogue of Benjamin Heywood Bright, Esq. (June 18th, 1844) :

'240. Sidney (Sir Philip), Astrophel and Stella, Sonnets, 4to ; *injured by damp.*

' °₀° The following is Mr. Bright's note in this manuscript :

" I suspect that this MS. volume belonged to Wilton—that there is in it the writing of Sir P. S. and his sister. The Sonnets are with corrections made after the first edition, 1591, which is very incorrect. This MS., if I am right, is quite inestimable.—B. H. B."

' Inserted is an autograph letter of Mary Sidney, Countess of Pembroke, intended to show the similarity of portions of the manuscript, which is in various hands, to her writing. Mr. Bright supposes that a part of it is the autograph of Sam. Daniel. The volume contains sixteen of the Sonnets, and some of the Songs of Astrophel and Stella, with other poems not there printed.'

In our priced copy of the Catalogue there is placed against this MS. 4*l*. 14*s*. 6*d*. (Sir F. Madden), a price in such contrast with Mr. Bright's 'inestimable' as to indicate that experts stood in doubt of the manuscript. Nor can it be wondered at ; for a collation speedily reveals errors in the ' Astrophel and Stella' Sonnets that could only belong to a transcript, and that a very careless one : *e.g.* in Sonnet i. l. 2, 'thee' (deer thee) for 'the dear She' (2 quartos); 'she' (dear She), A (see our note *in loco*) ; Sonnet i. l. 8, ' showers' (2 qu. and A) begun as ' flowers ;' Sonnet ii. l. 3, ' mind' (' tract,' Q 1) for 'mine' (Q 2 and A) ; Sonnet iv. l. 4, ' with that it' (' that' impossible); Sonnet iv. l. 10, 'in thee' for 'in me' (2 qu. and A) ; Sonnet vii. l. 13, ' even' for ' ever' (2 qu. and A) ; Sonnet viii. l. 2, ' First' for ' Forst' (2 qu. and A) ; Sonnet x. l. 5, ' in sight' for ' unused' (Q 1) ; ' inside' (Q 2 and A) ; Sonnet xv. l. 7, ' dcessed' for 'de-cessed'=deceased ; Sonnet xviii. l. 12, ' doth'—first two letters begun wrongly—query as ' to' and then altered ; ibid. ' bent' and altered to ' bend ;' Sonnet xix. l. 3, ' witts' for ' fruits' (2 qu. and A ; see our note *in loco*); Sonnet cv. l. 1, ' light' for ' sight' (2 qu. and A; and see our note *in loco*) ; ibid. l. 12 ' did *drive so fast* resist'—the italics erased, being taken in error from next line ; Son-net cvi. l. 13, ' bald' (erased)—bad ; Sonnet cvii. l. 7, on—where an error was about to be committed and the pen drawn down.

These may suffice. With reference to Sonnet i. l. 2, it will be observed that if the first ' thee' stand for ' the' (a spelling found nowhere else in the MS.), then the ( ) is ridiculous, this being only required with the variant read-ing ' she' (dear she, A). This first ' thee' is perfectly dis-tinct in the MS.; but the paper having been stained and injured, there remains only -hee of the second, th- being just in the position of the thick cross-stroke of the *t*. It does not correspond with the transcriber's ' s,' and had an ' s' been there, some more of it would have remained. This

error and that of Sonnet ii. l. 3, 'mind' for ' mine,' settles
to us the non-authority of the 'Astrophel and Stella' portion of the MS. Its transcriber copied, in all probability,
from a scribbled and confused prior transcript. A glance
shows that it is not in Sidney's autograph, neither in the
Countess of Pembroke's ; and the same holds of the songs
introduced into 'Astrophel and Stella.' The 'variations,'
called by Mr. Bright 'corrections,' of 1591 are either
errors or inferior and conjectural. The only exception is in
Song viii. st. ii. l. 1, 'Astrophil' for 'Astrophel,' which is certainly more accurate as=lover of Stella ; but ' Astrophel,'
as it was Spenser's, so was it Sidney's spelling, no doubt to
disguise the ' love.' These Songs in the MS. are unintelli-
gently left unpunctuated.

Mr. Bright suggests that Daniel's handwriting is in the
MS. ; but a comparison of the MS. in the British Museum to
which he refers (lxxii. not xxii.) satisfies us that this is a
mistake. The handwritings are quite distinct. The undoubted autograph-letter of the Countess of Pembroke
inserted has nothing resembling it in the MS. ; nor in all
the six handwritings of the MS. am I certain of any being
Sidney's own, with the (somewhat doubtful) exception
of a poem (at least verse) on folio 19 as onward. The
water-mark looks here and throughout like

W

P S

If the W be not simply a part of the shield, it might be
=Wilton, and P S=Philip Sidney. But would Sir Philip
Sidney have paper specially marked thus for himself ? The
handwriting of the now to be noticed Verse has a certain
resemblance to Sidney's more careless hand, as in his Letters at Hatfield and elsewhere, examined by myself. But
it seems almost impossible that he could be the author (or
copyer) of such Verse. We have done our utmost to de-
cipher the MS., and it follows literally :

Iffe that [stained] [p]ynes and dyes
Bye dasling of your Eys,
  humblye entreatethe
To staye your selfe, soe lounge
Till you haue harde his songe,
  Whom Cupid beatethe.
Licke to the sillye swanne,
When Line noe more she Cane,   *sing*
  Settes fourthe her voyce,
Soe I a simple swanne,   *swaine*
thoughe mortall be my name,
  seeme to rejoice.
When you haue hard his dittie
Whose faythe maye drawe your pittie
  because vnfayned,
Judge then Whatte he dothe saye
and beare his name a waye
  [illegible] as disdained.
Your eies, licke starres, hathe wroughte
dirrections on my thoughte,
  Thoughte true to you.
O [stained and illegible] the desiers
Wʰ to my [illegible] aspiers
  tend all to you,
The cares wᶜʰ nighte dothe bringe
beginne and end one thinge.
  Would Silvya knowe,
Woulde Silvya knowe his faythe
that sundrie sorrowes hathe,
  Or Silvyas Loue.
Woulde Silvya harde his mone,
Who comeforte findeth none
  But Silvyas gloue.
But when he moste dothe murne,
then moste she seames to scorne,
  destinie dismale.
I followe, but she flies,
Neuertheless to please her eyes,
  thancke fortune for all.
Blame not her mynde divyne
Whoe sees wᵗʰ Wisdome eyen
  howe to make choise.

Thye selfe a waveringe yoothe,
She thinkes thoughte all not trueth,
        that woemens wise.
Whome your beautie and his owne
    fortune hath madde forlorne
Bye wch I for [stained]
my woorke of everaie daye
        Wourke to you done.
Your Lookes more fyner seene,
Then of the silkworme ben,
        Careles and comelie.
folde me soe faste all waie
I cannotte breake awaie
        Simple and homelye.
your voice still devidinge,
pearles and rubies shininge,
        a wondrous glorie.
[illegible] sweeter smelles by farre
then flowers ever bare
        in field or storie.
To wch voyce line [?] heuenlye ever
moste humblye shall p'sever
        in all obedience.
Mye selfe my flocke I keepe,
Whether I wake or sleepe,
        Wth out resistance.

Turning back to st. ii. 1. 5, can the line, ' thoughe mortall be my name,' carry in it a play on the name of Sidney's friend *Dye*-r? The poem is unworthy even of him; most certainly has no sign of Sidney in it.

If this Poem be in Sidney's own handwriting, then it is all of his handwriting in the MS.; and if it be not, then most assuredly there is not a single line or word of his handwriting in the whole MS. In our Notes and Illustrations in the places, we make occasional references to the readings of this MS.; but we cannot regard it as at all authoritative. Further details were supererogatory.

So far as I have been able to ascertain, there does not appear to be known a single MS. of the Poems of Sidney

in his own autograph, with the small exception of the
Lines with Queen Elizabeth's lock of hair, preserved at
Wilton. Letters abound in many collections (British Mu-
seum, Penshurst, Hatfield), but no MS. of his Poetry.
I proceed to consider

III. *The story of Lady Rich and Sidney in the* morale
of it, with hitherto unprinted Letters.

To the Biographer rather than to an Editor belong
most of the facts and problems (not to say paradoxes) of
the love-story of Sidney and the dazzling 'Stella.' But
interpenetrated as are the Sonnets of Astrophel and Stella
and the Sidera set of Poems, with the passion of their love
and disappointment, joy and most tragic sorrow, it seems
an inevitable task even to an Editor to touch on certain
points, seeing that our great and good memories are too
few to be lightly left to traditionary mistake and miscon-
struction, if these be removable.

Fundamentally it must never be forgotten that the
chronology of these Love-Sonnets and Poems is at present perplexing ; that is to say, they have from the first
been put together without regard to their *nexus,* very
much apparently as the scattered originals or transcripts
came into the hands of their first publisher, Thomas Newman—for his order (or dis-order) was scarcely departed
from afterwards. They thus came to be printed merely
as so many Sonnets and Poems, as an addition to the
Poetry of England—then meagre—with no reference to the
two hearts that were laid bare in them. It is of the last
importance to remember this ; for upon the dates of these
Sonnets and Poems is contingent our verdict of shame or
praise ; and shame has been too readily pronounced. *E.g.*
there are Sonnets that, though placed onward, seem to
belong to a very early period, while 'Stella' in heart and
hand was still free and to be wooed. Others similarly
placed, that is misplaced, onward, self-revealingly belong

to the inter-space during which only the sacred memory
of her father's dying prayer for their union held them ;
when Sidney was not 'enthralled' by her, nor she by him.
Others, placed hither and thither, belong to a time when
Sidney's heart was filled to its utmost capacity with his
love for Stella, though Leicester's marriage made him fear
she was being removed by circumstances beyond his win-
ning. Then there are others that were born of the un-
explained fact that she had married another, unworthy of
her ; and coördinate with these, others that belong to the
discovery of a *forced* marriage, of a hand-loss without a
heart-loss, and all the consequent anguish and tumult.
Finally, there is a double set, also misarranged hither and
thither, belonging to (*a*) the struggle with a love known
to be in her heart and his own inextinguishable and burning love ; (*b*) the recovery and victory of both, after a
keen, intense discipline. So too with the 'Sidera' set :
they seem to have been intentionally intermixed and
sundered.

Some day surely something of the thought and love
given to Shakespeare's Sonnets will be dedicated to those
of Sidney ; and if so, the story hidden in them be relieved of stains and shadows at present resting on it.[1]

---

[1] Sonnets xxiv. xxxv. and xxxvii. are much too early placed
in the series: xxv., again, is too late. So too v. xxx. xl. and xli.
are self-evidently misplaced. A very noticeable Letter to Languet, in
the 'Zurich Letters' of the Parker Society, shows that in March 1578
Sidney was not yet 'enthralled' by his love for Stella. I must find
room for a short extract, premising that the Editor (Dr. Robinson)
supplies Lady Penelope Devereux's name in the place as the 'illa:'
'But I wonder, my very dear Hubert, what has come into your mind,
that when I have not as yet done anything worthy of me, you would
have me bound in the chains of matrimony; and yet without pointing
out any individual lady, but rather seeming to extol the state itself,
which, however, you have not as yet sanctioned by your own example. Respecting her, of whom I readily acknowledge how unworthy
I am, I have written you my reasons long since; briefly indeed, but

Throughout, a study of these Sonnets and Poems impresses us not merely with the brilliant beauty and splendid intellectual gifts of ' Stella,' but profoundly with her self-restraint and her restraint of Sidney. The rebuke of her adorer for a stolen kiss (Sonnet lxxiii.) is only one of very many semi-unconscious admissions on Sidney's part that Stella, while owning her kindred ' love' for him, stood true and inviolate. This does not appear to have been sufficiently weighed in behalf of Essex's radiant daughter. Neither has the fact of that kindred love been sufficiently weighed on behalf of Sidney. It must have been a terrible discovery on each side. Terrible to Stella, that she was the enforced wife of Rich, while her ' love' was still Sidney's; terrible to Sidney, that he had that ' love,' while she was Rich's. Leicester's marriage had cut off his presumptive inheritance of *his* wealth and position, and apparently Sidney had concluded that the love was only on his side, and that, infinitely deeper than he ever suspected until it was ' too late;' and when he did dis-

---

yet as well as I was able. At this present time, indeed, I believe you have entertained some other notion; which I earnestly entreat you to acquaint me with, whatever it may be: for everything that comes from you has great weight with me; and to speak candidly, I am in some measure doubting whether some one, more suspicious than wise, has not whispered to you something unfavourable concerning me, which, though you did not give entire credit to it, you nevertheless prudently, and as a friend, thought right to suggest for my consideration. Should this have been the case, I entreat you to state the matter to me in plain terms, that I may be able to acquit myself before you, of whose good opinion I am most desirous ; and should it only prove to have been a joke, or a piece of friendly advice, I pray you nevertheless to let me know immediately, since everything from you will always be no less acceptable to me than the things that I love most dear.' (Zurich Letters, 2d series, p. 297 ; Latin, p. 182: dated 1st March 1578.) Sidney seems to suspect that even thus early he was being talked of in relation to Stella—to suspect, indeed, that it was regarded as a moral necessity that he should marry some one.

cover that the love was co-equal in her, and that nevertheless she could not now be his, very awful must have been
the conflict between honour and love, heart and conscience.   There was an enormous amount of justification
of the struggle, of the slowness utterly to yield each
other up.   I cannot apportion the praise of the ultimate
triumph as between Stella and Sidney.   I find in Sonnets lxxxvii. lxii. and elsewhere, demonstration that the
triumph was not all on one side, and that side Sidney's.
One line is laden with pathos : ' Alas, I found that she
with me did smart !'   I have an abiding conviction that
while Sidney lived, ' Stella' was true and pure and noble,
after no common ideal, and in every way worthy of Sidney.   I give to Stella without reserve the glory of having
' kept' Sidney true to his best self.   She opened his eyes to
discern the wrong path he was taking in still seeking to
cherish a hopeless love for her.   She drew from him that
great cry of pain — to me unutterably piercing — ' *nowe
of the basest.*'[1]   It was a love-tragedy more lamentable
than ever even Shakespeare or Philip Massinger (Sidney's
' Philip') imagined ; and over the after-years of Stella, for
myself I have infinite pity and nothing but tears.   I fear
the ' fine bells' grew ' jangled' under the terrible sorrow of

---

[1] See our relative note on pages 123-4. I am satisfied that Sonnet
xiv. belongs to the same period, and is much too early placed in the
series. Lines 4-8 are profoundly suggestive of a consciousness of
wrong-feeling, not the less so that there is a semitone of defiance in
the answer :
> ' ye must contend
> To grieue me worse, in saying that Desire
> Doth plunge my wel-form'd soule euen in the mire
> Of sinfull thoughts, which do in ruin end.'

Like internecine heart-struggles are revealed all through the later
Sonnets. I note the following as worthy of study : v. ll. 1-4, 13-14;
x. ll. 7-11 ; xvi. l. 10 ; xviii. ll. 8-12 ; xix. ll. 3-6 ; xx. l. 14 ; xxi.
l. 4 and 7 ; xxv. l. 14; xxviii. l. 8 ; xxxiv. l. 2 and 14; xxxvii. l.
11 ; xlvii. l. 12-14 ; l. lii. lxi. lxii. lxvi. lxix. lxx. lxxii. lxxiv.
lxxxiv. lxxxvii. xc. xci. xcii. xciii. civ. and cix.

her brother's death.　For Sidney, I dare not say with Shelley in ' Adonais,'

> ' Sidney, as he fought
> And as he fell, and as he lived and loved,
> Sublimely mild, a spirit without spot;'

echo of Spenser's earlier,

> ' Nor Spite itself, that all good things doth spill,
> Found aught in him that she could say was ill.'
> -　　　　　　　　　　　　　(Astrophel.)

He was human, and therefore there were 'spot' and 'ill ;' but it is as though one caught the music of the spheres amid the dissonance of a thunderstorm and comet-haunted air to find Sidney, released of his unwarranted and impossible 'love,' thus singing at last :

> ' Leave me, O Love, which reaches but to dust,
> And thou, my mind, aspire to higher things ;
> Grow rich in that which never taketh rust ;
> Whatever fades, but fading pleasure brings.
> Draw in thy beams, and humble all thy might
> To that sweet yoke where lasting freedoms be;
> Which breaks the clouds, and opens forth the light,
> That doth both shine, and give us eyes to see.
> O, take fast hold ; let that light be thy guide
> In this small course which birth draws out to death ;
> And think how ill becometh him to slide,
> Who seeketh heav'n, and comes of heavenly breath.
> Then farewell, world ; thy uttermost I see :
> *Eternal Love, maintain thy life in me !'*　　(A. and S. cx.)

Looking a little closer to the Sonnets of ' Astrophel and Stella,' certain dates are recoverable.　Bourne (p. 286) fixes Stella's marriage in 1580; but, as Lloyd has very well shown (pp. ix. x.), the Letter of Lord Huntingdon, on which he relies in departing from 1581, corrects his error.　It is indorsed ' 10th March 1580,' which by our calendar is 1581.　Consequently Stella could not have been married till after the 10th March 1581—it may have been well on in 1581. ' The error,' observes Lloyd (p. x.), 'is the more grave that Mr. Bourne's estimate of Sidney's moral character depends upon it.' By the true date we have an enlarged period for the Love-Sonnets as having been composed while ' wooing' was still innocent.[1]

Turning to Sonnet xxxiii., it is usually supposed that Sidney here speaks of Stella's marriage, and laments his error in not marrying her. I ask the student-reader to open at this Sonnet and read it slowly. This interpretation seems altogether opposed to facts and to the wording of the Sonnet itself. There was no ' might be.' Leicester's marriage had rendered Sidney unacceptable to her friends, and it is nonsensical to suppose a 'might be' when they so ' forced' her marriage that she proclaimed her dislike at the very altar, and—in vain. This too being the case, how, if Sidney meant to refer to the marriage, could he have written of himself :

> 'No force, no fraud rob'd thee of thy delight,
> Nor Fortune of thy fortune author is'?

Besides, while there is only very conjectural evidence that Sidney was so smitten with her before the marriage, or that he himself knew the power she held over him until the shock of the marriage came, there is the evidence of the larger proportion of the Sonnets to show that it was not till late in the period comprised in the Sonnets that he was aware she loved him. The tone of the Sonnet, the word ' day' in l. 4, explained as it is by its repetition in ll. 12-14, the ' respects' spoken of in l. 11, and most of all ll. 12-14, show that he is merely lamenting that slanderers should talk that he showed so much respect to her and to himself as to absent himself on some especial occasion when he

---

[1] Lloyd's proof is incomplete, because 10th March 1580 by Lord Huntingdon might have been our 10th March 1580. The official indorsement X March 1580 decides it, because officials kept to the official commencement of the year. The copy of Constable's letter in Cotton MSS. is in point. Constable dates 9th Jan. 1604, and we learn that he dated as we would, by the official indorsement 1603.

might have met her. ' Fitly-punisht eyes' agrees with this, but is an absurd phrase if he were lamenting his loss in not marrying her ; and the whole of this early Sonnet— except in so far as ' In respects' shows an early phase of her love—is similar to, and may be profitably compared with, Sonnet cv. on a somewhat similar occasion. Very trivial things in love were then magnified.

In Sonnet xxiii. l. 1, the ' some' and ' others' and l. 7 show this to have been composed after his return to Court in or about October 1580. How long after is another question.

Sonnet xli. is a very noticeable one chronologically. On Whit-Monday 15th May 1581, after hasty but great preparations, a gorgeous tournament was held by and before Queen Elizabeth, in honour of the French Ambassadors who had arrived to treat of her marriage with the Duke of Anjou. Sidney was one of the challengers who attacked the fortress in which Queen Elizabeth, as the Queen and Virgin Beauty, was enthroned. The Sonnet may not, it is just possible, refer to this time and event ; and unfortunately, though a long account of it was printed, neither the Author, nor Holinshed, who copied from it, mention the prize-winners. But, looking to the greatness of the occasion, it is most probable that the Sonnet does refer to it ; for had Sidney been vanquished, then he would hardly boast of those French and English having been spectators and awarders of the minor prize of some ordinary tilting, the very mention of which has not come down to us.

Sonnet xxx. is dated by Pears and others in the Spring of 1580, thus placing it several months earlier than Sonnet xxxiii., even on the supposition that the latter was written on Stella's marriage. But Languet's letters to Sidney are decisive as to a later date. Writing on the 28th October 1580, he says : ' The Archduke Mathias has heard from Vienna that peace is made between the Turks and

Persians, and letters from Constantinople imply the same, but do not directly affirm it. They add that the Sultan has commanded Ochiali to have a number of new galleys built, so that it is expected he will make some attempt against the Spaniards next Summer. It certainly concerns him in the highest degree that the Spaniards should not conquer Portugal, lest they should deprive Egypt of their traffic with India through the Red Sea,' &c. Now Languet's intelligence was likely to be as early, if not earlier than any that got abroad at Cork ; nor is it probable that the report as to the Turks would have got abroad earlier than the cessation of the year's campaign at the time of going into winter-quarters. So long as the Persian war lasted, the Sultan could not have undertaken a European one, and, as it turned out, the Persian war did go on ; and therefore the intention, if intention there were, of going to war with Spain came to nothing. Hence the date of the Sonnet necessarily falls between the middle, say, of Nov. 1580 and June 1581, and the words ' this year' rather point to some early month in 1581. With regard to the Polish war, Languet's news of 21st November 1579 shows that Stephen could not then have been meditating invasion, as he had only just recovered Polotzk, and was besieging Smolensk. Similarly, on 6th February 1580 he writes (Pleskow being then besieged by Stephen) : ' The Muscovite prince is said to be at Pleskow (*i.e.* for its relief) with a large force, with which it is expected he will invade Livonia.' Late in the year, I think on 24th September, he mentions a report that Stephen had been killed by his own people ; and in October, immediately after the quotation about the Turks, adds : ' What we heard about the death of the King of Poland is not true. They say he has penetrated with his victorious army into the heart of Muscovy, and that the Muscovite is suing to him for peace.' The query therefore that Sidney alludes to was probably whether Stephen would again enter Muscovy or make peace.

'Muscovy' seems to have had a strange interest for Sidney. It is introduced into the earliest of the Sonnets. Had he a prophetic glimpse of the after-offer of Poland's crown to him ?

These remarks may go to show the need of a very thorough revision of the chronology of 'Astrophel and Stella' and related Poems.

It is now my privilege to print for the first time no fewer than five letters from Stella as Lady Rich and as Countess of Devonshire. I found these at Hatfield while pursuing other researches there by the unreserved permission of the Marquis of Salisbury. Such letters, if intrinsically not very remarkable, cannot but be of interest to all who care to get nearer to great historic names; and certainly 'Stella' has 'for all time' taken her place in the heaven of Literature beside not merely the Geraldine of Surrey earlier, or the Mary of Robert Burns later, but the Laura of Petrarch, and Beatrice of Dante, and Rosalind and Elizabeth of Spenser, and Celia of Carew, and Castara of Habington, and Leonora of Milton, and Sacharissa of Waller.

These Letters, and a very touching and noble one to Elizabeth in behalf of her brother (Essex), published by us in 'The Farmer Chetham MS.,' for the Chetham Society, are exceedingly characteristic in their gracious light-heartedness and kindly interest in the humblest.

The first is addressed to the Earl of Southampton— Shakespeare's Southampton[1]—as follows :

'Noble S^r, I hope my first letter will excuse some parte of my faulte, and I assure you nothinge shall make me neglecte to yealde you all the ernest assurances I can of my affection and desires to be helde deare in your fa-

[1] I have for some years been collecting materials for an adequate Life of Shakespeare's Southampton. These prove more abundant than has been supposed.

uour, whose worthy kindnes I will striue to merit by the
faithfullest endeuors my loue can performe towards you,
who shall euer finde me vnresumably,

'Your Lo. faithfull cosin and true frende,

'PENELOPE RICH.

'Your Lo. Daughter is exceeding faire and well, and
I hope by your sonn to winn my wager.

'Chartly, this 10 of May.'

It is indorsed 'The La. Rich : to yᵉ E. of Southampton ;' and has a note, ' This alludes to the expectation the
Earl had of a son at this time. See Lodge.' The seal
is a 'deer,' very much resembling that used by Andrew
Marvell later.

Our next Letter is also addressed to Southampton :

'The exseeding kindnes I resue [receive] from your
Lo. in hering often from you doth geue me infinite contentment, bothe in refering assurance of your health and
that I remaine in your constant fauor, which I well en-
duour to merit by my affection unto your Lo. my Lo.
Riche doth so importune me dayly to retorne to my owne
house as I can not stay here longar then bartelmentide,
which I do against his will, and the cause of his ernest
desire to haue me come vp is his being so persecuted for his
lande, as he is in feare to loose the greatest parte he hath
and his next terme, who would haue me a soliseter to beare
parte of his trobles, and is much discontented with my
staing so longe : wherefore I beseche your Lo. to speeke
with my brother, since I am lothe to leue my La. here
alone, and if you resolue shee shall go with me into Essex,
which I very much desire, then you were best to write to
me that you would haue her go with me, which will make
my Lo. Riche the more willing, though I know he will be
well contented, to whom I haue writen that I will come as
soone as I knowe what my Brother and your selfe deter-
mins for my Lo.   I am sorry for Sir Hary Bauers hurte,

though I hope it is so littel as it will not marr his good face; and so in hast I wishe your Lo. all the honor and hapines you desire.

'Your Lo. most affectionat cosin,

'PENELOPE RICHE.

'Chartly, this 9 of iuly.

' To the most honorable the Earle of Southamton.'

'Chartley,' it will be remembered, was the first meeting-place between Stella and Sidney.

Our third Letter is far onward, being indorsed 'La. Rich, 1604.' It follows :

'Mr. Renalls, my ould woman harny hath a sute to my brother, which I would not haue her troble him with ; but that it is only his letter to my Lo. Maire [Mayor] for a meane place that is fallen in his gifte, which she desires for her sonn White. Let me intreate you to drawe a letter, and that some body may go if you haue no laisor [leisure] your selfe, that will be ernest with the Maire, since it is like he will excuse it if he can for some creature of his owne ; and so in haste I rest,

' Your very assured frende,   PENELOPE RICHE.

' To my frende Mr. Renalles.'

Our next is to the Earl of Salisbury, and thus runs :

' Noble Lo., this Jentell woman hath intreted me to recomende her sute vnto you, of whose good sucses I should be very glade, because she is on [one] I haue bine longe aquainted with, and is of the best disposition that euer I founde any of her nation. I beseche your Lo. to fauour her, that if it be possible she may obtaine some satisfaction if her desires be not vnreasonable ; and so wishing your Lo. all happines and contentment, I remaine,

'Your Lo. most affectionate frende to do you seriuce,

'PENELOPE RICHE.

'Ennile[?], this last of May. [Indorsed ' 1605.']'

' To the right honorable my Lo. the Earle of Salisburye.'

Our last Letter is of peculiar interest, as being from Stella as the Countess of Devonshire. It is as follows, and is also addressed to Salisbury :

'Noble Lo., the rumers of your sicknes I confes hath made me hast to this place, wher I might resue [receive] better satisfaction by the knowledge of your health, and had the good fortune this day to meet with the messenger you sente to my Lo. of Clanricarde, whereby I was assured of your safe recouery, beseeching your Lo. to beleue that no frende you haue liuing doth participate more of your grefe or ioye then my selfe, whose affection you haue so infinitly obliged with your constante fauours. while I was at draiton with my mother, the yonge hunters came very well pleased, vntill your seruant came with your co-mission to gide my Lo. of Cranborne to my La. of Darbye, which discont'ment for feare of parting three days made them all loose their suppers, and became extreeme mali-ciouse, till it was concluded that ther traine should staye at Draiton, and they go to gether with to [two] seruants a peece. I feare nothing but ther riding so desperately, but your sonn is a perfett horse man, and can nether be out riden nor matched any waye. my mother, I thinke, will growe yonge with ther companye : so longinge to here of your safe and perfect health, I remaine

'Your Lo. most faithfull to do you seruice,
                                    P. DEUONSHIERE.
'Wansted, this Monday.'

It is indorsed ' Lady Deuonshire, 1606,' and addressed ' To the right honorable my Lo. the Earle of Salisburye.'[1]

[1] By the kindness of the Marquis of Westminster I was favoured with a contemporary transcript (1616) of Mountjoy's, i.e. Devonshire's, defence of his marriage with Lady Rich. It proved to be a mere technical and scholastic defence of marriage of a divorced wife dur-ing the lifetime of her former husband. There is not a scintillation of personal reference. Numbers of copies are extant.

These Letters and the whole story of Stella, earlier and later, strongly tempt to commentáry and ' Apology'—in its old sense. I cannot too emphatically utter my conviction, after anxious study of it under no common advantages, that Stella in her relations with Sidney was, if' anything, the truer and nobler. Spenser saw nothing but glory in the passionate story :

> ' To her he vow'd the service of his days;
>   On her he spent the riches of his wit;
> For her he made hymns of immortal praise;
>   Of only her he sung, he thought, he writ;
> Her, and but her, of love he worthy deem'd;
> For all the rest but little he esteem'd.'

(Astrophel, ll. 61-66.)

It seems to me about the shallowest of criticism imaginable that says, as does the Archbishop of Dublin in his Notes to his charming ' Household Book of English Poetry' (as before): ' Sir Philip Sidney's sonnets may be " vain and amatorious," as Milton has called his fine romance of The Arcadia, but they possess grace, fancy, and a passion which makes itself felt even under the artificial forms of a Platonic philosophy ;' and then emptying out the meaning of the right word ' passion,' goes on : ' They are addressed to one who, if the course of true love had run smooth, should have been his wife. When, however, through the misunderstanding of parents, or through some other cause, she had become the wife of another, Platonic as they are, they would far better have remained unwritten' (pp. 390-1). Nay, verily ! Our early Literature is not so rich as to afford the loss of ' Astrophel and Stella' and related Poems, while ' Platonic' is about the most inept and false description of the ' passion' one could conceive. It was, I believe, a tragedy of Conflict, and the Love went down to the very roots of both in their deepest. Earlier there was pastime and intellectual exercise, or, as Sonnet i. (Astrophel and Stella) puts it, ' studying inuentions fine her wits to entértain ;' but as you read you find yourself borne on a molten stream of love-passion. I know nothing grander than the double overcoming of it. To call such a struggle of Love and Honour, Heart and Conscience 'Platonic' shows—with the profoundest respect for his Grace—in our estimate, a revelation of sad ignorance or momentary forgetfulness of the facts and the persons. To the last, Sidney was ' bound' to Stella ; for I fear she who became his wife was utterly unworthy of him, whether regarded intellectually or womanly. Perhaps Mrs. Craik in her passionate 'Head of the Family' has best put the feeling that I imagine to have remained with Sidney, as follows : ' Let no one say that passion is unconquerable. It can never be so in a pure heart. Inevitable necessity—the stern sense of right—the will at last bent to that holier Will which maps out human life—can in time crush-down the individual longing that would wholly appropriate to itself what seems fairest both to its spiritual and visual eye. Yet nothing can obliterate tenderness—that hallowed lingering of memory which seems to say, " Thou art not mine,—I have ceased to hope or even wish it so ; but no one can ever be to me in thy stead, and at any time I would give my life to pour out blessings upon thee and thine." With this sort of feeling, strangely intense though calm, Ninian went to see Mrs. Ulverston' (c. xxxiii.). I pass finally to

IV. *The characteristics of Sidney's Poetry, with the praises of it by his contemporaries and onward.*

We have already called attention to the *posthumous* publication of the entire Writings of Sidney. To this falls now to be added the undoubted fact that ' Astrophel and Stella' and the 'Sidera' and kindred Poems never were intended for the public—were for 'Stella' alone, save in the earlier and lighter, wherein Sidney played with her love after the manner of his age. No one ought to come to the study of his Poetry without an abiding recollection of this. There are things in every man's life which are not for the world's eyes. There are things especially that lose their subtlest edge of meaning—as a handled peach or plum its bloom—when read as mere written words. There are things too that grow unconsecrate if their inner message be made outer.

Regarded broadly, the Poetry of Sir Philip Sidney has three characteristics that I wish briefly to set forth : (*a*) Passion; (*b*) Thought; (*c*) Fineness of art.

(*a*) *Passion.* This requires only a very few additional sentences to what has been already submitted. The man just as he was is self-painted as in a diary in ' Astrophel and Stella ;' and throughout, Sidney was intense in all he did. His Letters—as the memorable one to ' Mr. Moly- neux' and the imperishable one to Queen Elizabeth—in especial show this ; but most of all, his Poetry. You miss the sweetest music of ' Astrophel and Stella,' if you do not steep your own spirit in the passion of its Sonnets and Songs. And so is it everywhere. You have the throbbing heart, the quick conscience in its tremor and disturbance and seeking of the right, the shifting moods, the sudden freaks of fancy, the overbearing grief, the as overbearing ardour, the frank penitence, the as frank avowal of failure to master, and, sounding out like a muffled buoy-bell, cries of absolute distress that are to me awful. The Poetry of Sidney is marked by this Passion because into his Poetry he has put the most of his own very self, at his best and worst, noblest and basest—for there was the ' base' too. Occasionally the Passion hides itself in strangely artificial forms—just as a splendour of tree-blossom and tree-fragrance was often and often found while the trees were clipped and over-trimmed in very fan- tastique of gardening art ; but taken all in all, there is Passion in this Poetry, that informs it as the blood does our body ; and hence a life, a mobility, an electric excita- tion of sympathy, almost unique.

d

(*b*) *Thought.* This Sidney shared with his friend Fulke Greville, Lord Brooke, and indeed all his foremost con- temporaries. [The reserve of power in these Poems is ✓ something wonderful. You feel that what is uttered is as nothing to what is left unuttered. You are held by a sense of Thought ‘ too deep’ for words. If Passion, *i.e.* Feeling, as distinguished from Thought be the predomin- ant characteristic, certainly Thought in quantity and qua- lity is a second characteristic that the most cursory reader of these Poems cannot fail to be struck with.] You have it in most unlooked-for places. As a whole—but only as a whole—the Poems of ‘ Arcadia’ are not up to the high intellectual level of ‘ Astrophel and Stella’ and ‘ Sidera’ set. Yet as you ‘ search’ and ponder them you are as- tonished at the superficiality and haste of that criticism which has read so poorly the ‘ thoughts that breathe in words that burn’ of these ‘ Arcadia’ poems. [There is, apart from their brilliance imaginatively and vivid nature- portraiture, some of Sidney’s deepest and most unique thinking in them.] Take this blending of affection and aspiration in his celebration of Stephen Languet :

> ‘ The song I sang old Languet had me taught,.
> Languet, the shepherd best swift Ister knew ;
> For clarkly read, and hating what is naught,
> For faithful heart, clean hands, and mouth as true,
> With his sweet skill my sailless youth he drew
> To have a feeling taste of Him *that sits*
> *Beyond the heaven, far more beyond our wits.*’

(vol. ii. p. 154.)

Or take this glimpse of his sounding of the ‘ depths of things’ in a snatch burdened with thick-coming question- ings :

> ‘ What essence destiny hath! if fortune be or no ;
> Whence our immortal souls to mortal earth do stow;
> What life it is, and how that all these lives do gather
> With outward maker’s force, or like an inward father.

Such thoughts, methought, I thought, and shamed my single mind,
Then void of nearer cares, the depths of things to find.'
(vol. ii. p. 116.)

I have cited these in preference to others marked and remarked by the score, that I might adduce Dr. George
Macdonald's comment on them (in 'Antiphon,' p.
79), as follows : 'Lord Bacon was not the only one, in such an
age, to think upon the mighty relations of physics and
metaphysics, or, as Sidney would say, "of naturall and
supernaturall philosophie." For a man to do his best, he
must be upheld, even in his speculations, by those around
him. In the specimen just given, we find that our religious
poetry has gone down into the deeps. There are indica-
tions of such a tendency in the older times, but neither
then were the questions so articulate, nor were the ques-
tioners so troubled for an answer. The alternative expressed in the middle couplet seems to me the most
imperative of all questions, both for the individual and
for the Church. Is man fashioned by the hand of God,
as a potter fashioneth his vessel ; or do we indeed come
from His heart ? Is power or love the making might of
the universe ? He who answers this question aright
possesses the key to all righteous [query—religious ?]
questions.'
The Poetry of Sir Philip Sidney is packed with
Thought of this deep, interrogative-speculative type ; nor
does he fail to suggest the true answers. The poorer and
most artificial of the 'Arcadia' poems come first. We
felt constrained to adhere to the original order of the
pieces ; but it is a disadvantage. Let the reader simply
read and pass on from No. i. to vi. and other after-poems
of considerable extent. These will yield unexpected
treasure of aphoristic thoughts, epigrammatic sayings,
proverb-like condensations of trains of observation,
felicitous compliments, dainty-coloured epithets, arresting
metaphors, and many celebrations of old English manners

and customs pricelessly valuable.] I cull from literally
hundreds of marked passages these, which are all in a single
poem:

A RURAL BEAUTY.

'Neuer the Earth on her round shoulders bare
A maid train'd up from high or low degree,
That in her doings better could compare   *equal*
Mirth with respect, few words with curtesie,
A carelesse comlinesse with comely care,
Selfe-gard with mildnesse, sport with majestie.'

(x. Lamon, ll. 209-14.)

PURSUED LION.

'Strephon so chas'd did seeme in milke to swimme;
He ran, but ran with his eye ore shoulder cast,   .
More marking her than how himselfe did goe:
Like Numid lyons by the hunter chas'd,
Though they doe flie, yet backwardly do glowe
With proud aspect, disdaining greater haste.'

(Ibid. ll. 288-93.)

LOVE-SMITTEN.

'A shot unheard gave me a wound unseene.' (Ibid. l. 455.)

'Mine eyes had their curse from blessèd eyne.' (Ibid. l. 497.)

Cf. this, 'Who where she went bare in her forehead Morning' (xxx. Strephon, &c. l. 70). Again, and deeper:

GOD.

'To harme vs wormes should that high Iustice leaue
His nature? nay, Himselfe? for so it is:
What glory from our losse can He receaue?
   But still our dazled eyes their way do misse;
While that we do at His sweete scourge repine,—
The kindly way to beate vs on to blisse.'

(xviii. Plangus, &c. ll. 67-70.)

These must suffice. Finally here—Nowhere have you the
high*est* genius without some sense of humour. I should
have liked to have dwelt on this additional characteristic of Sidney's thought. I must content myself by referring to the 'Mopsa' (i. and lxxviii.) pieces. These will

satisfy that, with all his loftiness and gravity, Sir Philip
could and did discern the ' wit' in men and things—exactly
as a close study of even Milton and Dante, George Herbert
and Cowper, show that they had this faculty of humour,
and could laugh at as well as with the ' humours' of their
fellows.

(c) *Fineness of art.* I have no intention to intermeddle
with the ' Areopagus,' as Spenser called it, wherein Gabriel
Harvey, Sir Edward Dyer, Fulke Greville Lord Brooke,
Sidney, and Spenser, sought to found a new school of poetry.
We are not as yet sufficiently furnished with information
on either the design or the methods contemplated. The
merest fragments of detail have reached us. The actual
specimens of ' classical rhythms,' as distinguished from the
' encumbrance of rhyme,' are puzzles on all sides. Nor are
the hexameters of the ' Arcadia' the least incomprehensible.
Certes it had been a poor exchange to have given the
' Faerie Queen' for Spenser's iambics, or ' Astrophel and
Stella' for Sidney's hexameters and other vagaries. Thomas
Nash, who had wealth of admiration for Sidney and
Spenser, if contemptuous hate for Harvey, adjudged well,
when he pronounced in the well-known quotation, that
though the hexameter verse ' be a gentleman of an ancient
home, yet this clime of ours he cannot thrive in. Our
speech is too craggy for him to set his plough in. He
goes twitching and hopping in our language, like a man
running upon quagmires, up the hill in one syllable and
down the dale in another ; retaining no part of that
stately smooth gait which he vaunts himself with amongst
the Greeks and Latins.' Even Spenser himself could poke
fun at the experiment, ultimately ; *e.g.* it is ' either like a
lame gosling that draweth one leg after, or like a lame
dog that holdeth one leg up.'

Passing these ' experiments'—which neither Southey
nor Longfellow have been able to revive—our Notes and
Illustrations of ' Astrophel and Stella' and the ' Psalms'

demonstrate in the amount of various readings with what insistence of care and with what daintiness and fastidiousness of election Sidney matured his Verse. If the reader will keep a look-out for it, he will again and again be arrested by the exquisite art and delicacy of many of these Poems. Even his most rapturous as his most troubled Sonnets of 'Astrophel and Stella' have cunning workmanship. It were idle to point out examples. I wish to suggest study, and to guide to insight.

Considering that when the well-nigh innumerable Elegies were issued upon his death scarcely a line of his Poems had been printed, it is noticeable that, with hardly an exception, he is celebrated preëminently as a POET. 'He was the Muses' joy ;' give him 'the laurell, *with the bay ;*' 'crowned with lasting bays ;' and

> 'Did never Muse inspire beneath
> A Poet's brain with finer store ;'

and the like, perpetually occur. Then Spenser in his plaintive Pastoral thus sang :   .

> 'He could pipe, and dance, and carol sweet,
> Amongst the shepherds on their shearing feast ;
> As summer's lark, that with her song doth greet
> The dawning day, forthcoming from the East.
> And lays of love he also could compose :
> Thrice happy she whom he to praise did choose.'

And his sister, in her inestimable 'Doleful Lay of Clorinda,' calling on the shepherd-lasses to wear 'cypress' instead of flower-garland, asks 'Who ever made such lays of love as he ?' Ben Jonson has celebrated similarly,

> 'That taller tree, which of a nut was set
> At his great birth, *where all the Muses met ;*' .

and Thomson caught up the flying echo :

> 'Nor can the Muse the gallant Sidney pass.
> The plume of war ! with early laurels crowned,
> The lover's myrtle, and *the Poet's bay.*'

It were easy to multiply recognition of Sidney as a Poet by the foremost of our Literature—to trace Shakespeare's reading of him with wondrous assimilative sympathies, and so others ; and yet ours is the first collective edition of his Poetry. This, while among the ' British Poets' and ' Lives of the Poets' the merest rhymesters have found an apparently irremovable place.

I cannot more fitly close our Essay than with Charles Lamb on ' Some Sonnets of Sir Philip Sydney.' It is ex- cursive in the outset, and I excise a digression on Milton ; but give all the rest, as follows :

' Sydney's Sonnets—I speak of the best of them—are among the very best of their sort. They fall below the plain moral dignity, the sanctity, and high yet modest spirit of self-approval of Milton, in his compositions of a similar structure. They are, in truth, what Milton, cen- suring the Arcadia, says of that work (to which they are a sort of after-tune or application), " vain and amatori- ous" enough, yet the things in their kind (as he confesses to be true of the romance) may be " full of worth and wit." They savour of the courtier, it must be allowed, and not of the Commonwealthman. But Milton was a courtier when he wrote the Masque at Ludlow Castle, and still more a courtier when he composed the Arcades. When the national struggle was to begin, he becomingly cast these vanities behind him ; and if the order of time had thrown Sir Philip upon the crisis which preceded the Revolution, there is no reason why he should not have acted the same part in that emergency which has glori- fied the name of a later Sydney. He did not want for plainness or boldness of spirit. His letter on the French match may testify he could speak his mind freely to princes. The times did not call him to the scaffold. The Sonnets which we oftenest call to mind of Milton were the compositions of his maturest years. These of Sydney, which I am about to produce, were written in the very

heyday of his blood. [They are stuck full of amorous
fancies, far - fetched conceits, befitting his occupation ;
for true love thinks no labour to send out thought upon
the vast and more than Indian voyages, to bring home
rich pearls, outlandish wealth, gums, jewels, spicery, to
sacrifice in self - depreciating similitudes, as shadows of
true amiabilities in the beloved. We must be lovers—or
at least the cooling touch of time, the *circum præcordia
frigus* must not have so damped our faculties as to take
away our recollection that we were once so—before we
can duly appreciate the glorious vanities and graceful
hyperboles of the passion. The images which lie before
our feet (though by some accounted the only natural) are
least natural for the high Sydnean love to express its
fancies.]They may serve for the loves of Tibullus, or the
dear Author of the Schoolmistress [Shenstone], for passions that weep and whine in Elegies and Pastoral Ballads.
I am sure Milton never loved at this rate.' The word
' Sydnean' reminds us to intercalate that Richard Cra-
shaw in his marvellous 'Wishes to his supposed Mistresse'
dedicates one vivid stanza in it to our Sidney :

> ' Sydnæan showers
> Of sweet discourse, whose powers
> Can crown old Winter's head with flowers.'

After quoting and criticising one of Milton's addresses
(in Latin), ' Ad Leonaram,' Elia proceeds : ' I am sure Sydney has no flights like this. His extravaganzas do not
strike at the sky, though he takes leave to adopt the pale
Dian into a fellowship with his mortal passion.' He then
gives Sonnet xxxi., remarking, ' The last line of this poem
is a little obscured by transposition. He means, Do they
call ungratefulness there a virtue ?' The further sonnets
quoted are xxxix. xxiii. xxvii. xli. liii. lxiv. lxxiii. lxxiv.
lxxv. ciii. and lxxxiv. And the reader will do well to
follow Elia's guidance, and give an hour to the studying

of these sonnets. He continues: 'Of the foregoing, the first [xxxix.], the second [xxiii.], and the last [lxxxiv.] sonnet, are my favourites. But the general beauty of them all is, that they are so perfectly characteristical. The spirit of "learning and of chivalry"—of which union Spenser has entitled Sydney to have been the "president" —shines through them. I confess I can see nothing of the "jejune" or "frigid" in them ; much less of the "stiff" and "cumbrous"—which I have sometimes heard objected to the Arcadia. The verse runs off swiftly and gallantly. It might have been tuned to the trumpet, or tempered (as himself expresses it) to "trampling horses' feet." They abound in felicitous phrases :

> "O heav'nly Fool, the most kiss-worthy face."
>
> "Sweet pillows, sweetest bed ;
> A chamber deaf of noise, and blind of light ;
> A rosy garland, and a weary head."
>
> "that sweet enemy,—France."

But they are not rich in words only, in vague and un-localised feelings—the failing too much of some poetry of the present day; they are full, material, and circum-stantiated. Time and place appropriates every one of them. It is not a fever or passion wasting itself upon a thin diet of dainty words, but a transcendent passion per-vading and illuminating actions, pursuits, studies, feats of arms, the opinions of contemporaries, and his judgment of them. An historical thread runs through them, which almost affixes a date to them ; marks the *when* and *where* they were written. It needeth not *now* that we add Lamb's reply to Hazlitt's paradox of insult.

And so it is a joy to me to invite the constituents of the Fuller Worthies' Library to give days and nights to the noble Verse of Sir Philip Sidney, now collected for them. Mary, Countess of Pembroke, as she wept over that 'immortal spirit,' sobbed :

> 'Ah, me, can so divine a thing be dead?'

and answered, of faith :

> 'Ah, no! it is not dead, nor can it die,
> But lives for aye in blissful paradise.'

Nor in a 'blissful paradise' only. ⌈For long as England
lasts will Sir Philip Sidney's name be her boast and or-
nament.⌋ My work for the present has been mainly on
his Poetry, and I close with Matthew Roydon's prescient
as loving estimate of the Man and the Poet :

> 'You knew—who knew not Astrophel?
> (That I should live to say I knew,
> And have not in possession still!)—
> Things known permit me to renew—
>   Of him you know his merit such,
>   I cannot say—you hear—too much.
>
> Within these woods of Arcady
> He chief delight and pleasure took ;
> And on the mountain Partheny,
> Upon the crystal liquid brook,
>   *The Muses met him every day,*
>   *That taught him sing, to write, and say.*
>
> When he descended down the mount,
> His personage seemed most divine :
> A thousand graces one might count
> Upon his lovely cheerful eyne.
>   To hear him speak, and sweetly smile,
>   You were in Paradise the while.
>
> A sweet attractive kind of grace ;
> A full assurance given by looks ;
> Continual comfort in a face ;
> The lineaments of Gospel books—
>   I trow that count'ance cannot lye,
>   Whose thoughts are legible in the eye.
>
>   *   *   *   *   *
>
> Alas, all others this is he,
> Which erst approvèd in her song,

That love and honour might agree,
And that pure love will do no wrong.
  Sweet saints, it is no sin or blame
  To love a man of virtuous name.

Did never love so sweetly breathe
In any mortal breast before;
Did never Muse inspire beneath
A Poet's brain with finer store.
  He wrote of Love with high conceit,
  And Beauty rear'd above her height.'

ALEXANDER B. GROSART.

°ₐ° I add here two of Henry Constable's Sonnets on Lady Rich, prefacing that Ben Jonson thus praised him:

  ' Hath our great Sydney Stella set
  Where never star shone brighter yet?
  Or Constable's ambrosiac muse
  Made Diana not his notes refuse?'

I. TO THE LADIE RICH.

Heralds at armes doe three perfections quote,
  To wit—most faire, most rich, most glittering;
  So when these three concurre within one thing,
Needs must that thing of honour be, of note.
Lately did I behold a rich faire coate,
  Which wishèd fortune to mine eyes did bring:
  A lordly coate—but worthy of a king:
Wherein all these perfections one might note--
A field of lilies, roses proper bare,
  To stars in chiefe, the crest was waves of gold;
How glittering was the coate the starrs declare,
  The lilies made it faire for to behold;
And rich it was, as by the gold appears,
So happy he which on his armes it beares.' (Diana: Son. x.)

II. TO MY LADYE RICH.

O that my songe like to a ship might be,
  To beare aboute the world my Ladie's fame;
  That, chargèd with the riches of her name,
The Indians might our countrye's treasure see.

No treasure, they would say, is rich but she;
    Of all theyre golden parts they would have shame,
    And haplye, that they might but see the same,
To give theyre gold for nought they would agree.
This wishèd voyage, though it I begin,
    Without your beautie's helpe cannot prevayle:
For as a ship doth beare the men therein,
    And yet the men doe make the ship to sayle,
Youre beauties so, which in my verse apeare,
Doe make my verse and it your beauties beare.'

(Sonnets from Todd's MS. p. 6 : Hazlitt's edition of Con-
table, 1859, pp. 7, 39-40.) There are other two Sonnets
on Lady Rich by Constable: (*a*) 'A calculation upon the
birth of an honourable Ladie's daughter, borne in the
yeere 1588, and on a Friday' (p. 18); (*b*) 'Of the death of
my Ladie Riche's daughter : shewing the reason of her
untimelye death hindred her effecting those things which
by the former calculation of her nativitye he foretold'
(p. 44).

I.

ASTROPHEL AND STELLA.

VOL. I.   B

The Student-Reader will find in our Essay in the present volume full details on the following points:

(*a*) The original and after-editions, and the Bright MS. (of a portion) of Astrophel and Stella.

(*b*) The text of our edition, line-arrangement and rhyme-structure, punctuation, &c.

(*c*) The chronology and arrangement of the Sonnets, and the admixture of the eleven Songs (so-called) with them—removed to end in our edition.

(*d*) The story of Lady Rich and Sidney—with hitherto unprinted Letters—in the *morale* of it.

At the close of the series are placed Notes and Illustrations of the CX. Sonnets and XI. Songs; and at the end of these, 1. the Epistle-dedicatory of the Publisher of the first edition of Astrophel and Stella, 1591; 2. the Epistle-prefatory of Thomas Nash in the same; 3. the Preface to Arcadia, &c. of 1593.

Throughout I have supplied headings for the successive Sonnets, drawn from the leading thought of each, and in the Poet's own words. It is found that the absence of headings is inexpedient in the case of most readers. I have also printed these and the after-Sonnets in solid, not after the erratic arrangement of lines in the early Arcadia editions and others. But see a critical account of the line-arrangement, &c., as *supra*. G.

Of louers neuer knowne, a grieuous case,
Pitie thereof gate in her breast such place,
That, from that sea deriv'd, teares' spring did flow.
Alas, if Fancie, drawne by imag'd things
Though false, yet with free scope, more grace doth breed
Than seruants' wracke, where new doubts honor brings;
Then thinke, my deare, that you in me do reed
Of louers' ruine some thrise-sad tragedie.
I am not I; pitie the tale of me.

XLVI.

'Blind-hitting Boy.'

I curst thee oft, I pitie now thy case,
Blind-hitting Boy, since she that thee and me
Rules with a becke, so tyranniseth thee,
That thou must want or food or dwelling-place,
For she protests to banish thee her face:
Her face! O Loue, a roge thou then shouldst be,   rogue
If Loue learne not alone to loue and see
Without desire to feed of further grace.
Alas, poor wag, that now a scholler art
To such a schoolemistresse, whose lessons new
Thou needs must misse, and so thou needs must smart.
Yet, deare, let me his pardon get of you,
So long, though he from book myche to desire,
Till without fewell you can make hot fire.

XLVII.

'Gaine to misse.'

What, haue I thus betrayed my libertie !
Can those blacke beames such burning markes engraue
In my free side; or am I borne a slaue,
Whose necke becomes such yoke of tyrannie !
Or want I sense to feele my miserie,
Or sprite, disdaine of such disdaine to haue !
Who for long faith, tho' daily helpe I craue,
May get no almes, but scorne of beggerie.
Vertue, awake ! Beautie but beautie is;
I may, I must, I can, I will, I do
Leaue following that which it is gaine to misse.
Let her goe ! Soft, but here she comes ! Goe to,
Vnkind, I loue you not ! O me, that eye
Doth make my heart to giue my tongue the lie !

XLVIII.

'Sweete cruell shot.'

Soule's ioy, bend not those morning starres from me,
Where Vertue is made strong by Beautie's might ;
Where Loue is chastnesse, Paine doth learne delight,
And Humblenesse growes on with Majestie.   one
Whateuer may ensue, O let me be
Copartner of the riches of that sight;
Let not mine eyes be hel-driv'n from that light;
O looke, O shine, O let me die, and see.

For though I oft my selfe of them bemone
That through my heart their beamie darts be gone,
Whose curelesse wounds euen now most freshly bleed,
Yet since my death-wound is already got,
Deere killer, spare not thy sweete-cruell shot;
A kinde of grace it is to slaye with speed.

XLIX.

'I on my horse.'

I on my horse, and Loue on me, doth trie
Our horsmanships, while by strange worke I proue
A horsman to my horse, a horse to Loue,
And now man's wrongs in me, poor beast! descric.
The raine wherewith my rider doth me tie
Are humbled thoughts, which bit of reuerence moue,
Curb'd-in with feare, but with guilt bosse aboue   gil[
Of hope, which makes it seeme faire to the eye:
The wand is will; thou, Fancie, saddle art,
Girt fast by Memorie; and while I spurre
My horse, he spurres with sharpe desire my hart;
He sits me fast, howeuer I do sturre;
And now hath made me to his hand so right,
That in the manage my selfe take delight.   menage

L.

'Fulnesse of thoughts.'

Stella, the fulnesse of my thoughts of thee
Cannot be staid within my panting breast,

But they do swell and struggle forth of me,
Till that in words thy figure be exprest:
And yet, as soone as they so formèd be,
According to my lord Loue's owne behest,
With sad eies I their weake proportion see
To portrait that which in this world is best.
So that I cannot chuse but write my mind,
And cannot chuse but put out what I write,
While these poore babes their death in birth do find;
And now my pen these lines had dashèd quite,
But that they stopt his furie from the same,
Because their fore-front bare sweet Stella's name.

LI.

'Pardon mine eares.'

Pardon mine eares, both I and they do pray,
So may your tongue still flauntingly proceed,
To them that do such entertainment need;
So may you still haue somewhat new to say.
On silly me do not the burthen lay
Of all the graue conceits your braine doth breed;
But find some Hercules to beare, insteed
Of Atlas tyrd, your wisedom's heav'nly sway.
For me,—while you discourse of courtly tides,
Of cunningst fishers in most troubled streames,
Of straying waies, when valiant Errour guides,—
Meanewhile my heart confers with Stella's beames,

And is e'en woe that so sweet comedie
By such vnsuted speech should hindred be.

LII.

'Vertue and Loue.'

A strife is growne between Vertuè and Loue,
While each pretends that Stella must be his :
Her eyes, her lips, her all, saith Loue, do this,
Since they do weare his badge, most firmely proue.
But Vertue thus that title doth disproue,
That Stella,—O deare name ! that Stella is
That vertuous soule, sure heire of heav'nly blisse,
Not this faire outside, which our heart doth moue :
And therefore, though her beautie and her grace
Be Loue's indeed, in Stella's selfe he may
By no pretence claime any manner place.
Well, Loue, since this demurre our sute doth stay,
Let Vertue haue that Stella's selfe ; yet thus,
That Vertue but that body graunt to vs.

LIII.

'What now, Sir Foole !'

In martiall sports I had my cunning tride,
And yet to breake more staues did mee adresse,
While, with the people's shouts, I must confesse,
Youth, lucke, and praise euen fil'd my veines with pride;
When Cupid, hauing me, his slaue, describe

In Marses liuery prauncing in the presse :
What now, Sir Foole ! said he,—I would no lesse :
Looke here, I say ! I look'd, and Stella spide,
Who, hard by, made a window send forth light.
My heart then quak'd, then dazled were mine eyes,
One hand forgat to rule, th' other to fight,
Nor trumpet's sound I heard, nor friendly cries :
My foe came on, and beate the aire for me,
Till that her blush taught me my shame to see.

LIV.

' They love indeed who quake to say they love.'

Because I breathe not loue to euery one,
Nor doe not vse sette colours for to weare,
Nor nourish speciall locks of vowèd haire,
Nor giue each speech a full point of a grone,
The Courtly nymphes, acquainted with the mone
Of them which in their lips Loue's standard beare :
What, he ! (say they of me) : now I dare sweare
He cannot loue ; no, no, let him alone.
And thinke so still, so Stella know my minde ;
Profess in deede I do not Cupid's art ;
But you, fair maides, at length this true shall find,
That his right badge is but worne in the hart :
Dumbe swans, not chattring pies, do louers proue ;
They loue indeed who quake to say they love.

LV.

' Muses . . . holy ayde.'

Muses, I oft inuoked your holy ayde,
With choisest flowers my speech to' engarland so,
That it, despisde, in true but naked shew
Might winne some grace in your sweet grace arraid;
And oft whole troupes of saddest words I staid,
Striuing abroad a-foraging to go,
Vntill by your inspiring I might know
How their blacke banner might be best displaid.
But now I meane no more your helpe to try,
Nor other sugring of my speech to proue,
But on her name incessantly to cry;
For let me but name her whom I doe loue,
So sweet sounds straight mine eare and heart do hit,
That I well finde no eloquence like it.

LVI.

' Patience.'

Fy, schoole of Patience, fy ! your lesson is
Far, far too long to learne it without booke :
What, a whole weeke without one peece of looke,
And thinke I should not your large precepts misse !
When I might reade those letters faire of blisse
Which in her face teach vertue, I could brooke
Somwhat thy lead'n counsels, which I tooke
As of a friend that meant not much amisse.

But now that I, alas, doe want her sight,
What, dost thou thinke that I can euer take
In thy cold stuffe a flegmatike delight?
No, Patience; if thou wilt my good, then make
Her come and heare with patience my desire,
And then with patience bid me beare my fire.

LVII.

'My paines me reioyce.'

Wo hauing made, with many fights, his owne
Each sence of mine, each gift, each power of mind;
Growne now his slaues, he forst them out to find
The thorowest words fit for Woe's selfe to grone,
Hoping that when they might finde Stella 'alone,
Before she could prepare to be vnkind,
Her soule, arm'd but with such a dainty rind,
Should soone be pierc'd with sharpnesse of the mone.
She heard my plaints, and did not onely heare,
But them, so sweet is she, most sweetly sing,
With that faire breast making Woe's darknesse cleare.
A pretie case; I hopèd her to bring
To feele my griefe; and she, with face and voyce,
So sweets my paines, that my paines me reioyce.

LVIII.

'Soueraignty.'

Doubt there hath beene when with his golden chaine
The orator so farre men's hearts doth bind,

That no pace else their guidèd steps can find
But as he them more short or slack doth raine;
Whether with words this souraignty he gaine,
Cloth'd with fine tropes, with strongest reasons lin'd,
Or else pronouncing grace, wherewith his mind
Prints his owne liuely forme in rudest braine.
Now iudge by this: in piercing phrases late
Th' anatomy of all my woes I wrate ;
Stella's sweet breath the same to me did reed.
O voyce, O face ! maugre my speeche's might,
Which wooèd wo, most rauishing delight
Euen those sad words euen in sad me did breed.

LIX.

'More of a dog then me.'

Deere, why make you more of a dog then me?
If he doe loue, I burne, I burne in loue;
If he waite well, I neuer thence would moue;
If he be faire, yet but a dog can be;
Little he is, so little worth is he ;
He barks, my songs thine owne voyce oft doth proue;
Bidd'n, perhaps he fetchèd thee a gloue,
But I, vnbid, fetch euen my soule to thee.
Yet, while I languish, him that bosome clips,
That lap doth lap, nay lets, in spite of spite,
This sowre-breath'd mate taste of those sugred lips.
Alas, if you graunt onely such delight

To witlesse things, then Loue, I hope—since wit
Becomes a clog—will soone ease me of it.

LX.

' Blest in my curse.'

When my good angell guides me to the place
Where all my good I doe in Stella see,
That heau'n of ioyes throwes onely downe on me
Thundring disdaines and lightnings of disgrace ;
But when the ruggedst step of Fortune's race
Makes me fall from her sight, then sweetly she,
With words wherein the Muse's treasures be,
Shewes loue and pitie to my absent case.
Now I, wit-beaten long by hardest fate,
So dull am, that I cannot looke into
The ground of this fierce loue and lovely hate.
Then, some good body, tell me how I do,
Whose presence absence, absence presence is ;
Blest in my curse, and cursèd in my blisse.

LXI.

' Angel's sophistrie.'

Oft with true sighes, oft with vncallèd teares,
Now with slow words, now with dumbe eloquence,
I Stella's eyes assaid, inuade her eares ;
But this, at last, is her sweet-breath'd defence :
That who indeed in-felt affection beares,
So captiues to his saint both soule and sence,
That, wholly hers, all selfenesse he forbeares.

Then his desires he learnes, his liue's course thence.
Now, since her chast mind hates this loue in me,
With chastned mind I straight must shew that she
Shall quickly me from what she hates remoue.
O Doctor Cupid, thou for me reply;
Driu'n else to graunt, by angel's sophistrie,　　=through
That I loue not without I leaue to loue.

LXII.

'Watred was my wine.'

Late tyr'd with wo, euen ready for to pine
With rage of loue, I cald my Loue vnkind;
She in whose eyes loue, though vnfelt, doth shine,
Sweet said, that I true loue in her should find.
I ioyed; but straight thus watred was my wine:
That loue she did, but loued a loue not blind;
Which would not let me, whom shee loued, decline
From nobler course, fit for my birth and mind:
And therefore, by her loue's authority,
Wild me these tempests of vaine loue to flie,
And anchor fast my selfe on Vertue's shore.
Alas, if this the only mettall be
Of loue new-coin'd to helpe my beggery,
Deere, loue me not, that you may loue me more.

LXIII.

' No, no.'

O grammer-rules, O now your vertues show;
So children still reade you with awfull eyes,

As my young doue may, in your precepts wise,
Her graunt to me by her owne vertue know:
For late, with heart most hie, with eyes most lowe,
I crau'd the thing which euer she denies;
Shee, lightning loue, displaying Venus' skies,
Least once should not be heard, twise said, No, no.
Sing then, my Muse, now Io Pæan sing;
Heau'ns enny not at my high triumphing,
But grammer's force with sweete successe confirme:
For grammer says,—O this, deare Stella, say,—
For grammer sayes,—to grammer who sayes nay ?—
That in one speech two negatiues affirme !

LXIV.

'Do not will me from my loue to flie.'

No more, my deare, no more these counsels trie ;
O giue my passions leaue to run their race ;
Let Fortune lay on me her worst disgrace ;
Let folke orecharg'd with braine against me crie ;
Let clouds bedimme my face, breake in mine eye ;
Let me no steps but of lost labour trace ;
Let all the earth with scorne recount my case,—
But do not will me from my loue to flie.
I do not enuie Aristotle's wit,
Nor do aspire to Cæsar's bleeding fame;
Nor ought do care though some aboue me sit ;
Nor hope nor wish another course to frame,

But that which once may win thy cruell hart:
Thou art my wit, and thou my vertue art.

LXV.

' Loue . . . vnkind.'

Loue, by sure proofe I may call thee vnkind,
That giu'st no better ear to my iust cries;
Thou whom to me such my good turnes should bind,
As I may well recount, but none can prize:　　price
For when, nak'd Boy, thou couldst no harbour finde
In this old world, growne now so too-too wise,
I lodg'd thee in my heart, and being blind
By nature borne, I gaue to thee mine eyes;
Mine eyes! my light, my heart, my life, alas!
If so great seruices may scornèd be,
Yet let this thought thy tygrish courage passe,
That I perhaps am somewhat kinne to thee;
Since in thine armes, if learnd fame truth hath spread,
Thou bear'st the arrow, I the arrow-head.

LXVI.

' Hope to feede.'

And do I see some cause a hope to feede,
Or doth the tedious burd'n of long wo
In weakened minds quick apprehending breed
Of euerie image which may comfort show?
I cannot brag of word, much lesse of deed,

Fortune wheeles still with me in one sort slow;
My wealth no more, and no whit lesse my need;
Desier still on stilts of Feare doth go.
And yet amid all feares a hope there is,
Stolne to my hart since last faire night, nay day,
Stella's eyes sent to me the beames of blisse,
Looking on me while I lookt other way:
But when mine eyes backe to their heau'n did moue,
They fled with blush which guiltie seem'd of loue.

LXVII.

'More truth, more paine.'

Hope, art thou true, or doest thou flatter me?
Doth Stella now beginne with pitious eye
The ruines of her conquest to espie?
Will she take time before all wrackèd be?
Her eyes-speech is translated thus by thee,
But failst thou not in phrase so heau'nly hye?
Looke on againe, the faire text better prie;
What blushing notes dost thou in margine see?
What sighes stolne out, or kild before full-borne?
Hast thou found such and such-like arguments,
Or art thou else to comfort me forsworne?
Well, how-so thou interpret the contents,
I am resolu'd thy errour to maintaine,
Rather then by more truth to get more paine.

LXVIII.

' Planet of my light.'

Stella, the onely planet of my light,
Light of my life, and life of my desire,
Chiefe good whereto my hope doth only 'aspire,
World of my wealth, and heau'n of my delight;
Why dost thou spend the treasures of thy sprite
With voice more fit to wed Amphion's lyre,
Seeking to quench in me the noble fire
Fed by thy worth, and kindled by thy sight?
And all in vaine : for while thy breath most sweet
With choisest words, thy words with reasons rare,
Thy reasons firmly set on Vertue's feet,
Labour to kill in me this killing care :
O thinke I then, what paradise of ioy
It is, so faire a vertue to enjoy !

LXIX.

' Couenant.'

O ioy too high for my low stile to show !
O blisse fit for a nobler state then me!
Enuie, put out thine eyes, least thou do see
What oceans of delight in me do flowe !
My friend, that oft saw through all maskes my wo,
Come, come, and let me powre my selfe on thee.
Gone is the Winter of my miserie !
My Spring appeares; O see what here doth grow :

For Stella hath, with words where faith doth shine,
Of her high heart giu'n me the monarchie :
I, I, O I, may say that she is mine!
And though she giue but thus <u>conditionly,</u>
This realme of blisse while vertuous course I take,
No kings be crown'd but they some couenants make.

LXX.

'Wise silence.'

My Muse may well grudge at my heau'nly ioy,
Yf still I force her in sad rimes to creepe :
She oft hath drunk my teares, now hopes to enioy
Nectar of mirth, since I Ioue's cup do keepe.
Sonets be not bound prentise to annoy ;
Trebles sing high, so well as bases deepe ;
Griefe but Loue's winter-liuerie is ; the boy
Hath cheekes to smile, so well as eyes to weepe.
Come then, my Muse, shew thou height of delight
In well-raisde notes ; my pen, the best it may,
Shall paint out ioy, though but in blacke and white.
Cease, eager Muse ; peace, pen, for my sake stay,
I giue you here my hand for truth of this,—
Wise silence is best musicke vnto blisse.

✻ LXXI.

'Inward sunne.'

Who will in fairest booke of Nature know
How vertue may best lodg'd in beautie be,

Let him but learne of Loue to reade in thee,
Stella, those faire lines which true goodnesse show.
There shall he find all vices' ouerthrow,
Not by rude force, but sweetest soueraigntie
Of reason, from whose light those night-birds flie,
That inward sunne in thine eyes shineth so.
And, not content to be Perfection's heire
Thy selfe, doest striue all minds that way to moue,
Who marke in thee what is in thee most faire :
So while thy beautie drawes the heart to loue,
As fast thy vertue bends that loue to good :
But, ah, Desire still cries, Giue me some food.

LXXII.

'My onely Deare.'

Desire, though thou my old companion art,
And oft so clings to my pure loue that I
One from the other scarcely can discrie,
While each doth blowe the fier of my hart ;
Now from thy fellowship I needs must part ;
Venus is taught with Dian's wings to flie;
I must no more in thy sweet passions lie ;
Vertue's gold now must head my Cupid's dart.
Seruice and honour, wonder with delight,
Feare to offend, well worthie to appeare,
Care shining in mine eyes, faith in my sprite ;
These things are left me by my onely Deare :

But thou, Desire, because thou wouldst haue all,
Now bauisht art; but yet, alas, how shall?

LXXIII.

'Kisse.'

Loue, still a Boy, and oft a wanton is,
School'd onely by his mother's tender eye;
What wonder then if he his lesson misse,
When for so soft a rodde deare play he trye?
And yet my Starre, because a sugred kisse   = Stella
In sport I suckt while she asleepe did lye,
Doth lowre, nay chide, nay threat for only this.
Sweet, it was saucie Loue, not humble I.
But no 'scuse serues; she makes her wrath appeare
In Beautie's throne: see now, who dares come neare
Those scarlet Iudges, threatning bloudie paine.
O heau'nly foole, thy most kisse-worthy face
Anger invests with such a louely grace,
That Anger's selfe I needs must kisse againe.

LXXIV.

'I am no pickpurse of another's wit.'

I neuer dranke of Aganippe well,
Nor euer did in shade of Tempe sit,
And Muses scorne with vulgar brains to dwell;
Poore layman I, for sacred rites vnfit.
Some doe I heare of poets' furie tell,

But, God wot, wot not what they meane by it;
And this I sweare by blackest brooke of hell,
I am no pick-purse of another's wit.
How falles it then, that with so smooth an ease
My thoughts I speake; and what I speake doth flow
In verse, and that my verse best wits doth please?
Ghesse we the cause? What, is it this? Fie, no.
Or so? Much lesse. How then? Sure thus it is.
My lips are sweet, inspired with Stella's kisse.

LXXV.

'Edward IV.'

Of all the kings that euer here did raigne,
Edward, named fourth, as first in praise, I name:
Not for his faire outside, nor well-lined braine,
Although lesse gifts impe feathers oft on fame. join, add on
Nor that he could, young-wise, wise-valiant, frame
His sire's reuenge, ioyn'd with a kingdome's gaine;
And gain'd by Mars, could yet mad Mars so tame,
That balance weigh'd, what sword did late obtaine.
Nor that he made the floure-de-luce so 'fraid,
Though strongly hedg'd of bloudy lyons' pawes,
That wittie Lewes to him a tribute paid: wise
Nor this, nor that, nor any such small cause;
But only for this worthy knight durst proue
To lose his crowne, rather then faile his loue.

LXXVI.

' Gentle force.'

She comes, and streight therewith her shining twins do
    moue
Their rayes to me, who in their tedious absence lay
Benighted in cold wo; but now appears my day,
The onely light of ioy, the only warmth of loue.
She comes with light and warmth, which, like Aurora,
    proue
Of gentle force, so that mine eyes dare gladly play
With such a rosie morne, whose beames, most freshly
    gay,
Scorch not, but onely doe dark chilling sprites remoue.
But, lo, while I do speake, it groweth noone with me,
Her flamie-glistring lights increase with time and place,
My heart cries, ah! it burnes, mine eyes now dazled be;
No wind, no shade can coole : what helpe then in my
    case?
But with short breath, long looks, staid feet, and aching
    hed,
Pray that my sunne goe downe with meeker beames to
    bed.

LXXVII.

' A meane price.'

Those lookes, whose beames be ioy, whose motion is
    delight;
That face, whose lecture shews what perfect beauty is;

That presence, which doth giue darke hearts a liuing
    light;·   [misse;
That grace, which Venus weeps that she her selfe doth
That hand, which without touch holds more then Atlas
    might;   than
Those lips, which make death's pay a meane price for
    a kisse;
That skin, whose passe-praise hue scornes this poor
    tearm of white;
Those words, which do sublime the quintessence of
    bliss;
That voyce, which makes the soule plant himselfe in
    the eares;
That conuersation sweet, where such high comforts be,
As, consterd in true speech, the name of heav'n it
    beares;
Makes me in my best thoughts and quietst iudgments
    see
That in no more but these I might be fully blest:
Yet, ah, my mayd'n Muse doth blush to tell the best.

LXXVIII.

·'Ielousie.'

O how the pleasant ayres of true loue be
Infected by those vapours which arise
From out that noysome gulfe, which gaping lies
Betweene the iawes of hellish Ielousie!
A monster, others' harme, selfe-miserie,

Beautie's plague, Vertue's scourge, succour of lies ;
Who his owne ioy to his owne hurt applies,
And onely cherish doth with injurie :
Who since he hath, by Nature's speciall grace,
So piercing pawes as spoyle when they embrace ;
So nimble feet as stirre still, though on thornes ;
So many eyes, ay seeking their owne woe ;
So ample eares as neuer good newes know :
Is it not euill that such a diuell wants hornes ?

LXXIX.

' Sweetnesse.'

Sweet kisse, thy sweets I faine would sweetly' endite,
Which, euen of sweetnesse sweetest sweetner art ;
Pleasingst consort, where each sence holds a part ;
Which, coupling doues, guides Venus' chariot right.
Best charge, and brauest retrait in Cupid's fight ;
A double key, which opens to the heart,
Most rich when most his riches it impart ;
Nest of young ioyes, schoolmaster of delight,
Teaching the meane at once to take and giue ;
The friendly fray, where blowes both wound and heale,
The prettie death, while each in other liue.
Poore hope's first wealth, ostage of promist weale ;
Breakefast of loue.   But lo, lo, where she is,
Cease we to praise ; now pray we for a kisse.

LXXX.

'Sweet lipp.'

Sweet-swelling lip, well maist thou swell in pride,
Since best wits thinke it wit thee to admire;
Nature's praise, Vertue's stall; Cupid's cold fire,
Whence words, not words but heav'nly graces slide;
The new Pernassus, where the Muses bide;
Sweetner of musicke, Wisedome's beautifier,
Breather of life, and fastner of desire,
Where Beautie's blush in Honor's graine is dide.
Thus much my heart compeld my mouth to say;
But now, spite of my heart, my mouth will stay,
Loathing all lies, doubting this flatterie is :
And no spurre can his resty race renewe,
Without, how farre this praise is short of you,
Sweet lipp, you teach my mouth with one sweet kisse.

LXXXI.

'Still, still kiss.'

O kisse, which dost those ruddie gemmes impart,
Or gemmes or fruits of new-found Paradise,
Breathing all blisse, and sweetning to the heart,
Teaching dumbe lips a nobler exercise ;—
O kisse, which soules, euen soules, together ties
By linkes of loue and only Nature's art,
How faine would I paint thee to all men's eyes,
Or of thy gifts at least shade out some part!

But she forbids; with blushing words she sayes
She builds her fame on higher-seated praise.
But my heart burnes; I cannot silent be.
Then, since, dear life, you faine would haue me peace,
And I, mad with delight, want wit to cease,
Stop you my mouth with still, still kissing me.

LXXXII.

'Cherries.'

Nymph of the gard'n where all beauties be,—
Beauties which do in excellencie passe
His who till death lookt in a watrie glasse,
Or hers whom nakd the Troian boy did see;　　Venus
Sweet-gard'n-nymph, which keepes the cherrie-tree
Whose fruit doth farre th' Esperian tast surpasse,
Most sweet-faire, most faire-sweete, do not, alas,
From comming neare those cherries banish mee.
For though, full of desire, empty of wit,
Admitted late by your best-gracèd grace,
I caught at one of them, and hungry bit;
Pardon that fault; once more grant me the place;
And I do sweare, euen by the same delight,
I will but kisse; I neuer more will bite.

LXXXIII.

To a Sparrow.

Good brother Philip, I haue borne you long;
I was content you should in fauour creepe,
While craftely you seem'd your cut to keepe,

As though that faire soft hand did you great wrong:
I bare with enuie, yet I bare your song,
When in her necke you did loue-ditties peepe;
Nay—more foole I—oft suffered you to sleepe
In lillies' neast where Loue's selfe lies along.
What, doth high place ambitious thoughts augment?
Is sawcinesse reward of curtesie?
Cannot such grace your silly selfe content,
But you must needs with those lips billing be,
And through those lips drinke nectar from that toong?
Leaue that, Syr Phip, least off your neck be wroong!

LXXXIV.

' My Muse.'

High way, since you my chiefe Pernassus be,
And that my Muse, to some eares not vnsweet,
Tempers her words to trampling horses' feete
More oft then to a chamber-melodie.
Now, blessèd you beare onward blessèd me
To her, where I my heart, safe-left, shall meet;
My Muse and I must you of dutie greet
With thankes and wishes, wishing thankfully.
Be you still faire, honourd by publicke heed
By no encrochment wrong'd, nor time forgo
Nor blam'd for bloud, nor sham'd for sinfull need;
And that you know I enuy you no lot
Of highest wish, I wish you so much bliss,—
Hundreds of yeares you Stella's feet may kisse.

LXXXV.
'Kingly tribute.'

I see the house,—my heart thy selfe containe!
Beware full sailes drowne not thy tottring barge,
Least ioy, by nature apt sprites to enlarge,
Thee to thy wracke beyond thy limits straine;
Nor do like lords whose weake confusèd braine,
Not 'pointing to fit folkes each vndercharge,   =appointing
While euerie office themselues will discharge,
With doing all, leaue nothing done but paine.
But giue apt seruants their due place: let eyes
See beautie's totall summe summ'd in her face;
Let eares heare speach which wit to wonder ties;
Let breath sucke vp those sweetes; let armes embrace
The globe of weale, lips Lou's indentures make;
Thou but of all the kingly tribute take.

LXXXVI.
'Sweet Iudge.'

Alas, whence came this change of lookes? If I
Haue chang'd desert, let mine owne conscience be
A still-felt plague to selfe-condemning mee;
Let woe gripe on my heart, shame loade mine eye:
But if all faith, like spotlesse ermine, ly
Safe in my soule, which only doth to thee,
As his sole obiect of felicitie,
With wings of loue in aire of wonder flie,
O ease your hand, treate not so hard your slave

In iustice paines come not till faults do call:
Or if I needs, sweet Iudge, must torments haue,
Vse something else to chast'n me withall
Then those blest eyes, where all my hopes do dwell:
No doome should make one's heau'n become his hell.

LXXXVII.

'Duetie to depart.'

When I was forst from Stella euer deere—
Stella, food of my thoughts, hart of my hart—   heart
Stella, whose eyes make all my tempests cleere—
By Stella's lawes of duetie to depart;
Alas, I found that she with me did smart;
I saw that teares did in her eyes appeare;
I sawe that sighes her sweetest lips did part,
And her sad words my sadded sense did heare.
For me, I wept to see pearles scattered so;
I sigh'd her sighes, and wailèd for her wo;
Yet swam in ioy, such loue in her was seene.
Thus, while th' effect most bitter was to me,
And nothing then the cause more sweet could be,
I had bene vext, if vext I had not beene.

LXXXVIII.

'Absence.'

Ont, traytor Absence, darest thou counsell me
From my deare captainesse to run away,

Because in braue array heere marcheth she,
That, to win mee, oft shewes a present pay?
Is faith so weake? or is such force in thee?
When sun is hid, can starres such beames display?
Cannot heav'n's food, once felt, keepe stomakes free
From base desire on earthly cates to pray?   prey
Tush, Absence; while thy mistes eclipse that light,
My orphan sense flies to the inward sight,
Where memory sets foorth the beames of loue;
That, where before hart loued and eyes did see,
In hart both sight and loue now couplèd be:
Vnited powers make each the stronger proue.

LXXXIX.

'Day and Night.'

Now that of absence the most irksom night
With darkest shade doth ouercome my day;
Since Stella's eyes, wont to giue me my day,
Leauing my hemisphere, leaue me in night;
Each day seemes long, and longs for long-staid night;
The night, as tedious, wooes th' approch of day:
Tired with the dusty toiles of busie day,
Languisht with horrors of the silent night;
Suffering the euils both of day and night,
While no night is more darke then is my day,
Nor no day hath lesse quiet then my night:
With such bad mixture of my night and day,

That liuing thus in blackest Winter night,
I feele the flames of hottest Sommer day. .

XC.

'Fame.'

Stella, thinke not that I by verse seeke fame,
Who seeke, who hope, who loue, who liue but thee;
Thine eyes my pride, thy lips mine history :
If thou praise not, all other praise is shame.
Nor so ambitious am I, as to frame
A nest for my young praise in lawrell tree :
In truth, I sweare I wish not there should be
Graued in my epitaph a Poet's name.
Ne, if I would, could I iust title make,
That any laud thereof to me should growe,
Without my plumes from others' wings I take :
For nothing from my wit or will doth flow, -
Since all my words thy beauty doth endite,
And Loue doth hold my hand, and makes me write.

XCI.

' You in them I love.'

Stella, while now, by Honour's cruell might,
I am from you, light of my life, misled,
And whiles,—faire you, my sunne, thus ouerspred
With Absence' vaile,—I liue in Sorrowe's night ;
If this darke place yet shewe like candle-light,

Some beautie's peece, as amber-colour'd hed,   head
Milke hands, rose cheeks, or lips more sweet, more red;
Or seeings jet-blacke but in blacknesse bright;
They please, I do confesse they please mine eyes.
But why? because of you they models be;
Models, such be wood-globes of glist'ring skies.
Deere, therefore be not iealous ouer me,
If you heare that they seeme my heart to moue;
Not them, O no, but you in them I loue.

XCII.

' All said, still say the same.'

Be your words made, good Sir, of Indian ware,
That you allow me them by so small rate?
Or do you curtted Spartanes imitate?
Or do you meane my tender eares to spare,
That to my questions you so totall are?
When I demaund of Phœnix-Stella's state,
You say, forsooth, you left her well of late:
O God, thinke you that satisfies my care?
I would know whether she did sit or walke;
How cloth'd; how waited on; sigh'd she, or smilde;
Whereof,—with whom,—how often did she talke;
With what pastimes Time's iourney she beguilde;
If her lips daignd to sweeten my poore name.
Saie all; and all well sayd, still say the same.

XCIII.

'Tho' worlds 'quite me, shall I my selfe forgiue?'

O fate, O fault, O curse, child of my blisse !
What sobs can giue words grace my griefe to show ?
What inke is blacke inough to paint my woe?
Through me—wretch me—euen Stella vexèd is.
Yet, truth—if caitif's breath may call thee—this
Witnesse with me, that my foule stumbling so,
From carelesnesse did in no maner grow ;
But wit, confus'd with too much care, did misse.
And do I, then, my selfe this vaine 'scuse giue?
I haue—live I, and know this—harmèd thee;
Tho' worlds 'quite me, shall I my selfe forgiue?
Only with paines my paines thus easèd be,
That all thy hurts in my hart's wracke I reede;
I cry thy sighs, my deere, thy teares I bleede.

XCIV.

'Griefe.'

Griefe, find the words; for thou hast made my braine
So darke with misty vapours, which arise
From out thy heauy mould, that inbent eyes
Can scarce discerne the shape of mine owne paine.
Do thou, then—for thou canst—do thou complaine
For my poore soule, which now that sicknesse tries,
Which euen to sence, sence of it selfe denies,
Though harbengers of death lodge there his traine.

Or if thy loue of plaint yet mine forbeares,
As of a caitife worthy so to die;
Yet waile thy selfe, and waile with causefull teares,
That though in wretchednesse thy life doth lie,
Yet growest more wretched then thy nature beares
By being placed in such a wretch as I.

XCV.

' Sighes.'

Yet sighes, deare sighs, indeede true friends you are,
That do not leaue your left friend at the wurst,
But, as you with my breast I oft haue nurst,
So, gratefull now, you waite vpon my care.
Faint coward Ioy no longer tarry dare,
Seeing Hope yeeld when this wo strake him furst;
Delight exclaims he is for my fault curst,
Though oft himselfe my mate in arms he sware;
Nay, Sorrow comes with such maine rage, that he
Kils his owne children—teares—finding that they
By Loue were made apt to consort with me.
Only, true sighs, you do not goe away:
Thanke may you haue for such a thankfull part,
Thank-worthiest yet when you shall breake my hart.

           [heart

XCVI.

' Thought.'

Thought, with good cause thou likest so well the night,
Since kind or chance giues both one liuerie,

Both sadly blacke, both blackly darkned be;   [barred
Night bard'from sun, thou from thy owne sunlight;
Silence in both displaies his sullen might ;
Slow heauinesse in both holds òne degree—
That full of doubts, thou of perplexity;
Thy teares expresse Night's natiue moisture right ;
In both amazeful solitarinesse :
In night, of sp'rites the gastly powers do stur ;   ghastly
In thee, or sp'rites or sp'rited gastlinesse.
But, bùt, alas, Night's side the ods hath fur;   far
For that, at length, yet doth inuite some rest ;
Thou, though still tired, yet still doost it detest.

XCVII.

' Dian's peere.'

Dian, that faine would cheare her friend the Night,
Shewes her oft, at the full, her fairest face,
Bringing with her those starry nymphs, whose chace
From heauenly standing hits each mortall wight.
But ah, poore Night, in loue with Phœbus' light,
And endlesly dispairing of his grace,
Her selfe—to shewe no other ioy hath place—
Sylent and sad, in mourning weedes doth dight.
Euen so, alas, a lady, Dian's peere,
With choise delights and rarest company
Would faine driue cloudes from out my heavy cheere;
But, wo is me, though Ioy her selfe were she,

Shee could not shew my blind braine waies of ioy,
While I despaire my sunne's sight to enioy.

XCVIII.

' Loue's Spur.'

Ah, bed ! the field where Ioye's peace some do see,   *o*
The field where all my thoughts to warre be train'd, *b*
How is thy grace by my strange fortune strain'd ! *b*
How thy lee-shores by my sighes stormèd be! *a*
With sweete soft shades thou oft inuitest me   *a*
To steale some rest ; but, wretch, I am constrained—
Spurd with Loue's spur, though gald, and shortly
            rain'd   reined
With Care's hard hand—to turne and tosse in thee, *a*
While the blacke horrors of the silent night   *c*
Paint Woe's blacke face so liuely to my sight, *c*
That tedious leasure markes each wrinkled line: *d*
But when Aurora leades out Phœbus' daunce,   *e*
Mine eyes then only winke; for spite, perchaunce, *e*
That wormes should haue their sun, and I want mine.

XCIX.

' Sleep's Armory.'

When far-spent Night perswades each mortall eye, *a*
To whome nor Art nor Nature graunteth light, *b*
To lay his then marke-wanting shafts of sight, *b*
Clos'd with their quiuers, in Sleep's armory ; *b*

With windowes ope, then most my mind doth lie, *a*
Viewing the shape of darknesse, and delight *b*
Takes in that sad hue, which, with th' inward night *b*
Of his mazde powers, keepes perfet harmony : *a*
But when birds charme, and that sweete aire which is *c*
Morne's messenger, with rose-enameld skies *d*
Cals each wight to salute the floure of blisse ; *c*
In tombe of lids then buried are mine eyes, *d*
Forst by their lord, who is asham'd to find *e*
Such light in sense, with such a darkned mind. *e*

C.

' All mirth farewell.'

O teares ! no teares, but raine, from Beautie's skies,
Making those lillies and those roses growe,
Which ay most faire, now more then most faire show,
While gratefull Pitty Beautie beautifies.
O honied sighs ! which from that breast do rise,
Whose pants do make vnspilling creame to flow,
Wing'd with whose breath, so doth zephires blow,
As might refresh the hell where my soule fries.
O plaints ! conseru'd in such a sugred phrase,
That Eloquence itself enuies your praise,
While sobd-out words a perfect musike giue.
Such teares, sighs, plaints, no sorrow is, but ioy :
Or if such heauenly signes must proue annoy,
All mirth farewell, let me in sorrow liue.

CI.

'Stella is sicke.'

Stella is sicke, and in that sicke-bed lies
Sweetnesse, which breathes and pants as oft as she :
And Grace, sicke too, such fine conclusion tries,
That Sickenesse brags it selfe best graced to be.
Beauty is sicke, but sicke in so faire guise,
That in that palenesse Beautie's white we see ;
And Ioy, which is inseparate from those eyes,
Stella, now learnes, strange case, to weepe in me.
Loue mones thy paine, and like a faithfull page,
As thy lookes sturre, runs vp and downe, to make
All folkes prest at thy will thy paine to swage ;
Nature with care sweates for her darling's sake,
Knowing worlds passe, ere she enough can finde,
Of such heauen-stuffe to cloath so heauenly a minde.

CII.

'It is but loue.'

Where be those roses gone, which sweetned so our eyes?
Where those red cheeks, which oft, with faire encrease,
            did frame
The height of honour in the kindly badge of shame?
Who hath the crimson weeds stolne from my morning
            skies?
How doth the colour vade of those vermilion dies,

Which Nature' selfe did make, and self-ingrain'd the
  same?
I would know by what right this palenesse ouercame
That hue, whose force my hart still unto thraldome
  ties?
Galen's adoptiue sonnes, who by a beaten way
Their iudgements hackney on, the fault of sicknesse
  lay;
But feeling proofe makes me say they mistake it furre :
It is but loue which makes this paper perfit white,
To write therein more fresh the storie of delight,
Whiles Beautie's reddest inke Venus for him doth
  sturre.

CIII.

' Golden Haire.'

O happie Thames, that didst my Stella beare !
I saw thee with full many a smiling line
Vpon thy cheerefull face, Ioye's liuery weare,
While those faire planets on thy streames did shine.
The boate for ioy could not to daunce forbear,
While wanton winds, with beauties so diuine
Rauisht, staid not, till in her golden haire
They did themselues, O sweetest prison, twine.
And faine those Æol's youth there would their stay
Haue made, but forst by Nature still to flie,
First did with puffing kisse those lockes display :
She, so disheuld blusht : from window I   disheuelled

With sight thereof cride out, 'O faire disgrace,
Let Honor' selfe to thee grant highest place.'

CIV.

'Enuious wits.'

Enuious wits, what hath bene mine offence,
That with such poysonous care my lookes you marke,
That to each word, nay sigh of mine, you harke,
As grudging me my sorrowe's eloquence?
Ah, is it not enough, that I am thence,
Thence, so farre thence, that scantly any sparke
Of comfort dare come to this dungeon darke,
Where Rigour's exile lockes vp al my sense?
But if I by a happie window passe,
If I but stars vppon mine armour beare;
Sicke, thirsty, glad (though but of empty glasse):
Your morall notes straight my hid meaning teare
From out my ribs, and, puffing, proues that I
Doe Stella loue: fooles, who doth it deny?

CV.

'Unhappie.'

Vnhappie sight, and hath shee vanisht by
So nere, in so good time, so free a place!
Dead glasse, dost thou thy obiect so imbrace,
As what my hart still sees thou canst not spie!   heart
I sweare by her loue and lacke, that I

Was not in fault, who bent thy dazling race
Onely vnto the heau'n of Stella's face,
Counting but dust what in the way did lie.
But cease, mine eyes, your teares do witnesse well
That you, guiltlesse thereof, your nectar mist :
Curst be the page from whome the bad torch fell :
Curst be the night which did your strife resist :
Curst be the coachman that did driue so fast,
With no lesse curse then absence makes me tast.

CVI.

'Absent presence.'

O absent presence! Stella is not here ; ‿
False-flattering hope, that with so faire a face ♭
Bare me in hand, that in this orphane place, ♪
Stella, I say my Stella, should appeare : ‿
What saist thou now? where is that dainty cheere ～
Thou told'st mine eyes should helpe their famisht case ? ♭
But thou art gone, now that selfe-felt disgrace ‿
Doth make me most to wish thy comfort neere. ～
But heere I do store of faire ladies meete, ‿
Who may with charme of conuersation sweete ‿
Make in my heauy mould new thoughts to grow. ⌐
Sure they preuaile as much with me, as he ‿
That bad his friend, but then new maim'd to be ‿ bade
Mery with him, and so forget his woe. ⌐

CVII.

'See what it is to loue.'

Stella, since thou so right a princesse art
Of all the powers which life bestowes on me,
That ere by them ought vndertaken be,
They first resort vnto that soueraigne part;
Sweete, for a while giue respite to my heart,
Which pants as though it stil should leape to thee:
And on my thoughts giue thy lieuetenancie
To this great cause, which needes both use and art.
And as a queene, who from her presence sends
Whom she imployes, dismisse from thee my wit,
Till it haue wrought what thy owne will attends.
On seruants' shame oft maister's blame doth sit:
O, let not fooles in me thy workes reproue,
And scorning say, 'See what it is to loue!'

CVIII.

'Dead Despaire.'

When Sorrow (vsing mine owne fier's might)
Melts downe his lead into my boyling brest,
Through that darke furnace to my hart opprest,
There shines a ioy from thee my only light:
But soone as thought of thee breeds my delight,
And my yong soule flutters to thee his nest,
Most rude Despaire, my daily 'vnbidden guest,
Clips streight my wings, streight wraps me in his night,

And makes me then bow downe my heade, and say,
Ah, what doth Phœbus' gold that wretch auaile
Whom iron doores doe keepe from vse of day ?
So strangely, 'alas, thy works in me preuaile,
That in my woes for thee thou art my ioy,
And in my ioyes for thee my onely 'anoy.

CIX.

' Desire.'

Thou blind man's marke, thou foole's self-chosen snare,
Fond fancie's scum, and dregs of scattered thought:
Band of all euils; cradle of causelesse care;
Thou web of will, whose end is neuer wrought:
Desire! Desire! I haue too dearly bought,
With prise of mangled mind, thy worthlesse ware;
Too long, too long, asleepe thou hast me brought,
Who shouldst my mind to higher things prepare.
But yet in vaine thou hast my ruine sought;
In vaine thou madest me to vaine things aspire;
In vaine thou kindlest all thy smokie fire;
For Vertue hath this better lesson taught,—
Within myselfe to seeke my onelie hire,
Desiring nought but how to kill Desire.

CX.

' Aspire to higher things.'

Leaue me, O Loue, which reachest but to dust;
And thou, my mind, aspire to higher things;

Grow rich in that which never taketh rust; ⌣
Whateuer fades, but fading pleasure brings. ♭
Draw in thy beames, and humble all thy might ⌣
To that sweet yoke where lasting freedomes be; ⌣
Which breakes the clowdes, and opens forth the light,
That doth both shine, and giue us sight to see. ⌣
O take fast hold; let that light be thy guide ⌣
In this small course which birth drawes out to death, ⌣
And thinke how euill becommeth him to slide, ⌣
Who seeketh heau'n, and comes of heau'nly breath. ⌣
Then farewell, world; thy vttermost I see: ⌣
Eternall Loue, maintaine thy life in me. ⌣

Splendidis Longum Valedico Nugis.

SONGS

IN

ASTROPHEL AND STELLA.

FIRST SONG.

I. Doubt you to whom my Muse these notes en-
   tendeth,
   Which now my breast, surcharg'd, to musick
   lendeth!
   To you, to you, all song of praise is due,
   Only in you my song begins and endeth.

II. Who hath the eyes which marrie state with plea-
    sure!
    Who keeps the key of Nature's chiefest treasure!
    To you, to you, all song of praise is due,
    Only for you the heau'n forgate all measure.

III. Who hath the lips, where wit in fairenesse raign-
     eth!
     Who womankind at once both deckes and stayn-
     eth!
     To you, to you, all song of praise is due,
     Onely by you Cupid his crowne maintaineth.

IV. Who hath the feet, whose step all sweetnesse
    planteth!
    Who else, for whom Fame worthy trumpets want-
    eth!

To you, to you, all song of praise is due,
Onely to you her scepter Venus granteth.

v. Who hath the breast, whose milk doth patience
    nourish !
Whose grace is such, that when it chides doth
    cherish !
To you, to you, all song of praise is due,
Onelie through you the tree of life doth flourish.

vi. Who hath the hand which, without stroke, sub-
    dueth !
Who long-dead beautie with increase reneueth !
To you, to you, all song of praise is due,
Onely at you all enuie hopelesse rueth.

vii. Who hath the haire, which, loosest, fastest tieth !
Who makes a man liue, then glad when he dieth!
To you, to you, all song of praise is due,
Only of you the flatterer neuer lieth.

viii. Who hath the voyce, which soule from sences
    sunders !
Whose force, but yours, the bolts of beautie thun-
    ders !
To you, to you, all song of praise is due,
Only with you not miracles are wonders.

ix. Doubt you, to whome my Muse these notes in-
    tendeth,

Which now my breast, orecharged, to musicke
    lendeth !
To you, to you, all song of praise iȘ due :
Only in you my song begins and endeth.

SECOND SONG.

  I. Haue I caught my heau'nly iewell,
     Teaching Sleepe most faire to be!
     Now will I teach her that she,
     When she wakes, is too-too cruell.

  II. Since sweet Sleep her eyes hath charmèd,
     The two only darts of Loue,
     Now will I, with that Boy, proue,
     Some play, while he is disarmèd.

  III. Her tongue, waking, still refuseth,
     Giuing frankly niggard no:
     Now will I attempt to know
     What no her tongue, sleeping, vseth.

  IV. See the hand that, waking, gardeth,   guardeth
     Sleeping, grants a free resort :
     Now will I inuade the fort,
     Cowards Loue with losse rewardeth.

  V. But, O foole, thinke of the danger
     Of her iust and high disdaine;
     Now will I, alas, refraine ;
     Loue feares nothing else but anger.

VI. Yet those lips, so sweetly swelling,
Do inuite a stealing kisse.
Now will I but venture this ;
Who will reade, must first learne spelling.

VII. Oh, sweet kisse! but ah, she's waking;
Lowring beautie chastens me :
Now will I for feare hence flee;
Foole, more foole, for no more taking.

THIRD SONG.

I. If Orpheus' voyce had force to breathe such mu-
sick's loue
Through pores of senceles trees, as it could make
them moue ;
If stones good measure daunc'd, the Theban walles
to build
To cadence of the tunes which Amphion's lyre did
yeeld;
More cause a like effect at least-wise bringeth :
O stones, O trees, learne hearing,—Stella singeth.

II. If loue might sweet'n so a boy of shepheard brood,
To make lyzard dull, to taste loue's dainty food;
If eagle fierce could so in Grecian mayde delight,
As her eyes were his light, her death his endlesse
night,—

Earth gaue that loue; heav'n, I trow, loue re-
fineth,—

O beasts, O birds, looke loue,—lo, Stella shineth.

III. The beasts, birds, stones, and trees feele this, and,
feeling, loue;

And if the trees nor stones stirre not the same to
proue,

Nor beasts nor birds do come vnto this blessèd
gaze,

. Know that small loue is quicke, and great loue
doth amaze;

They are amaz'd, but you with reason armed,

O eyes, O eares of men, how are you charmed!

FOURTH SONG.

I. Onely Ioy, now here you are,
Fit to heare and ease my care,
Let my whispering voyce obtaine
Sweete reward for sharpest paine;
Take me to thee, and thee to mee:
' No, no, no, no, my Deare, let bee.'

II. Night hath closde all in her cloke,
Twinkling starres loue-thoughts prouoke,
Danger hence, good care doth keepe,
Iealouzie himselfe doth sleepe;
Take me to thee, and thee to mee:
' No, no, no, no, my Deare, let bee.'

III. Better place no wit can finde,
Cupid's knot to loose or binde ;
These sweet flowers our fine bed too,
Vs in their best language woo :
Take me to thee, and thee to mee : ~
' No, no, no, no, my Deare, let bee.'

IV. This small light the moone bestowes
Serues thy beames but to disclose ;
So to raise my hap more hie,
Feare not else, none can vs spie ;
Take me to thee, and thee to mee :
' No, no, no, no, my Deare, let bee.'

V. That you heard was but a mouse,
Dumbe Sleepe holdeth all the house :
Yet asleepe, me thinkes they say,
Yong fooles take time while you may ;
Take me to thee, and thee to mee :
' No, no, no, no, my Deare, let bee.'

VI. Niggard time threates, if we misse
This large offer of our blisse,
Long stay, ere he graunt the same :
Sweet, then, while ech thing doth frame,
Take me to thee, and thee to mee :
' No, no, no, no, my Deare, let bee.'

VII. Your faire mother is a-bed,
Candles out and curtaines spread ;

She thinkes you do letters write;
Write, but first let me endite;
Take me to thee, and thee to mee:
' No, no, no, no, my Deare, let bee.'

VIII. Sweete, alas, why striue you thus?
Concord better fitteth vs;
Leaue to Mars the force of hands,
Yonr power in your beautie stands;
Take thee to me, and me to thee:
' No, no, no, no, my Deare, let bee.'

IX. Wo to mee, and do you sweare
Me to hate? but I forbeare;   unless
Cursèd be my destines all,   destinies
That brought me so high to fall;
Soone with my death I will please thee:
' No, no, no, no, my Deare, let bee.'

FIFT SONG.

I. While fauour fed my hope, delight with hope was
    brought,
Thought waited on delight, and speech did follow
    thought;
Then grew my tongue and pen records vnto thy
    glory,
I thought all words were lost that were not spent
    of thee,

I thought each place was darke but where thy
lights would be,
And all cares worse then deafe that heard not out
thy storie.

ii. I said thou wert most faire, aud so indeed thou
art;
I said thou wert most sweet, sweet poison to my
heart;
I said my soule was thine, O that I then had lyed;
I said thine eyes were starres, thy breast the milk'n
way,
Thy fingers Cupid's shafts, thy voyce the angels'
lay:
And all I said so well, as no man it denied.

iii. But now that hope is lost, vnkindnesse kils delight;
Yet thought and speech do liue, though metamorphos'd quite,
For rage now rules the raines which guided were
by pleasure;
I thinke now of thy faults, who late thought of
thy praise,
That speech falles now to blame, which did thy
honour raise,
The same key ope'n can, which can locke up a
treasure.

IV. Then thou, whom partiall heauens conspir'd in
    one to frame
The proofe of Beautie's worth, th' inheritrix of
    fame,
The mansion state of blisse, and iust excuse of
    louers;
See now those feathers pluckt, wherewith thou
    flewest most high:
See what cloudes of reproch shall dark thy hon-
    our's skie:
Whose owne fault cast him downe hardly high
    state recouers.

v. And, O my Muse, though oft you luld her in your
    lap,
And then a heau'nly child, gaue her ambrosian
    pap,
And to that braine of hers your kindest gifts
    infused ;
Since she, disdaining me, doth you in me disdaine,
Suffer not her to laugh, while both we suffer paine.
Princes in subiects' wrong must deeme themselves
    abused.

VI. Your client, poore my selfe, shall Stella handle so!
Reuenge! reuenge! my Muse! defiance' trumpet
    blow;
Threat'n! what may be done, yet do more then
    you threaten ;

Ah, my sute granted is, I feele my breast doth
swell;
Now, child, a lesson new you shall begin to spell,
Sweet babes must babies haue, but shrewd gyrles
must be beat'n.   dolls

VII. Thinke now no more to heare of warme fine-
odour'd snow,
Nor blushing lillies, nor pearles' ruby-hidden row,
Nor of that golden sea, whose waues in curles are
brok'n ;
But of thy soule, so fraught with such vngratefulnesse,
As where thou soone might'st helpe, most faith
dost most oppresse;
Vngratefull, who is cald, the worst of euils is
spok'n ;

VIII. Yet worse then worst, I say thou art a theefe—
A theefe !
Now God forbid ! a theefe ! and of worst theeues
the cheefe :
Theeues steal for need, and steale but goods which
paine recouers,
But thou, rich in all ioyes, dost rob my ioyes from
me,
Which cannot be restor'd by time or industrie:
Of foes the spoile is euill, far worse of constant
louers.

Of herbes or beasts which Inde or Affrike hold.
For me, in sooth, no Muse but one I know;
Phrases and problemes from my reach do grow;
And strange things cost too deare for my poore sprites:
How then? euen thus,—in Stella's face I reed   read
What Loue and Beautie be; then all my deed
But copying is, what, in her, Nature writes.

IV.

'Vertue, thou thy selfe shalt be in loue.'

Vertue, alas, now let me take some rest;
Thou set'st a bate betweene my will and wit;
If vaine Loue haue my simple soule opprest,
Leaue what thou likest not, deale not thou with it.
Thy scepter vse in some olde Catoe's brest,
Churches or Schooles are for thy seat more fit;
I do confesse—pardon a fault confest—
My mouth too tender is for thy hard bit.
But if that needes thou wilt vsurping be
The little reason that is left in me,
And still th' effect of thy perswasions prooue,
I sweare, my heart such one shall shew to thee,
That shrines in flesh so true a deitie,
That, Vertue, thou thy selfe shalt be in loue.

V.

'True beautie vertue is.'

It is most true that eyes are form'd to serue
The inward light, and that the heauenly part

Ought to be King, from whose rules who do swerue,
Rebels to nature, striue for their owne smart.
It is most true, what we call Cupid's dart
An image is, which for ourselues we carue,
And, fooles, adore in temple of our hart,
Till that good god make church and churchman starue.
True, that true beautie vertue is indeed,
Whereof this beautie can be but a shade,
Which, elements with mortall mixture breed.
True, that on earth we are but pilgrims made,
And should in soule vp to our countrey moue:
True, and yet true—that I must Stella loue.

VI.

'I do Stella love.'

Some louers speake, when they their Muses entertaine,
Of hopes begot by feare, of wot not what desires,
Of force of heavnly beames infusing hellish paine,
Of liuing deaths, dere wounds, faire storms, and frees-
          ing fires: [tires,
Some one his song in Ioue and Ioue's strange tales at-
Bordred with buls and swans, powdred with golden
          raine:
Another, humbler wit, to shepheard's pipe retires,
Yet hiding royall bloud full oft in rurall vaine.   vein
To some a sweetest plaint a sweetest stile affords,
While teares poure out his inke, and sighes breathe out
          his words,

His paper pale despaire, and pain his pen doth moue.
I can speake what I feele, and feele as much as they,
But thinke that all the map of my state I display
When trembling voyce brings forth, that I do Stella loue.

VII.

'Stella's eyes in colour black.'

When Nature made her chiefe worke, Stella's eyes,   *a*
In colour blacke why wrapt she beames so bright?   *b*
Would she, in beamy blacke, like Painter wise,   *a*
Frame daintiest lustre, mixt of shades and light?   *b*
Or did she else that sober hue deuise,   *a*
In obiect best to knitt and strength our sight;   *b*
Least, if no vaile these braue gleames did disguise,   *a*
They, sunlike, should more dazle then delight?   *b*
Or would she her miraculous power show,   *c*
That, whereas blacke seemes Beautie's contrary,   *d*
She euen in blacke doth make all beauties flow?   *c*
Both so, and thus,—she, minding Loue should be   *d*
Placed euer there, gaue him this mourning weede   *e*
To honor all their deathes who for her bleed.   *e*

VIII.

'Love . . . in my close heart.'

Loue, borne in Greece, of late fléd from his nátiue pláce,
Forct, by a tedious proofe, that Turkish hardned hárt
Is nót fit márke to pierce with his fiñe-póinted dárt;

And, pleas'd with our soft peace, staide here his flying
race:
But, finding these north clymes too coldly him embrace,
Not vsde to frozen clips, he straue to finde some part
Where with most ease and warmth he might employ
his art;
At length he perch'd himselfe in Stella's ioyfull face,
Whose faire skin, beamy eyes, like morning sun on snow,
Deceiu'd the quaking boy, who thought, from so pure
light,
Effects of liuely heat must needs in nature grow :
But she, most faire, most cold, made him thence take
his flight
To my close heart; where, while some firebrands he
did lay,
He burnt vn'wares his wings, and cannot flie away.

IX.

' Vertue's Court.'

Queen Vertue's Court, which some call Stella's face,
Prepar'd by Nature's choysest furniture,
Hath his front built of alabaster pure;
Gold is the couering of that stately place.
The doore, by which sometimes comes forth her grace,
Red porphir is, which locke of pearle makes sure,
Whose porches rich—which name of chekes indure—
Marble, mixt red and white, doe enterlace.
The windowes now, through which this heav'nly guest

Looks ouer the world, and can finde nothing such,
Which dare claime from those lights the name of best,
Of touch they are, that without touch doe touch,
Which Cupid's selfe, from Beautie's minde did draw:
Of touch they are, and poore I am their straw.

X.

'Reason and Love.'

Reason, in faith thou art well seru'd, that still
Wouldst brabbling be with Sense and Loue in me;
I rather wisht thee clime the Muses' hill;
Or reach the fruite of Nature's choysest tree;
Or seeke heav'n's course or heav'n's inside to see:
Why shouldst thou toyle our thornie soile to till?
Leaue Sense, and those which Sense's obiects be;
Deale thou with powers of thoughts, leaue Loue to Will.
But thou wouldst needs fight both with Loue and
        Sence,
With sword of wit giuing wounds of dispraise,
Till downe-right blowes did foyle thy cunning fence;
For, soone as they strake thee with Stella's rayes,
Reason, thou kneeld'st, and offered'st straight to proue,
By reason good, good reason her to loue.

XI.

'Love, thou leav'st the best behinde.'

In truth, O Loue, with what a boyish kind   =nature
Thou doest proceed in thy most serious wayes,
That when the heav'n to thee his best displayes,

Yet of that best thou leau'st the best behinde!
For, like a childe that some faire booke doth find,
With gilded leaues or colourd velume playes,   vellum
Or, at the most, on some fine picture stayes,
But neuer heeds the fruit of Writer's mind;
So when thou saw'st, in Nature's cabinet,
Stella, thou straight lookt'st babies in her eyes,
In her chekes' pit thou didst thy pitfold set,
And in her breast bo-peepe or crouching lies,
Playing and shining in each outward part;
But, fool, seekst not to get into her heart.

XII.

' Cupid.'

Cvpid, because thou shin'st in Stella's eyes—
That from her locks thy day-nets none scapes free—
That those lips sweld so full of thee they be—
That her sweet breath makes oft thy flames to rise—
That in her breast thy pap well sugred lies—
That her grace gracious makes thy wrongs—that she,
What words soere shee speake, perswades for thee—
That her cleere voice lifts thy fame to the skies,—
Thou countest Stella thine, like those whose powers
Hauing got vp a breach by fighting well,
Crie ' Victorie, this faire day all is ours!'
O no; her heart is such a cittadell,
So fortified with wit, stor'd with disdaine,
That to win it is all the skill and paine.

XIII.

' Phœbus.'

Phœbus was iudge betweene Ioue, Mars, and Loue,
Of those three gods, whose armes the fairest were.—
Ioue's golden shield did eagle sables beare,
Whose talons held young Ganimed aboue:
But in vert field Mars bare a golden speare,
Which through a bleeding heart his point did shoue:
Each had his creast, Mars caried Venus' gloue,
Ioue on his helme the thunderbolt did reare.
Cupid then smiles, for on his crest there lies
Stella's faire haire, her face he makes his shield,
Where roses gueuls are borne in siluer field.   gules
Phœbus drew wide the curtaines of the skies,
To blaze these last, and sware devoutly then,   =blazon
The first, thus matcht, were scantly gentlemen.

XIV.

' Alas, haue I not paine enough !'

Alas, haue I not paine enough, my friend,
Vpon whose breast a fiercer Gripe doth tire
Then did on him who first stale down the fire,
While Loue on me doth all his quiuer spend,—
But with your rubarbe words ye must contend,   rhubarb
To grieue me worse, in saying that Desire
Doth plunge my wel-form'd soule euen in the mire
Of sinfull thoughts, which do in ruin end?
If that be sinne which doth the manners frame,

Well staid with truth in word and faith of deede,
Ready of wit, and fearing nought but shame;
If that be sin, which in fixt hearts doth breed
A loathing of all loose vnchastitie,
Then loue is sin, and let me sinfull be.

For gods sake, hold your peace & let me

XV.

' Dictionarie's methode.'

You that do search for euery purling spring
Which from the ribs of old Parnassus flowes,
And euery flower, not sweet perhaps, which growes
Neere thereabouts, into your poesie wring;
Ye that do dictionarie's methode bring
Into your rimes, running in ratling rowes;
You that poore Petrarch's long-deceasèd woes
With new-borne sighes and denisen'd wit do sing;
You take wrong wayes; those far-fet helps be such
As do bewray a want of inward tuch,   touch [far-fetch'd
And sure, at length stolne goods doe come to light:
But if, both for your loue and skill, your name
You seeke to nurse at fullest breasts of Fame,
Stella behold, and then begin to endite.

XVI.

' Loue's pain.'

In nature, apt to like, when I did see
Beauties which were of many carrets fine,   carats
My boiling sprites did thither then incline,

And, Loue, I thought that I was full of thee:
But finding not those restlesse flames in mee,
Which others said did make their soules to pine,
I thought those babes of some pinne's hurt did whine,
By my soule judging what Loue's paine might be.
But while I thus with this young lyon plaid,
Mine eyes—shall I say curst or blest?—beheld
Stella: now she is nam'd, neede more be said?
In her sight I a lesson new haue speld;
I now haue learnd loue right, and learnd euen so
As they that being poysoned poyson know.

XVII.

' Cupid offending.'

His mother deere, Cupid offended late,
Because that Mars, growne slacker in her loue,
With pricking shot he did not throughly moue
To keepe the place of their first louing state.
The boy refusde for feare of Marses hate,   · Mars'
Who threatned stripes, if he his wrath did proue;
But she, in chafe, him from her lap did shoue,
Brake bowe, brake shafts, while Cupid weeping sate;
Till that his grandame Nature, pittying it,
Of Stella's browes made him two better bowes,
And in her eyes of arrowes infinit.
O how for ioy he leapes! O how he crowes!
And straight therewith, like wags new got to play,
Fals to shrewd turnes; and I was in his way.

XVIII.

'Bankrout.'

With what sharpe checkes I in my selfe am shent
When into Reason's audite I do goe,
And by iust 'counts my selfe a bankrout know
Of all those goods which heau'n to me hath lent;
Vnable quite to pay euen Nature's rent,
Which vnto it by birthright I do ow;
And, which is worse, no good excuse can showe,
But that my wealth I haue most idly spent!
My youth doth waste, my knowledge brings forth toyes;
My wit doth striue those passions to defende,
Which, for reward, spoile it with vaine annoyes.
I see, my course to lose my selfe doth bend;
I see—and yet no greater sorrow take
Than that I lose no more for Stella's sake.

XIX.

'Words . . . vainely spent.'

On Cupid's bowe how are my heart-strings bent,
That see my wracke, and yet embrace the same!
When most I glory, then I feele most shame;
I willing run, yet while I run repent;
My best wits still their owne disgrace inuent:
My very inke turnes straight to Stella's name;
And yet my words, as them my pen doth frame,
Auise themselues that they are vainely spent:
For though she passe all things, yet what is all

That vnto me, who fare like him that both
Lookes to the skies, and in a ditch doth fall?
O let me prop my mind, yet in his growth,
And not in nature,—for best fruits vnfit.
Scholler, saith Loue, bend hitherward your wit.

XX.

'My death's wound.'

Fly, fly, my friends; I haue my death's wound, fly;
See there that boy, that murthring boy, I say,
Who, like a theefe hid in darke bush, doth ly,
Till bloudy bullet get him wrongfull pray.   prey
So, tyran he, no fitter place could spie,
Nor so faire leuell in so secret stay,
As that sweet black which vailes the heav'nly eye;
There himselfe with his shot he close doth lay.
Poore passenger, passe now thereby I did,
And staid, pleasd with the prospect of the place,
While that black hue from me the bad guest hid:
But straight I saw motions of lightning grace;
And then descried the glistrings of his dart:
But ere I could flie thence, it pierc'd my heart.

XXI.

'Aught so faire as Stella is?'

Your words, my friend (right healthfull caustiks), blame
My young mind marde, whom Loue doth windlas so;
That mine owne writings, like bad seruants, show

My wits quicke in vaine thoughts, in vertue lame;
That Plato I read for nought but if he tame   =unless
Such coltish yeeres; that to my birth I owe
Nobler desires, least else that friendly foe,
Great expectation, weare a traine of shame :
For since mad March great promise made to mee,
If now the May of my yeeres much decline,
What can be hoped my haruest-time will be ?
Sure, you say well, ' Your wisedome's golden myne
Dig deepe with Learning's spade.' Now tell me this—
Hath this world aught so faire as Stella is ?

XXII.

'The Sunne . . . did her but kisse.'

In highest way of heav'n the sunne did ride,
Progressing then from faire Twinnes' gold'n place,
Hauing no maske of clowds before his face,
But streaming forth of heate in his chiefe pride ;
When some faire ladies, by hard promise tied,
On horsebacke met him in his furious race ;
Yet each prepar'd with fannes' wel-shading grace
From that foe's wounds their tender skinnes to hide.
Stella alone with face vnarmèd marcht,
Either to do like him which open shone,
Or carelesse of the wealth, because her owne.
Yet were the hid and meaner beauties parcht ;
Her dainties bare went free : the cause was this,—
The sunne, that others burn'd, did her but kisse.

XXIII.

'Pensiuenesse.'

The curious wits, seeing dull pensiuenesse
Bewray it selfe in my long-settled eies,
Whence those same fumes of melancholy rise,
With idle paines and missing ayme, do guesse.
Some, that know how my spring I did addresse,
Deem that my Muse some fruit of knowledge plies;
Others, because the prince of seruice tries,
Thinke that I thinke State errours to redress:
But harder iudges iudge ambition's rage—
Scourge of it selfe, still climing slipperie place—
Holds my young braine captiv'd in golden cage.
O fooles, or ouer-wise: alas, the race
Of all my thoughts hath neither stop nor start
But only Stella's eyes and Stella's hart.

XXIV.

'Rich, more wretched.'

Rich fooles there be whose base and filthie heart
Lies hatching still the goods wherein they flow,
And damning their owne selues to Tantal's smart,
Wealth breeding want—more rich, more wretched
        growe:
Yet to those fooles Heav'n doth such wit impart,
As what their hands do hold, their heads do know,
And knowing, loue, and louing lay apart.

As sacred things, far from all danger's show.
But that rich foole, who by blind Fortune's lot
The richest gemme of loue and life enioyes,
And can with foule abuse such beauties blot;
Let him, depriu'd of sweet but vnfelt ioyes,
Exild for ay from those high treasures which
He knowes not, grow in only folly rich!

XXV.
' Loue . . . takes Stella's shape.'

The wisest scholler of the wight most wise
By Phœbus' doome, with sugred sentence sayes,
That vertue, if it once met with our eyes,
Strange flames of loue it in our soules would raise;
But for that man with paine this truth descries,   =only
Whiles he each thing in Sense's ballance wayes,
And so nor will nor can behold those skies
Which inward sunne to heroick minde displaies.
Vertue of late, with vertuous care to ster   stir
Loue of herselfe, tooke Stella's shape, that she —
To mortall eyes might sweetly shine in her.
It is most true; for since I her did see,
Vertue's great beauty in that face I proue,
And find th' effect, for I do burne in loue.

XXVI.
' Astrologie.'

Though dustie wits dare scorne Astrologie,
And fooles can thinke those lampes of purest light—

Whose numbers waies, greatnesse, eternity,
Promising wonders, wonder do inuite—
To haue for no cause birthright in the sky
But for to spangle the blacke weeds of Night ;
Or for some braule, which in that chamber hie,
They should still daunce to please a gazer's sight.
For me, I do Nature vnidle know,
And know great causes great effects procure ;
And know those bodies high raigne on the low.
And if these rules did faile, proofe makes me sure,
Who oft fore-see my after-following race,
By only those two starres in Stella's face.

XXVII.

' Most alone in greatest company.'

Because I oft in darke abstracted guise
Seeme most alone in greatest company,
With dearth of words, or answers quite awrie,
To them that would make speech of speech arise ;
They deeme, and of their doome the rumour flies,
That poison foule of bubbling pride doth lie
So in my swelling breast, that only I
Fawne on my selfe, and others do despise.
Yet pride I thinke doth not my soule possesse
(Which looks too oft in his vnflattering glasse) :
But one worse fault, ambition, I confesse,
That makes me oft my best friends ouerpasse,

Vnseene, vnheard, while thought to highest place
Bends all his powers, euen vnto Stella's grace.

XXVIII.

'Allegorie.'

You that with Allegorie's curious frame
Of others' children changelings vse to make,
With me those paines, for God's sake, do not take ;
I list not dig so deepe for brasen fame.
When I say Stella, I doe meane the same
Princesse of beauty, for whose only sake
The raines of Loue I loue, though neuer slake,   slack
And ioy therein, though Nations count it shame.
I beg no subiect to vse eloquence,
Nor in hid wayes do guide philosophie ;
Looke at my hands for no such quintessence ;
But know that I in pure simplicitie
Breathe out the flames which burne within my heart,
Loue onely reading unto me this arte.

XXIX.

'Given vp for a slaue.'

Like some weak lords neighbord by mighty kings,
To keep themselues and their chiefe cities free,
Do easly yeeld that all their coasts may be
Ready to store their campes of needfull things ;
So Stella's heart, finding what power Loue brings,

To keep it selfe in life and liberty,
Doth willing graunt that in the frontiers he
Vse all to helpe his other conquerings.
And thus her heart escapes; but thus her eyes
Serue him with shot, her lips his heralds are, ,
Her breasts his tents, legs his triumphall carre, .
Her flesh his food, her skin his armour braue ;
And I, but for because my prospect lies   only
Vpon that coast, am giv'n vp for a slaue.

XXX.

'Questions.'

Whether the Turkish new moone minded be
To fill her hornes this yeere on Christian coast ?
How Poles' right king means without leaue of hoast
To warme with ill-made fire cold Muscouy ?   [host
If French can yet three parts in one agree ?
What now the Dutch in their full diets boast ?
How Holland hearts, now so good townes be lost,
Trust in the shade of pleasant Orange-tree ?
How Vlster likes of that same golden bit
Wherewith my father once made it halfe tame ?
If in the Scotch Court be no weltring yet ?
These questions busie wits to me do frame :
I, cumbred with good maners, answer doe,
But know not how; for still I thinke of you.

XXXI.

in writing of Charles Friend.

'The Moone.'

With how sad steps, O Moone, thou clim'st the skies!
How silently, and with how wanne a face!
What, may it be that euen in heau'nly place
That busie archer his sharpe arrowes tries!
Sure, if that long-with-loue-acquainted eyes
Can iudge of loue, thou feel'st a louer's case,
I reade it in thy lookes; thy languisht grace,
To me, that feele the like, thy state discries.
Then, eu'n of fellowship, O Moone, tell me,
Is constant loue deem'd there but want of wit?
Are beauties there as proud as here they be?
Do they aboue loue to be lou'd, and yet
Those louers scorne whom that loue doth possesse?
Doe they call vertue there vngratefulnesse?

XXXII.

'Morpheus.'

Morpheus, the liuely sonne of deadly Sleepe,
Witnesse of life to them that liuing die,
A prophet oft, and oft an historie,
A poet eke, as humours fly or creepe;
Since thou in me so sure a power doest keepe,
That neuer I with clos'd-vp sense do lie,
But by thy worke my Stella I discrie,
Teaching blind eyes both how to smile and weepe;

Vouchsafe, of all acquaintance, this to tell,
Whence hast thou iuorie, rubies, pearle, and gold,
To shew her skin, lips, teeth, and head so well?
Foole! answers he; no Indes such treasures hold;
But from thy heart, while my sire charmeth thee,
Sweet Stella's image I do steale to mee.

XXXIII.

'I might.'

I might!—vnhappie word—woe me, I might,
And then would not, or could not, see my blisse;
Till now wrapt in a most infernall night,
I finde how heau'nly day, wretch! I did misse.
Hart, rent thy selfe, thou dost thy selfe but right;
No louely Paris made thy Hellen his;
No force, no fraud robd thee of thy delight,
Nor Fortune of thy fortune author is;
But to my selfe my selfe did giue the blow,
While too much wit, forsooth, so troubled me,
That I respects for both our sakes must show:
And yet could not, by rysing morne fore-see
How faire a day was neare: O punisht eyes,
That I had bene more foolish, or more wise!

XXXIV.

'How can words ease?'

Come, let me write. And to what end? To ease
A burthened hart. How can words ease, which are

The glasses of thy dayly-vexing care?
Oft cruell fights well pictured-forth do please.
Art not asham'd to publish thy disease?
Nay, that may breed my fame, it is so rare.
But will not wise men thinke thy words fond ware?
Then be they close, and so none shall displease.
What idler thing then speake and not be hard?   than
What harder thing then smart and not to speake?
Peace, foolish wit! with wit my wit is mard.
Thus write I, while I doubt to write, and wreake
My harmes in ink's poore losse. Perhaps some find
Stella's great powrs, that so confuse my mind.

XXXV.

' Grow rich, meaning my Stella's name.'

What may words say, or what may words not say,
Where Truth it selfe must speake like Flatterie?
Within what bounds can one his liking stay,
Where Nature doth with infinite agree?
What Nestor's counsell can my flames alay,
Since Reason's selfe doth blow the coale in me?
And, ah, what hope that Hope should once see day,
Where Cupid is sworne page to Chastity?
Honour is honour'd, that thou doest possesse
Him as thy slaue, and now long-needy Fame
Doth euen grow rich, meaning my Stella's name.
Wit learnes in thee perfection to expresse,

Not thou by praise, but praise in thee is raisde :
It is a praise to praise, when.thou art praisde.

XXXVI.

'New assaults.'

Stella, whence doth these new assaults arise,
A conquerd yeelding ransackt heart to winne,
Whereto long since, through my long-battred eyes,
Whole armies of thy beauties entred in ?
And there, long since, Loue, thy lieuetenant, lies ;
My forces razde, thy banners raisd within :
Of conquest do not these effects suffice,
But wilt new warre vpon thine owne begin ?
With so sweet voyce, and by sweet Nature so
In sweetest strength, so sweetly skild withal
In all sweet stratagems sweete Art can show,
That not my soule, which at thy foot did fall
Long since, forc'd by thy beames : but stone nor tree,
By Sence's priuiledge, can scape from thee !

XXXVII.

'No misfortune but that Rich she is.'

My mouth doth water, and my breast doth swell,
My tongue doth itch, my thoughts in labour be :
Listen then, lordings, with good eare to me,
For of my life I must a riddle tell.
Towárd Aurora's Court a nymph doth dwell,.

Rich in all beauties which man's eye can see ;
Beauties so farre from reach of words, that we
Abase her praise saying she doth excell ;
Rich in the treasure of deserv'd renowne,
Rich in the riches of a royall hart,
Rich in those gifts which giue th' eternall crowne ;
Who, though most rich in these and euery part
Which make the patents of true worldly blisse,
Hath no misfortune but that Rich she is.

XXXVIII.

' The unkinde guest.'

This night, while sleepe begins with heauy wings
To hatch mine eyes, and that vnbitted thought
Doth fall to stray, and my chiefe powres are brought
To leaue the scepter of all subiect things ;
The first that straight my fancie's errour brings
Vnto my mind is Stella's image, wrought
By Loue's owne selfe, but with so curious drought
That she, methinks, not onely shines but sings.
I start, looke, hearke, but what in closde-vp sence
Was held, in opend sense it flies away,
Leauing me nought but wayling eloquence.
I, seeing better sights in sight's decay,
Cald it anew, and wooèd Sleepe againe ;
But him, her host, that vnkind guest had slaine.

XXXIX.

'Sleepe.'

Come, Sleepe ! O Sleepe, the certaine knot of peace,
The baiting-place of wit, the balme of woe,
The poore man's wealth, the prisoner's release,
Th' indifferent iudge betweene the high and low;
With shield of proofe shield me from out the prease
Of those fierce darts Despaire at me doth throw:
O make in me those ciuill warres to cease ;
I will good tribute pay, if thou do so.
Take thou of me smooth pillowes, sweetest bed,
A chamber deafe of noise and blind of light,
A rosie garland and a weary hed :
And if these things, as being thine in right,
Moue not thy heauy grace, thou shalt in me,
Liuelier then else-where, Stella's image see.

XL.

'Nowe of the basest.'

As good to write, as for to lie and grone.
O Stella deare, how much thy power hath wrought,
That hast my mind—nowe of the basest—brought
My still-kept course, while others sleepe, to mone ;
Alas, if from the height of Vertue's throne
Thou canst vouchsafe the influence of a thought
Vpon a wretch that long thy grace hath sought,
Weigh then how I by thee am ouerthrowne;

And then thinke thus—although thy beautie be
Made manifest by such a victorie,
Yet noble conquerours do wreckes auoid.
Since then thou hast so farre subduèd me,
That in my heart I offer still to thee,
O do not let thy temple be destroyd.

XLI.

'Stella lookt on.'

Hauing this day my horse, my hand, my launce
Guided so well that I obtain'd the prize,
Both by the iudgement of the English eyes
And of some sent from that sweet enemy Fraunce;
Horsemen my skill in horsemanship advaunce,
Towne folkes my strength; a daintier iudge applies
His praise to sleight which from good vse doth rise;
Some luckie wits impute it but to chance;
Others, because of both sides I doe take
My blood from them who did excell in this,
Thinke Nature me a man-at-armes did make.
How farre they shot awrie! the true cause is,
Stella lookt on, and from her hcau'nly face
Sent forth the beames which made so faire my race.

XLII.

'Eyes.'

O eyes, which doe the spheares of beautie moue;
Whose beames be ioyes, whose ioyes all vertues be;

Who, while they make Loue conquer, conquer Loue;
The schooles where Venus hath learn'd chastitie :
O eyes, where humble lookes most glorious proue,
Onely-lov'd tyrans, iust in cruelty;—
Do not, O doe not, from poore me remoue,
Keep still my zenith, euer shine on me :
For though I neuer see them, but straightwayes
My life forgets to nourish languisht sprites;
Yet still on me, O eyes, dart downe your rayes :
And if from maiestie of sacred lights
Oppressing mortall sense my death proceed,
Wrackes triumphs be which Loue hie set doth breed.

XLIII.

' Leaue to die.'

Faire eyes, sweet lips, deare heart, that foolish I
Could hope, by Cupid's helpe, on you to pray,   prey
Since to himselfe he doth your gifts apply,
As his maine force, choise sport, and easefull stay !
For when he will see who dare him gain-say,
Then with those eyes he lookes : lo, by and by   instantly
Each soule dothe at Loue's feet his weapons lay,
Glad if for her he giue them leaue to die.
When he will play, then in her lips he is,
Where blushing red, that Loue's selfe them doth loue,
With either lip he doth the other kisse;
But when he will, for quiet's sake, remoue

From all the world, her hart is then his rome,   =plac
Where well he knowes no man to him can come.

XLIV.

'Inward smart.'

My words I know do well set forth my minde ; ∟
My mind bemones his sense of inward smart ; ∟
Such smart may pitie claime of any hart ; ∟
Her heart, sweet heart, is of no tygre's kind ∠
And yet she heares, and yet no pitie I find, α
But more I cry, lesse grace she doth impart. ∟
Alas, what cause is there so ouerthwart, ∟
That Noblenesse it selfe makes thus vnkind ∩
I much do ghesse, yet finde no truth saue this, ć
That when the breath of my complaints doth tuch ⅾ
Those daintie dores vnto the Court of Blisse, c
The heav'nly nature of that place is such, ⅾ
That, once come there, the sobs of mine annoyes ć
Are metamorphos'd straight to tunes of ioyes. ⅾ

XLV.

'Imag'd things.'

Stella oft sees the very face of wo   ∩
Painted in my beclowded stormie face, ɦ
But cannot skill to pitie my disgrace, ɣ
Not though thereof the cause herself she know:
Yet hearing late a fable, which did show ⋀

IX. Yet—gentle English theeues do rob, but will not
    slay,
Thou English murdring theefe, wilt haue harts
    for thy prey :   pray
The name of murdrer now on thy faire forehead
    sitteth,
And euen while I. do speake, my death-wounds
    bleeding be,
Which, I protest, proceed from only cruell thee :
Who may, and will not saue, murder in truth
    committeth.

X. But murder, priuate fault, seemes but a toy to
    thee :
I lay then to thy charge vniustest tyrannie,
If rule, by force, without all claim, a tyran show-
    eth ;
For thou dost lord my heart, who am not borne
    thy slaue,
And, which is worse, makes me, most guiltlesse,
    torments haue :
A rightfull prince by unright deeds a tyran grow-
    eth.

XI. Lo, you grow proud with this, for tyrans make
    folke bow :
Of foule rebellion then I do appeach thee now,
Rebell by Nature's law, rebell by law of Reason :

Thou, sweetest subiect wert, borne in the realme
   of Loue,
And yet against thy prince thy force dost daily
   proue :
No vertue merits praise, once toucht with blot of
   treason.

XII. But valiant rebels oft in fooles' mouths purchase
   fame :
I now then staine thy white with vagabonding
   shame,
Both rebell to the sonne and vagrant from the
   mother;
For wearing Venus' badge in euery part of thee,
Vnto Dianae's traine thou, runnaway, didst flie :
Who faileth one is false, though trusty to another.

XIII. What, is not this enough ! nay, farre worse com-
   meth here;
A witch, I say, thou art, though thou so faire
   appeare;
For, I protest, my sight neuer thy face enioyeth,
But I in me am chang'd, I am aliue and dead,
My feete are turn'd to rootes, my hart becommeth
   lead :
No witchcraft is so euill as which man's mind
   destroyeth.

XIV. Yet witches may repent; thou art farre worse
   then they :

Alas that I am forst such euill of thee to say:
I say thou art a diuell, though cloth'd in angel's
    shining;
For thy face tempts my soule to leaue the heav'n
    for thee,
And thy words of refuse do powre euen hell on
    mee:
Who tempt, and tempting plague, are diuels in
    true defining.

xv. You, then, vngrateful theefe, you murdring tyran,
    you,
You rebell runaway, to lord and lady vntrue,
You witch, you diuell, alas, you still of me be-
    loued,
You see what I can say; mend yet your froward
    mind,
And such skill in my Muse, you, reconcil'd, shall
    find,
That all these cruell words your praises shalbe
    proued.

SIXT SONG.

i. O you that heare this voice,
  O you that see this face,
  Say whether of the choice
  Deserues the former place:

Feare not to iudge this bate,
For it is void of hate.

II. This side doth Beauty take,
For that doth Musike speake ;
Fit oratours to make
The strongest iudgements weake :
The barre to plead their right
Is only true delight.

III. Thus doth the voice and face,
These gentle lawyers, wage,
Like louing brothers' case,
For father's heritage ;
That each, while each contends,
It selfe to other lends.

IV. For Beautie beautifies
With heauenly hew and grace
The heauenly harmonies ;
And in this faultlesse face
The perfect beauties be
A perfect harmony.

V. Musick more loftly swels
In speeches nobly placed ;
Beauty as farre excels,
In action aptly graced :
A friend each party draws
To countenance his cause.

VI. Loue more affected seemes
To Beautie's louely light;
And Wonder more esteemes
Of Musicke's wondrous might;
But both to both so bent,
As both in both are spent.

VII. Musicke doth witnesse call
The eare his truth to trie;
Beauty brings to the hall
Eye-iudgement of the eye :
Both in their obiects such,
As no exceptions tutch.

VIII. The common sense, which might
Be arbiter of this,
To be, forsooth, vpright,
To both sides partiall is;
He layes on this chiefe praise,
Chiefe praise on that he laies.

IX. Then Reason, princesse hy,—
Whose throne is in the minde,
Which Musicke can in sky
And hidden beauties finde,—
Say whether thou wilt crowne
With limitlesse renowne ?

SEUENTH SONG.

I. Whose senses in so euill consort their step-dame
    Nature laies,
That rauishing delight in them most sweete tunes
    do not raise;
Or if they do delight therein, yet are so closde with
    wit,
As with sententious lips to set a title vaine on it;
O let them heare these sacred tunes, and learne in
    Wonders' scholes,
To be, in things past bounds of wit, fooles—if they
    be not fooles.

II. Who haue so leaden eyes, as not to see sweet Beau-
    tie's show,
Or, seeing, haue so wooden wits, as not that worth
    to know,
Or, knowing, haue so muddy minds, as not to be in
    loue,
Or, louing, haue so frothy thoughts, as eas'ly thence
    to moue;
O let them see these heauenly beames, and in faire
    letters reede
A lesson fit, both sight and skill, loue and firme
    loue to breede.

III. Heare then, but then with wonder heare, see, but
   adoring, see,
No mortall gifts, no earthly fruites, now here descended be :
See, doo you see this face ? a face, nay, image of the
   skies,
Of which, the two life-giuing lights are figured in
   her eyes :
Heare you this soule-inuading voice, and count it
   but a voice ?
The very essence of their tunes, when angels do re-
   joyce.

EIGHT SONG.

I. In a groue most rich of shade,
   Where birds wanton musicke made,
   May, then yong, his pide weedes showing,
   New-perfumed with flowers fresh growing :

II. Astrophel with Stella sweet
   Did for mutual comfort meete,
   Both within themselues oppressèd,
   But each in the other blessèd.

III. Him great harmes had taught much care,
   Her faire necke a foule yoke bare ;
   But her sight his cares did banish,
   In his sight her yoke did vanish :

IV. Wept they had, alas, the while,
But now teares themselues did smile,
While their eyes, by Loue directed;
Enterchangeably reflected.

V. Sigh they did; but now betwixt
Sighes of woe were glad sighes mixt;
With arms crost, yet testifying
Restlesse rest, and liuing dying.

VII. Their eares hungrie of each word
Which the deare tongue would afford ;
But their tongues restrain'd from walking,
Till their harts had ended talking.

VIII. But when their tougues could not speake,
Loue it selfe did silence breake ;
Loue did set his lips asunder,
Thus to speake in loue and wonder.

VIII. Stella, soueraigne of my ioy,
Faire triumpher of annoy ;
Stella, starre of heauenly fier,
Stella, loadstar of desier ;

IX. Stella, in whose shining eyes
Are the lights of Cupid's skies,
Whose beames, where they once are darted,
Loue therewith is streight imparted ;

X. Stella, whose voice, when it speakes,
Senses all asunder breakes ;

Stella, whose voice, when it singeth,
Angels to acquaintance bringeth ;

XI. Stella, in whose body is
Writ each caracter of blisse ;
Whose face all, all beauty passeth,
Saue thy mind, which yet surpasseth.

XII. Graunt, O graunt ; but speach, alas,
Failes me, fearing on to passe : ,
Graunt, O me : what am I saying ?
But no fault there is in praying.

XIII. Graunt—O deere, on knees I pray,
(Knees on ground he then did stay)
That, not I, but since I loue you,
Time and place for me may moue you.

XIV. Neuer season was more fit ;
Neuer roome more apt for it ;
Smiling ayre allowes my reason ;
These birds sing, ' Now vse the season.'

XV. This small wind, which so sweete is,
See how it the leaues doth kisse ;
Each tree in his best attiring,
Sense of loue to loue inspiring.

XVI. Loue makes earth the water drink,
Loue to earth makes water sinke ;
And, if dumbe things be so witty,
Shall a heauenly grace want pitty ?

XVII. There his hands, in their speech, faine
    Would haue made tongue's language plaine;
    But her hands, his hands repelling,
    Gaue repulse all grace excelling.

XVIII. Then she spake; her speech was such,
    As not eares, but hart did tuch :   heart
    While such-wise she loue denièd,
    And yet loue she signifièd.

XIX. Astrophel, sayd she, my loue,
    Cease, in these effects, to proue;
    Now be still, yet still beleeue me,
    Thy griefe more then death would grieue me.

XX. If that any thought in me
    Can tast comfort but of thee,
    Let me, fed with hellish anguish,
    Ioylesse, hopelesse, endlesse languish.

XXI. If those eyes you praisèd, be
    Halfe so deare as you to me,
    Let me home returne, starke blinded
    Of those eyes, and blinder minded;

XXII. If to secret of my hart, .
    I do any wish impart,
    Where thou art not formost placèd,
    Be both wish and I defacèd.

XXIII. If more may be sayd, I say,
    All my blisse in thee I lay;

If thou loue, my loue, content thee,
For all loue, all faith is meant thee.

xxiv. Trust me, while I thee deny,
In my selfe the smart I try;
Tyran Honour doth thus vse thee,
Stella's selfe might not refuse thee.

xxv. Therefore, deare, this no more moue,
Least, though I leaue not thy loue,
Which too deep in me is framèd,
I should blush when thou art namèd.

xxvi. Therewithall away she went,
Leauing him to passion rent,
With what she had done and spoken,
That therewith my song is broken.

NINTH SONG.

i. Go, my flocke, go, get you hence,
Seeke a better place of feeding,
Where you may haue some defence
Fro the stormes in my breast breeding,
And showers from mine eyes proceeding.

ii. Leaue a wretch, in whom all wo
Can abide to keepe no measure;
Merry flock, such one forego,
Vnto whom mirth is displeasure,
Onely rich in mischief's treasure.

III. Yet, alas, before you go,
    Heare your wofull maister's story,
    Which to stones I els would show :
    Sorrow only then hath glory
    When 'tis excellently sorry.

IV. Stella, fiercest shepherdesse,
    Fiercest, but yet fairest euer ;
    Stella, whom, O heauens still blesse,
    Though against me she perseuer,
    Though I blisse enherit neuer :

V. Stella hath refusèd me !
    Stella, who more loue hath prouèd,
    In this caitife heart to be,
    Then can in good eawes be mouèd   ewes
    Toward lambkins best belouèd.

VI. Stella hath refusèd me !
    Astrophel, that so well seruèd
    In this pleasant Spring must see,
    While in pride flowers be preseruèd,
    Himselfe onely Winter-steruèd.

VII. Why, alas, doth she then sweare
    That she loueth me so dearely,
    Seeing me so long to beare
    Coles of loue that burne so cleerly,
    And yet leaue me helplesse meerely ?

viii. Is that loue? forsooth, I trow,
    If I saw my good dog grieuèd,
    And a helpe for him did know,
    My loue should not be beleeuèd,
    But he were by me releeuèd.

ix. No, she hates me, well-away,
    Faining loue, somewhat to please me;
    For she knows, if she display
    All her hate, death soone would seaze me,
    And of hideous torments ease me.

x. Then adieu, deare flocke, adieu;
    But, alas, if in your straying
    Heauenly Stella meete with you,
    Tell her, in your pitious blaying,
    Her poore slaue's uniust decaying.

TENTH SONG.

i. O deare life, when shall it be
    That mine eyes thine eyes shall see,
    And in them thy mind discouer
    Whether absence haue had force
    Thy remembrance to diuorce
    From the image of thy louer?

ii. Or if I my self find not,
    After parting, aught forgot,

Nor debar'd from Beautie's treasure,
Let not tongue aspire to tell
In what high ioyes I shall dwell;
Only thought aymes at the pleasure.

iii. Thought, therefore, I will send thee
To take vp the place for me:
Long I will not after tary,
There, vnseene, thou mayst be bold,
Those faire wonders to behold,
Which in them my hopes do cary.

iv. Thought, see thou no place forbeare,
Enter brauely euerywhere,
Seize on all to her belonging;
But if thou wouldst garded be,
Fearing her beames, take with thee
Strength of liking, rage of longing.

v. Thinke of that most gratefull time
When my leaping heart will climb,
In my lips to haue his biding,
There those roses for to kisse,
Which do breathe a sugred blisse,
Opening rubies, pearles dividing.

vi. Thinke of my most princely power,
Which I blessèd shall devower
With my greedy licorous sences,
Beauty, musicke, sweetnesse, loue,

While she doth against me proue
Her strong darts but weake defences.

VII. Thinke, thinke of those dalyings,
When with doue-like murmurings,
With glad moning, passèd anguish,
We change eyes, and hart for hart,   heart
Each to other do depart,
Ioying till ioy makes vs languish.

VIII. O my thoughts, my thoughts surcease,
Thy delights my woes increase,
My life melts with too much thinking;
Thinke no more, but die in me,
Till thou shalt ruinèd be,
At her lips my nectar drinking.

ELEUENTH SONG.

I. ' Who is it that this darke night
Vnderneath my window playneth?'
It is one who from thy sight
Being, ah, exil'd, disdayneth
Euery other vulgar light.

II. ' Why, alas, and are you he?
Be not yet those fancies changèd?'
Deare, when you find change in me,
Though from me you be estrangèd,
Let my chaunge to ruine be.

III. 'Well, in absence this will dy.;
Leaue to see, and leaue to wonder.'
Absence sure will helpe, if I
Can learne how my selfe to sunder
From what in my hart doth ly.

IV. 'But time will these thoughts remoue;
Time doth work what no man knoweth.'
Time doth as the subiect proue;
With time still the affection groweth
In the faithful turtle-doue.

V. 'What if we new beauties see,
Will not they stir new affection?'
I will thinke they pictures be,
(Image-like, of saints' perfection)
Poorely counterfeting thee.

VI. 'But your reason's purest light
Bids you leaue such minds to nourish.'
Deere, do reason no such spite;
Neuer doth thy beauty florish
More then in thy reason's sight.

VII. 'But the wrongs Loue beares will make
Loue at length leaue undertaking.'
No, the more fooles it doth shake,
In a ground of so firme making
Deeper still they driue the stake.

viii. 'Peace, I thinke that some giue eare ;
　　　Come no more, least I get anger.'
　　　Blisse, I will my blisse forbeare ;
　　　Fearing, sweete, you to endanger ;
　　　But my soule shall harbour there.

　ix. 'Well, be gone ; be gone, I say,
　　　Lest that Argus' eyes perceiue you.'
　　　O vniust is Fortune's sway,
　　　Which can make me thus to leaue you ;
　　　And from lowts to run away.

NOTES AND ILLUSTRATIONS.

NOTES AND ILLUSTRATIONS.

THROUGHOUT these Notes, Q 1 is = Nash's edition of Astrophel and Stella (1591, 4to): Q 2=the second edition, without Nash's Epistle (1591, 4to): 2 qu.=the two editions of 1591: A=Arcadia edition of 1598, and A 1613=the Arcadia edition of that year. On these and other editions, see our Essay in the present volume.

Sonnet i. l. 2, ' she, deare Shee,' in 2 qu. 'the dere Shee,' earlier and less passionate : Bright MS., 'thee (deer thee)'. 2 qu. read ' my loue in verse.'

Sonnet i. l. 6, ' wits :' preferable to ' witte' Q 2, as including imagination, fancy, &c.

Sonnet i. l. 8, ' showers :' it was more than one ' shower' that he looked for, and the plural agrees with ' words' and 'inventions,' ll. 5-6 ; better, therefore, than ' shower' of 2 qu.

Sonnet i. l. 9, ' forth :' 2 qu. ' out.' Changes noted above indicate that this and l. 1 are later variants by the Author.

Sonnet i. l. 13, ' trewand.' ' You are no trewant in the Law, I see ;' Lod. Barrey's ' Ram Alley' (1636), act i. sc. 1.

Sonnet ii. l. 3, ' mine :' in Q 1 ' tract.' ' Mine' might perhaps be=mean, i.e. through the instrumentality of time ; but from the word ' conquest' the reference seems to be to the slow, unsuspected, yet very sure, advancé by mining, then as now much used in sieges. See Alexander of Parma's Campaigns in the Low Countries, &c. Hence it seems later than ' tract' of Q 1. The Bright MS. has ' mind,' which error A makes, ix. 13.

Sonnet ii. l. 1, ' Dribbed' = a term in archery, which has been ill explained (Measure for Measure, act i. sc. 4). As it appears to be the primitive of the frequentative ' dribble,' and allied to drip, drop, and droop, I agree with Mr. Collier's explanation, and take the sense here to be—not with a weak shot elevated that it may reach the mark during its fall, but with a straight-driven aim. Steevens' quotation from Ascham (Tox-

oph. p. 94, Arber's reprint) may be thus explanatorily filled in :
Ascham (Tox.) says that be a man never so apt to shoot, or
never so well taught in his youth, ' yet if he giue it ouer, and
not vse to shote,' [then when through pleasure or war he be-
takes himself to it again] 'he shall become, of a fayre archer,
a stark squyrter- and dribber.'   'Dribbed'='dribb'd,' is more
expressive of weakness than ' dribbèd' (A), and the tense agrees
better with ' gave' than Q 2.

Reverting to l. 1, we read :

' Not at | first sight | nor with | a drib $\begin{matrix} \text{bing} \ (\text{Q }2) \\ \text{bed} \ (\text{MS.}) \end{matrix}$ shot' |

' Not at | the first | sight nor | with a | dribbed (=dribb'd) shot.' (A)

' Not at | the first | sight nor | yet with | a dribbed shot.' (A, after editions.)

Of these I prefer A, because the second clause is lighter to
sound, and so more in agreement with the sense.   The third
reading seems to be one where ' yet' was inserted, but ' the' or
' a' inadvertently retained.

Sonnet ii. l. 10, ' slave-born Muscovite . . . . tyrannie.'   It
is the glory of the present Czar to have ended the long-con-
tinued serfdom of so many of his subjects.

Sonnet iii. l. 3, ' flaunt they in'=let them flaunt, may they.
Our modern taste would prefer A and Q2, ' flaunt in their:'
but the choice must be decided by l. 4.

Sonnet iii. l. 4, Q 2, ' their pride with flowers of golde,'
seems at first sight the better ; but there is the objection that
in the enamelled jewels of that day—the then style from which
this metaphor is taken—it was not the enamel that was enamelled with gold, but the gold that was enamelled with coloured
paste.   Hence Q 2 and A reading is a later alteration, though
not a happy one, the less so that ' Pindare's apes' was not altered.   This phrase we must take not in a depreciatory but
good sense, just as 'imp' was then used in a sense very different
from its present meaning. Cf. 'O sleep, thou ape of death' (Cymbeline, act ii. sc. 2), where there is no intended depreciation
of Sleep, but rather admiration of the resemblance to the calm
placidity into which the troubled features mould themselves.

Sonnet iii. l. 4, ' pied:' particoloured.

      ,,   l. 5, ' statelier :' i.e. more stately than mine, not
more stately than the style of Pindar and his imitators.   The
' statelyee' of Q 2 I take to be an error.

Sonnet iii. l. 7, ' enrich :' Q 1, 'inricht :' probably a blunder·
of tense, yet cf. ' maskt,' l. 2.

Sonnet iii. l. 8. Alluding to the style exemplified in Lyly's Court Comedies and Euphues (1579?).

Sonnet iv. l. 2, '*will and wit :*' Q 1 has '*love* and wit :' Q 2 and A ' will and wit.' As Love is an extern deity acting on him (l. 3), and making his ' will' wayward and an opponent of his wisdom or wit, ' will' is preferable.

Sonnet iv. l. 2, ' *bate*'=contention, strife—probably from Fr. '*battre.*' Cf. Song vi. l. 1, and Nares and Halliwell, *s.v.*, for examples: 2 Henry IV. act ii. sc. 4: Countess of Pembroke's Antonius, &c. I would add, that by taking the technical hawking term ' to bate' as allied to this, and as meaning not merely to flutter but to flutter strivingly, a much finer sense is given to the various passages where it is metaphorically employed.

Sonnet v. l. 1, '*form'd :*' Q 1, ' bound :' Q 2, ' found :' A, ' form'd.' ' That eyes are *found*' to serve the inward light and not the outward show, is contrary to fact, and besides is not his own (or his friend's) argument. ' Bound' is probably the earlier reading, though inferior to ' form'd.' The Bright MS. has ' form'd.'

Sonnet v. l. 3, ' *who.*' This is plural. Cf. ' rebels strive' and ' their' (l. 4); and though ' that,' as a collective, often took a verb singular, the examples of a plural ' who' so followed are very rare, and perhaps never when it precedes its own noun. Here the singular ' doth' of Q 2 necessarily makes a modern reader change the plural noun ' rebels' into a verb singular, to the utter confusion of the sense ; and as errors of ' do' and ' doth' occur throughout, and as A and the Bright MS., as well as A 1613, give ' do,' I adopt it. The archaic plural in -eth is not used by Sidney.

Sonnet v. l. 10, ' *be but :*' 2 qu. ' but be.'

    ,,   l. 14, '*yet :*' Q 2, ' most.' ' True,' says Sidney, ' all these arguments are true, yet my reply is—I must love Stella.' All previous to this reply are the dissuasions of his friend, or of his better sense. Hence I prefer ' yet' to ' most.' Cf. S. xiv. and xxi. and Letter of Languet.

Sonnet vi. l. 9, ' *some*' = some one. The construction is, A sweetest style affords to some [one] a sweetest plaint.

Sonnet vi. l. 10, ' *while :*' Q 2, ' whiles.'

    ,,   vii. l. 2, '*blacke.*' Cf. with this sonnet our SIR JOHN DAVIES, vol. i. pp. 469-70, two of his poems first printed by us.

Sonnet vii. l. 13, ' *euer :*' Bright MS. ' even.' The latter

perhaps under influence of ' euen' two lines above, with which
thought, however, this one has nothing to do, as shown by
' Both so, and thus.' ' Euer' is no doubt hyperbolical; but that
Love should be placed ' even' in Stella's eyes would be an insult and no compliment.

Sonnet viii. l. 2, ' *Forc't :*' the Bright MS. miswrites ' First.'
   „   l. 3, '*Is :*' Q 1, ' were'—a remnant of the 'hearts'
in the same, and not altered in Q 2, while altering to ' Is.'

Sonnet viii. l. 4, '*flying :*' 2 qu. 'fleeting:' the former
agrees better with the kind of ' race' noted than ' fleeting.'

Sonnet viii. l. 5, ' *too :*' this from Q 1 seems preferable to
' do,' Q 2 and A and A 1613.

Sonnet viii. l. 6, '*clips :*' this, from Q 2 and A and A 1613,
agrees better with ' embrace' than 'lippes,' Q 1, and shows a
more total coldness. Clip=embrace or hug.

Sonnet viii. l. 7, ' *art,*' sometimes misprinted ' dart,' as in
Gray's Misc. Works, and American reprint.

Sonnet viii. l. 8, '*perch'd :*' Q 2 misprints 'preach'd.'
   „   l. 9, ' *on :*' A 1613 has badly ' or.'
   „   l. 10, '*quaking :*' ibid. ' waking.'

Sonnet ix. l. 2, ' *choysest.*' Here and elsewhere 'chiefest'
is changed in A to ' choicest.' Cf. Sonnet x. l. 4.

Sonnet ix. l. 4, ' *gold.*' Stella's, therefore, was the strange
beauty of a golden-haired blonde with dark eyes. Cf. l. 12,
and Son. vii. viii. l. 9; xiii. ll. 10 -11.   Henry Constable in
' Diana' (Son. x.), ' To the Ladie Rich,' sings thus of her :

> ' A field of lilies, roses proper bare
> To stars in chiefe, the crest was waves of gold :'

and see that other to Mr. Hilliard upon occasion of a picture of
my Lady Rich, No. 6, p. 45 (Hazlitt's ed. 1859). It was perhaps this peculiarity of golden hair and fair rosy complexion
with dark eyes—a peculiarity which would give particular bril-
liancy and mark to the eyes—that caused Sidney to name her
Stella.

Sonnet ix. l. 5, ' *comes.*' Q 1 has ' runnes,' a mistake for
' romes' of Q 2 : but I prefer ' comes,' A and A 1613, as expressing better that she ' sent forth' her grace or graciousness.

Sonnet ix. l. 7, ' *which :*' 2 qu. misprint ' with,' a not un-
frequent mistake in these poems and elsewhere.

Sonnet ix. l. 11=dare claim for themselves the name of
' best,' and so dispossess Stella's eyes of that title.

Sonnet ix. ll. 12-14, '*Touch.*' There is a quibble here throughout. '*Touch*,' though used for any costly marble, is properly, says Nares, the *basanitis* of the Greeks, the hard black stone of the Rosetta inscription, and he refers to Dean Vincent's Commerce of the Anc. ii. 534. Hence its use here, for it will be remembered that Stella's eyes were a lustrous black. But in l. 14 he evidently uses the same word in its other meaning, and indicates that her eyes were like lighted tinder or matchlock match, and he the straw that they inflamed. Halliwell, *s.v.*, gives '*Touch-box*, a receptacle for lighted tinder carried by soldiers for matchlocks.' '*Touchwood*' is still in use; and cf. Son. xv. l. 10. Sir John Harington seems to have had these lines in mind when he says (Epigr. iv. 91), ' Of a Lady in a Straw Hat:

> '*What architect this work so strangely matcht*
> *An yvory house, doors, walls,—and windows tutch ;*
> *A gilded roof with straw all over-thatcht.*'

Sonnet ix. l. 13, '*mine :*' so in 2 qu., and the Bright MS. '*myne.*' '*Mind*' of A is repeated in A 1613. So also in Donne '*mind*' is miswritten for '*mine.*' The error here is continued by Gray and modern editors.

Sonnet x. l. 2, '*brabbling :*' in Bright MS. '*arguing.*' Looking to Sidney's frame of mind when he wrote the sonnet, and his view, that reason was intermeddling where not wanted, '*brabbling*' seems preferable.

Sonnet x. l. 3, '*wisht :*' 2 qu. '*wish.*'

„   l. 4, '*choysest :*' Q 2, '*cheefest.*' See note on Sonnet ix. l. 2.

Sonnet x. l. 5, '*inside :*' the Bright MS. has '*in sight*'—an error. The converse error is made in Sidney's Psalmes of Dauid, xvii. 3 : l. 2, where we read (from MS.) '*searching inside tride.*' See in the place.

Sonnet x. l. 12, '*For :*' 2 qu. '*so :*' the former agrees better with '*than.*'

Sonnet x. l. 13, '*kneeld'st :*' '*knewest*' in 2 qu.: '*kneeld'st,*' A. Both give good sense, and as the person is Reason, it is hard to say which is the better. But '*kneeld'st*' is perhaps the more forcible and the more agreeable to the custom of the Tiltyard, whence the whole metaphor is drawn, and it has the appearance of being an after-change, introducing a new image and thought in a passage where the '*knowing*' is sufficiently expressed by '*proving by reason good.*' I adopt '*kneeld'st.*'

Sonnet xi. In this sonnet nearly every alteration in A from the quartos is for the better, beginning with l. 1, ' O' for ' oh :' l. 7, the child has a ' faire,' *i.e.* excellently got-up book; but it is not so much a ' faire' (2 qu.) or beautifully limned picture that he would dwell on as on a ' fine' or gaudy one. Cf. ' gilded leaves,' &c.: l. 4, ' For' (A) is better than ' that' (2 qu.), because the answering clause begins ' So' (l. 9), and because ' that' seems to make the clause correlative with ' that' of l. 3, whereas it is not: l. 10. ' Lok'st,' present, requires to be ' lookd'st' (A). Cf. ' saw'st' (l. 9) and ' did'st set' (l. 11): l. 12, Cupid could hardly be in her breast without ' touching' (Q 2), and Sidney would hardly alter ' lowting'=bowing, or making obeisance, to ' touching.' I take it therefore to be an error for ' crouching' (A). For an example of ' lout,' used in this sense, see last line of Song xi., where it marks the obeisance on leaving ; also our Fraunce in Psalm xxix.:

> ' Kneele to the King of Kings, and bring your dutiful offrings
> *Lout* to the lyuing Lord.'

So too in the ' Return from Pernassus' (1606):

> ' his starres hath fauor'd him so ill
> As to debarre him by his dunghill thoughts
> Iustly to esteeme my verses *lowting* pitch.'   Act ii. sc. 4.

It is in every-day use in Scotland still. Line 11, ' pitfall' and ' pitfould.' Both meant not only what we call a pitfall, but also a gin or snare for small birds. See Halliwell *s.v.*, Cooper &c. *s.* Decipulum, Ryder *s.* pitfall=avicipula, Cotgrave *s.* Trebuchet. Our view therefore is, that as Cupids are little toying snares (cf. day-nets, Son. xii.), and as ' pitfall' (2 qu.) is suggestive of the true pitfall for wild-beasts, Sidney altered it to ' pitfold' (A). That ' pitfall' did mean sometimes a snare for birds is sufficiently evidenced by the following from Lod. Barrey's ' Ram Alley' (1636):

> ' like a bird in bird-lime or a *pit-fall*,
> The more a [=it] labours, still the deeper in.'   Act i. sc. 1.

On ' babies' in her eyes (l. 10) see our MARVELL, vol. i. p. 114. In l. 12, ' has' for ' hast' metri gratia.

Sonnet xii. l. 2, ' *locks* . . . *day-nets.*' For ' locks' 2 qu. has ' lookes :' for ' day-nets' of Q 2 we have in A and A 1613 ' daunces.' Either ' locks' as ' lookes' might be used as=Cupid's ' nets' (' day-nets'). For ' daunces' Q 1 misreads ' dimnesse,'. and the Bright MS. ' daynties' (which also has ' locks'). A MS. annotator 1674, in one of our copies of Arcadia, gives ' dancet,' a

line in heraldry; it is not wavy, but indented or notched or zig-
zag, and therefore scarcely applies. The curious thing is,
that the word of one agrees better with the opposite word of the
other:

$$\begin{matrix} \text{'looks} \\ \text{locks} \end{matrix} > < \begin{matrix} \text{day-nets} \\ \text{dances.'} \end{matrix}$$

As the hair is not otherwise mentioned, I adopt 'locks.'
'Daunces' (A) may be explained by the phrase of the eyes
'dancing with delight.' 'Day-nets' (Q 2) is given in Halliwell
on the authority of Diet. Rust [ique] as a net for catching small
birds. Query—a corruption of dare or daze-net, where mirrors
were used? These being necessarily 'day-nets' in opposition
to night-snares, the corruption was easy.

Sonnet xii. 1. 3, '*sweld*'= [are] swelled. Another of the not
infrequent instances of participles in -ed requiring some part
of the substantive verb to be supplied.

Sonnet xiii. 1. 12, '*curtaines :*' Q 1, Q 2, 'curtane.'

" 1. 13, '*these last :*' Q 1 and Q 2 and Bright MS.
'the last'—inferior.

Sonnet xiii. 1. 14, '*scantly :*' 'scarcely' (2 qu.). As they bore
arms, they were gentlemen. Hence A's 'scantly' is preferable,
as showing that they were on the borders, but only just within
the borders, of that rank. 'Scarcely' infers they had hardly
reached the rank.

Sonnet xiv. 1. 2, '*Gripe*'=(γρύψ), griffin or vulture, says
Nares. He should have said 'griffin or eagle,' both because it
is applied to the eagle of Prometheus, and because the vulture
neither tires with sharp claws nor feeds on living animals, but on
carrion; 'tire'=seize with the beak (Fr. tirer).

Sonnet xiv. 1. 5, '*rubarb*.' He says 'rubarb,' because its
various kinds, partly from its real effects, and partly from its
colour, were supposed to cleanse the liver, and the liver was the
supposed seat of desire and fleshly love.

Sonnet xiv. 1. 12, '*that :*' Q 2, ' it.' The former preferable.
Cf. 'that' in 1. 9. Mistake of y^t and yt common.

Sonnet xv. 1. 4, '*thereabouts :*' more substantival, and therefore better when 'near' is prefixed than 'thereabout.' 2 qu.
and Bright MS.

Sonnet xv. 11. 5-6. Alliteration is 'Dictionarie's or alpha-
betical method;' and 1. 6 sarcastically illustrates this. Dryden
has a similar conjunction of rhyming and rattling, though he is
not attacking Doeg-Settle on the score of alliteration:

> ' He was too warm on picking words to dwell,
> But fagoted his notions as they fell,
> And if they rhymed and rattled, all was well.'

(Abs. and Achit. pt. 2). Christie has no note hereon. Sidney himself is alliterative beyond what one would expect from these lines, as an observant reader will soon detect.

Sonnet xv. l. 8, '*denisend:*' Q 2 has ' deuised;' Q 1, ' disguised:' both errors. Denisened is=naturalised in English.

Sonnet xv. l. 10, '*tuch*'—not perhaps=touch in musical technical sense, but as if kindled tinder or coal=fire. See note on Son. ix. l. 14.

Sonnet xvi. l. 1=I being by nature apt to like. Hence ' nature,' not as usual ' Nature.'

Sonnet xvi. l. 8, '*soule:*' 2 qu. and Bright MS. ' loue.' As Love is an extraneous personified power (l. 4), and as it is other souls that pine with the pains of love, ' soule' is superior.

Sonnet xvi. l. 9. I accept here Q 2. In A 1613 'fool' is inserted in parentheses after I. In A it is not, nor ' young,' thus leaving the line imperfect.

Sonnet xvi. l. 14. Both for neatness of wording and metre I have preferred Q 1 to Q 2 and A; ' doth' is superfluous, and the trochee poïsŏnd is unpleasant, especially when dŏth poïson follows:

> 'As they | that be | ĭng poï | sŏn'd poï | son know
> As who | by being | poïsŏn'd | doth poi | son know.'

Moreover, that Q 1 is the better seems to be borne out by l. 3, where soon (Q 2 and A) is not so expressive of the effect of great beauty on a nature apt to like all things as is ' then' (Q 1).

Sonnet xvii. l. 2, '*growne:*' ' grew,' 2 qu., not English; the construction being not—that Mars ' grew' slacker; but—that Cupid did not move Mars, [now] ' grown' slacker (A).

Sonnet xvii. l. 4, '*place:*' ' pace' in Q 2 and A and A 1613. This seems justified by ' move' (l. 3). But in sense here used, a ' state' does not ' pace,' and in no sense otherwise than very measuredly; whereas the metaphorical use of the technical hawking term ' place' (Q 1), the height to which the falcon soars, is most common. Hence I adjudge ' pace' to have been an accidental error in MS. or type of Q 2 unwittingly perpetuated in A and A 1613, and so return upon Q 1 for ' place.'

Sonnet xvii. l. 6, '*proue*'=as we say, try.

    ,,   l. 8, '*while:*' ' where,' 2 qu. ' While' is so superior to ' where,' that I take the latter to be an error. The interchange is not uncommon.

Sonnet xviii. 1.1, '*sharpe :*' Q 2 '**strange.**' The '**checkes**' by which he in himself is '**shent**' are the considerations below, as in ll. 9-12; but these, though they might be and would be '**sharpe**' in one of Sidney's dispositions, could not in any way, to a man like him, be '**strange**' (2 qu.). Perhaps the latter was a misreading for '**strong**;' '**shent**'=scolded or punished.

Sonnet xviii. l. 11, '*spoile*'=despoil.

,, xix. l. 13, '*fruits*.' The Bright MS. has '**witts**,' but clearly by mistake. '**Wits**' do not grow in a mind as something new, the produce of the mind; and the verb '**prop**,' as one props an overladen branch fit by nature for best fruit, but unable in growth to support the weight, seems decisive.

Sonnet xix. l. 8, '*Auise*'=advise. In Q 1 '**accuse.**' '**Advise**' (=auise or warn) and '**accuse**' seem almost equal; but as the fault is not so much in the words as in the speaker, '**auise**' is better. We have the word in Hausted's Rivall Friends (1632), '**Are you avis'd of that?**' (*bis*, act v. sc. 4).

Sonnet xix. l. 14, '*your :*' '**thy**,' Q 1 and Bright MS.

,, xx. l. 3, '*darke*.' As the whole sonnet plays on the darkness of Stella's eyes, no-doubt '**darke**' of A and A 1613 is the later change for '**a**' of 2 qu.

Sonnet xx. l. 6, '*faire :*' 2 qu. '**farre**'—the latter an error for '**faire**' of A and A 1613. Cupid could get no such secret ambush, nor one where he could level so fairly=take so fair or excellent point-blank aim.

Sonnet xx. l. 8, '*himselfe . . . he*,' Q 2 and Bright MS. and A 1613: '**he himself**,' Q 1 and A.

Sonnet xx. l. 12, '*lightning :*' Q 2, '**lightning's grace.**' The latter is a strange grace and phrase, but '**lightning grace**' is not; and while there is a constant interchange in MSS. of '**then**' and '**there**' (Q1 and Q 2), the former agrees better with '**straight**'. (l. 12) and '**motions.**'

Sonnet xxi. l. 6, '*yeeres :*' in Q 2 '**giers**,' which, as=gears, can hardly be a variant reading, but=gyres, it might be right, and may have been made when or after '**windlas**' was substituted for '**menace**' of Q 1. But as '**yeeres**' of Q 1 is returned to in A and A 1613, it is safer to adhere to it. See also note on Sonnet xxxvi. l. 2, golden (A) yielding: and in Sonnet xcviii. l. 7, '**though gald**' of later Arcadias, Q 1 and Q 2, '**though gold**,' A and A 1605, and '**thus held**,' Q 1 and Q 2.

Sonnet xxi. l. 2, '*windlas*'=catch or ensnare craftily or by indirect acts, or perhaps envelop in snaring cords. A windlass (not the machine) is a circuitous course (see Golding's Cæsar, in Richardson, *s. v.*), and to 'windlas' .s to fetch a windlass or compass : and as such indirectness is generally taken, whether in words, hunting, or at bowls, or in anything else, for policy's sake and to ensnare or find out, the word is commonly used in passages involving these meanings. See Hamlet, act ii. sc. 1. Some examples, with the explanation of the word, are given in the Edinburgh Review, No. 187. It is a curious instance of the association of craft with indirect ways in the human mind, that the engine called a windlass, which by winding moves weights that could not be moved by the same force directly applied, is called in French *singe*, the crafty ape. It may be added, that though some of the Elizabethan spellings lead to the belief that they adopted the plausible etymology of wind-lace, to lace windingly, the verb is doubtless formed from the substantive, and that again is connected with ' windles.'

Sonnet xxi. l. 9, '*March :*' the misprint ' Mars,' Q 1 (but it is curious ' mad Mars' occurs in Sonnet lxxv.) led to ' promise made *to* me,' and the error of ' to' probably escaped notice in correcting for Q 2, but was altered to the right word ' of' in A.

Sonnet xxi. l. 10, '*May.*' See note on next sonnet, l. 2.

  „   l. 13, ' *dig :*' 2 qu. ' digs,' in error.

  „   xxii. l. 2. Q 1, in error, inserts ' in' after ' twinnes.'

  „   l. 3, '*maske.*' I accept this for ' scarf' of A and A 1613, seeing that as he compares the Sun's face with the ladies' and Stella's, it is more fitting, and probably later.

Sonnet xxii. l. 4, ' *streaming.*' I adopt this from Q 1 in preference to ' shining' of Q 2, A, and A 1613, as more forcible.

Sonnet xxii. l. 10, '*which open.*' Q 1 reads, not happily, ' as carelesse showne.'

Sonnet xxii. l. 13, '*dainties.*' Q 2, by ' dainties,' corrects the error of ' daintiest' in Q 1, A, A 1613, &c.

Sonnet xxii. l. 14, ' *that.*' I accept ' that' of Q 1, as better than ' which' of Q 2, A, and A 1613.

With reference to this sonnet, it is probable that in l. 10 of the preceding there was an intended double conceit, and that it was written in May. The present one was evidently so written, or shortly after May. We may here recall Spenser's brilliant portrait of May:

' Then came fair May, the fayrest mayd on ground,
Deckt all with dainties of her season's pryde,

And throwing flores out of her lap around :
Upon two brethren's shoulders she did ride,
The twinnes of Leda, which on either side
Supported her like to their soveraine Queene.'

Sonnet xxiii. l. 6, ' *deeme :*' Q 2 misreads ' deem'd.'

    ,,   l. 9, ' *ambition's :*' more poetic and Elizabethan than ' ambitious' of 2 qu.

Sonnet xxiii. l. 11, '*captiv'd.*' Cf. SOUTHWELL, *s.v.*

    ,,   l. 12, ' *race.*' Query—have ' case'? But I doubt whether any example of case=cause, can be found. The converse error is made by 2 qu. lxiv. l. 7, of ' race' for ' case,' where ll. 2, 3, 6, 7 rhyme together, and where, therefore, l. 7 cannot repeat the ' race' of l. 2, such repetition being unknown in these sonnets. Besides, the words ' stop' and ' start' seem imperative for ' race'—the quick progress that sees nothing but the goal; and this is confirmed by two parallel passages in the Countess of Pembroke's portion of the Psalms, *e. g.*

'While circling time, still ending and beginning,
Shall run the race when stop nor start appeares.'
                Ps. lxxxix. st. x. ll. 1, 2.

' Thou makest the sunne the chariot-man of light
Well knowe the start and stop of dayly race.'
                Ps. civ. st. ix. ll. 3, 4.

' Race' is used similarly in Sonnet xxii. l. 6 ; Sonnet xxvi. l. 13 (A), where it or ' case' (2 qu.) may be taken, but where ' race' seems better and more Sidneian; Sonnet lx. l. 5, ' Fortune's race:' Sonnet lxiv. l. 2, where the ' race' of the passions is spoken of instead of his thoughts; and, strangest use of all, Sonnet cv. l. 6,—on which see our note,—' the telescope's dazzling race.' May not most of these passages be quoted as strengthening the original reading of King John (act iii. sc. 3), ' into the drowsy race of night' ?

Sonnet xxiii. l. 13, ' *hath.*' 2 qu. read ' have.' As ' race of all my thoughts' may mean the race of each of various thoughts, one striving against the other, the plural verb might be justified; but having the choice between it and ' hath' (A and A 1613), we adopt the latter. Unless ' have' were determined in the plural by the accident of ' thoughts' coming just before it, it would go also to prove ' race' to be the true reading (as above) in l. 12, for ' case' could not take a verb plural.

Sonnet xxiv. l. 3, ' *Tantal's.*' Q 1 has ' Tantalus his'—probably a corrector's attempt to amend some error in his copy, for the genitival form ' Tantalus his' is not found elsewhere in A and S.

Sonnet xxiv. l. 4, '*rich :*' so in 2 qu. and preferable to 'blest' of A and A 1613, seeing the whole sonnet is a sarcastic play on the name of Lord 'Rich.'   See our Essay.

Sonnet xxiv. ll. 7, 8. This has been hitherto punctuated into puzzling nonsense. I have re-punctuated so as to bring out the sense = 'and knowing [what their hands hold], they lay love and loving apart (as they would sacred things) far from even the show of danger.'   'Scattered' of Q 2 is a misreading of ' sacred.'

Sonnet xxv. ll. 1, 2. I have deleted (,) [comma] after 'wise' as obscuring the sense. Socrates was pronounced by the oracle ' the wisest of men :' Plato, his scholar, spoke as in text.

Sonnet xxv. l. 3, '*met.*' 2 qu. misread 'meete'=if it once did meet.   So in l. 10 the past tense is required.

Sonnet xxv. l. 6, '*whiles :*' during the time when, more sub-stantival than 'while' (Q 1 and Q 2), and hence better here.

Sonnet xxv. l. 8, '*sunne :*' 2 qu. misread 'summe.'

        ,,   l. 10, '*herselfe :*' 2 qu. here and throughout read 'himselfe.'   Virtue (ἀρετή, *virtus*) is always personified as a female (even *virtus*, manly valour), and there is no neces-sity here for changing the sex.   Cf. also Sonnet ix. 'Queen Virtue.'

Sonnet xxv. l. 13, '*that :*' 2 qu. 'her.'   The 'her' may have come from 'her' just above, or may have been the Author's; but strictly speaking, 'that face' (A and A 1613) is more correct, seeing it was not Stella's face only, but *ex supp.* Virtue's and Stella's.   It is Virtue's great beauty that he sees.

The reference to Plato's saying concerning Virtue recalls an anecdote concerning Dr. Hugh Blair and his colleague Dr. Robert Walker. The former was what the Evangelicals re-garded as a mere Moralist, and grew eloquent after his prim sort on 'virtue' rather than on 'grace.' One forenoon, having discoursed on Virtue, he paraphrased Plato's saying to the effect that if She [Virtue] were now to appear on earth, all men would fall down and worship her. Dr. Walker, who was a thorough Evangelical, in the afternoon took up his colleague's words of the morning, and, with crushing effect and a rush of eloquence born of profoundest conviction, exclaimed, 'Virtue did appear on the earth, and they—crucified her !' and then went on to expatiate on the 'enmity' of the unrenewed heart to what is good. The anecdote seems to be well authenticated, although, for Walker, other names are sometimes given.

Sonnet xxv. 1. 14, '*th*' *effect :*' Q 1 has 'defect'—a curious instance of error from sound.

Sonnet xxvi. 1. 1, '*dustie :*' better than 'duskie' of Q 1 and Q 2, as=earth-low.

Sonnet xxvi. 1. 3, '*number, waies,*' &c. The blunders of editions after 1605 improvingly blundered in modern. 'Waies' is=ways, not 'weighs.'

Sonnet xxvi. 1. 4. 2 qu. read

'Promising wondrous wonders to inuite.'

I cannot see sense herein, while A is clear, which says—Whose number,.ways, &c., as they promise wonders to the inquirer, so do they invite wonder.

Sonnet xxvi. 1. 6, '*sky :*' 2 qu. 'skyes' — error. Cf. rhymes 'eternitie,' 1. 3, and 'hie,' 1. 7.

Sonnet xxvi. 1. 9, '*vnidle :*' here and elsewhere 'idle' does not mean wholly passive or resting, but frivolously or triflingly employed. Cf. 'idle toys.'

Sonnet xxvi. 1. 13, '*fore-see.*' I adopt this from Q 2 as more accurate than 'fore-iudge' (by the stars). Q 1 has 'bewraies.'

Sonnet xxvi. 1. 13, '*race.*' See note on xxiii. 1. 12. Looking well to it in itself and to the other examples quoted, while probably Sidney did write 'case' here as in Q 1 and Q 2, I think on revision he changed it to 'fore-see . . . race,' in the sense of progress of events. Thus taken it seems more poetic, and the sense more comprehensive.

Sonnet xxvii. 1. 3, '*or :*' 2 qu. 'and.'

,, 1. 8, '*and :*' 2 qu. 'all.' The latter is more taking, but it makes an ambiguous sentence (=it might be myself [whom] all others do despise—a meaning not the Author's); and by -ᴜ instead of ᴜ- the rhythm is worsened.

Sonnet xxvii. 1. 10, '*his :*' Q 1 and Q 2, 'this.' The soul looks in 'his vnflattering glass;' but it is difficult to see how he could look in 'this,' because there is nothing to which 'this' can refer. The error of interchange is a common one, as pointed out in our SOUTHWELL and DONNE.

Sonnet xxvii. 1. 13, '*place.*' See note on Sonnet xvii. 1. 4.

,, xxviii. 1. 3, '*God's sake :*' Q 2, 'good now' seems an attempt to soften down 'God's sake' (Q 1), to which A and A 1613 return.

Sonnet xxviii. 1. 5, '*say :*' 2 qu. 'see'—an evident error.

,, 1. 7=though the reins are never slack, and by their tight curbing pain me.

Sonnet xxviii. 1. 10, '*do :*' 2 qu. 'to.' Either might be with
Q 2 and A reading, but Q 1 reading 'hidden ways' rather requires ' do,' yet has 'to.' Hence, as frequently, we may take
this as an error which escaped correction in the altered copy
of Q 1, from which Q 2 was printed; fetched probably from
' to' of line above.

Sonnet xxviii. 1. 14, '*reading.*' Looking to the arts of eloquence (1. 9) and philosophy (1. 10), which were in technical
language 'read' in the Schools, I prefer the probably after-
change ' reading' (A and A 1613), and ' unto' to ' leading' . . .
' into' (Q 1 and Q 2).

Sonnet xxix. 1. 2, '*coasts*' (A) is more correct, as more than
one lord and one kingdom is spoken of; besides, the plural was
often used in this sense, even when one kingdom or province
was spoken of; witness our English Bible : *e.g.* 'all the *coasts* of
Egypt,' Exodus x. 14; ' all thy *coasts*,' Deut. xxviii. 40. So
that ' coast' of Q 1 and Q 2 is an error.

Sonnet xxix. 1. 4, '*store :*' 2 qu. 'serve.' One 'serves' a
meal or a guest, but ' stores' (A) a camp; and ' stores' is also
the stronger.

Sonnet xxix. 1. 7, '*frontiers :*' 2 qu. 'frontire.' Either might
be adopted; but as he enumerates different frontiers below (see
note on 1. 2), ' frontiers' (A) is adhered to.

Sonnet xxix. 1. 11, '*carre :*' 2 qu. 'chare,' old form of
' car.'

Sonnet xxix. 1. 12, '*flesh:*' 2 qu. ' selfe'—a mistake, of which
there are two examples in DONNE, for ' flesh.'

Sonnet xxix. 1. 14, ' *a :*' omitted in 2 qu.

,,   xxx. 1. 2, ' *her.*' The Author, thinking rather of the
Turk, has ' his' (A and A 1613); but ' her' (2 qu.) is more correct, and I adopt it. In like manner Shakespeare and the
author of Cock Lorell's Bote call Hesperus 'her,' because to
English Latinate ears Venus was the common and more personal name.

Sonnet xxx. 1. 3, ' *Poles :*' 2 qu. 'Poland's king.' The
Polish monarchy was elective, and when the foreigner, Henry
of Valois, left the throne of Poland to take that of France, the
nobles elected Stephen Bathori, a Pole (1575). Hence ' the
Poles' right king' of A and A 1613. Both, however, were probably written by Sidney, for the after-change of A was not a
prudent phrase in 1581, when ' Monsieur' came over to woo
Elizabeth, and when Sidney had already been outspoken be-

yond what seemed prudent, and could only await results. There
seems no doubt that, directly or indirectly, Sidney himself was
offered the throne of Poland.

Sonnet xxx. l. 7, '*be :*' 2 qu. '*are :*' English idiom allows
'be,' and with good effect.

Sonnet xxx. l. 8, '*pleasant :*' 2 qu. 'pleasing'—the former
(A and A 1613) the better epithet for a tree.

Sonnet xxx. l. 9, '*that same :*' 2 qu. 'the same.' Sidney's
father's successes were remarkable, and never more so than on
the third occasion of his being sent over; and 'that' seems to
call attention to this, and to be stronger, and therefore preferable.

Sonnet xxx. l. 11, '*no weltering*' is stronger and more
expressive of the turbulence and broils of the Scotch Court.
Hence I prefer A and A 1613 to 2 qu. 'If in the Scottish Court
be weltering yet.'

Sonnet xxx. l. 14, '*of :*' 2 qu. 'on :' 'of' is a favourite particle with Sidney, and to 'think *of*' is stronger and more
expressive of full-given thought than 'on.'

Sonnet xxxi. l. 2, '*wanne.*' So, in A, 'wan :' but in 2 qu.
and other Arcadia texts 'meane.' With our present sense
'meane' is intolerable; but in Sidney's time it may have been
an adjectival use of mean or mene=lamenting. See note on
Sonnet xxxv. l. 11.

Sonnet xxxi. ll. 7, 8. These lines, according to reading and
punctuation of 2 qu.—viz.

'I reade within thy lookes thy languisht grace,
    To mee that feele the like, my state discries:'

—form each a clause. But though one reads 'in' out of or
through, to read a thing within one's looks is a strange phrase,
and it is difficult, if not impossible, to understand how one can
read an outward and visible sign like the moon's languisht
grace, *i. e:* her 'wan face' of l. 2, 'within her looks.' Again,
if l. 8 be a distinct clause, the state descries—what? The
rhythm too agrees in making 'looks' end one clause, and 'descries' the other. But if so, 'I read within thy looks' is not
sense, whereas 'I read it in thy looks' (A and A 1613) is. And
again, in the next clause, the construction is, To me that feel
the like (my sympathy giving me the insight) thy languisht
grace, thy wan (pale) face, descries=points out 'thy' state.
Since, therefore, O Moon, I have rightly divined your state,
then of fellowship tell me, &c. 'My' is clearly one of those

frequent pronominal interchanges that transcribers make unwittingly, or to give a fancied sense of their own. It would be
absurd of the Moon to point out to Sidney his own state. 'Descries' is now used in the reflective sense of pointing out to
oneself, or rather perhaps in the sense of seeing out or beyond;
but in Sidney's day it had also the meaning of pointing out
to another, as here and as in the Countess of Pembroke's
Passion (Stanza lxxvi.):

> 'Behould the heavens what sorrowe they did showe,
> And how the earth her dolor did *discrye*.'

We have ' descry' used thus much later, *e. g.* in Lod. Barrey's
' Ram Alley' (1636), as follows :

> ' some scullion in a hole
> Begot thee on a gipsie, or
> Thy mother was some Collier's whore :
> "My rampant tricks!" you rogue, thou't be descride
> Before our plot be ended.
> *W. S.* What should *descry* him,
> Vnlesse it be his nose?'   Act ii. sc. 1.

The ' nose' is after the type of Bardolph's, and could not fail
to ' point out' its owner. See also Stanza viii. 1. 2, and Psalms
cxix. M, l. 3.

Sonnet xxxi. l. 11, ' *they*.' This is more indefinite and therefore better than ' there' (2 qu.). ' There' implies that there are
others in the world not proud; but in his love Stella is all the
world and all womankind to him, and so is she in his bitter-
ness and despair. That the correct reading is ' they' is also
shown by ' they' of ll. 12 and 14.

Sonnet xxxii. l. 1, ' *liuely*'=life-like or motioning.

     ,,   l. 4, ' *or :*' 2 qu. ' and'—a mistake.

     ,,   l. 13, ' *Sire*'=Somnus, l. 1. ' Fire,' a modern
error, as in Gray, &c. It is ' Sire' in 2 qu. and A 1613, &c.

Sonnet xxxiii. l. 2, ' *or :*' 2 qu. ' nor.' The former gives the
better sense, because Sidney represents himself as doubtful of
which might be the reason.

Sonnet xxxiii. l. 4, ' *I did*' (A and A 1613) better than ' did
I' of 2 qu.

Sonnet xxxiv. There are propositions and questioning answers here between his passion wit and his more essential or
intellectual wit. 1st Wit says, ' Come, let me write.' 2d Wit,
' To what end?' (1st) ' To ease . . . heart;' (2d) ' How . . .
care;' (1st) ' Oft . . . please,' l. 4; (2d) l. 5; (1st) l. 6; (2d)

l. 7; (1st) l. 8; (2d) l. 9; (1st) l. 10; (2d) l. 11. I have made the punctuation—hitherto mere confusion—accord herewith. So throughout.

Sonnet xxxiv. l. 8, 2 qu. read, 'Then be they close, and they shall none displease.' Cf. our text (A and A 1613). Both readings will suit, but A is the later; probably for this reason 2d Wit objects what 'wise men' will think. 1st Wit answers according to 2 qu. that if kept close none will be displeased; and Sidney seeing this makes him solicitous as to whether he displeases fools as well as wise—the multitude as well as the few —seems to have altered it to make ' none' a nominative agreeing with 'words.' The construction, however, is awkward. Indeed, after all, ' none' may be=not at all, and in such 2 qu. offer the better reading.

Sonnet xxxv. l. 6, 'coale in :' 2 qu. 'to.' As he speaks of ' his flames,' and as the coal is the love within him, and as he means his inward Reason itself increases the flame of love ' in' him, ' in' (A and A 1613) seems preferable, and so ' coale' (ib.) as generic rather than ' coals' (Q 1 and Q 2).

Sonnet xxxv. l. 11, ' rich.' Another play on ' Rich'—Stella being Lady Rich. So Henry Constable's Diana, Son. x. and Addl. Son. vi. p. 39.

Sonnet xxxv. l. 11, ' meaning.' I adopt this from 2 qu. in preference to ' naming.' Pinkerton has stated that ' mean' is still used in Scottish law phraseology as ' declaring,' or as we would say, setting forth; and it has been well remarked that in Midsummer-Night's Dream Shakespeare seems by the use of 'videlicet' to be using a law term in a burlesque sense :

' And thus she [Thisbe] means, videlicet.'

The present phrase of ' Fame meaning,' i.e. declaring or setting forth Stella's name, may be taken as the decisive phrase that was wanting to confirm this view. Only it must be added that Shakespeare probably made Demetrius pun, and use the word in the double sense of ' set forth' her case, and mean, moan or lament. For the later sense see our note on Sonnet xxxi, l. 2.

Sonnet xxxvi. l. 2, 'yeelding.' I adopt this from 2 qu., as ' golden' of A and A 1613 seems to be the same kind of mistake as ' giers' for ' years' (Q 1 and A) in Sonnet xxi. l. 6. Cf. also ' this held' (Q 1 and Q 2) for ' though gald,' later A : Sonnet xcviii. l. 7.

Sonnet xxxvi. l. 6. All the editions agree in [.] after ' in'

(l. 4), but 2 qu. have no stop after 'within' (l. 6)=thy banners of conquest, while A punctuates within :=effects of conquest. A continuation of the clause into the first part of the
next line is frequent in these sonnets, and the ' what' of 2 qu.
(l. 7) favours the view that Sidney meant banners of conquest,
and the plural ' assaults' (l. 1) and ' new' (l. 8) seem to approve
their readings of this sonnet. Accordingly I accept 'these
assaults' for ' this assault' (A and A 1613) : ' doth'=from what
'doth' arise these new assaults. I read in l. 7 ' do not,' else
there would be for these sonnets the unusual foot | Of conquest | ,
and besides, without 'not' (as in Q 1 and Q 2) the clause is
meaningless.

Sonnet xxxvi. l. 6, ' *My forces razde*' = erased from the
muster-roll, the word being chosen for its similarity in sound
to 'rais'd.' But had not the readings been unanimous, I should
have queried ' forces' as against 'fortress.'

Sonnet xxxvi. l. 9. The sense is at first sight obscure. The
construction is, ' with so sweet voice and by sweet Nature
[formed] so [*i.e.* so sweet] in sweetest strength. On the supposition that there is an ellipse, ' and by sweet Nature [formed]
so [sweet] in sweetest strength' we have tautology, albeit not
uncharacteristic of lingering over ' sweet.'

Sonnet xxxvi. ll. 10-11. The punctuation has been hitherto
ruined by the lavish use of commas. ' With . . . . strength' is
a clause telling what Nature did : ' so sweetly . . . . show' is
the clause telling what Art has done. I have punctuated accordingly.

Sonnet xxxvi. l. 13, '*but*.' This is supposed to contain the
negative expressed above and afterwards, and to be equal to
' but not' or ' but now.'

Sonnet xxxvii. See our Essay on this sonnet.

  ,,   xxxviii. l. 2, ' *hatch*'=shut or close—it is ' close' in
2 qu. For ' that' (A and A 1613) 2 qu. read ' the'—the former
far better=while that, because it separates ' his thought' from
the extraneous power ' sleep,' while ' the' rather connects them.
Cf. also ' my chief powres,' which is also against ' the.'

Sonnet xxxviii. l. 9 = was held in the closed-up senses.
2 qu. misread ' inclos'd-up,' which is not English ; nor does it
give sense in this passage.

Sonnet xxxviii. l. 10, ' *opend:*' 2 qu. ' open:' the former
almost demanded by ' clos'd;' and Sidney is speaking of awak-
ened, *i.e.* opened sense, not of open sense. There are at least

seven instances of the omission of a final *d* in the transcript of these poems, and several where *d* has been wrongly added.

Sonnet xxxviii. l. 12, '*sights :*' 2 qu. 'sighes'—the latter a mistake. He says that in sight's decay, *i.e.* in sleep, he sees better sights, that is, Stella's image, than when awake.

Sonnet xxxviii. l. 13, '*anew.*' Q 2, 'a new'—only one of the old ways of writing 'anew,' like 'a bed' for 'abed.'

Sonnet xxxviii. l. 13, '*Cald :*' '*conclude* anew,' Q 2. Probably variations like 'close' and 'hatch;' but 'conclude' =shut up [my lids] is strange and harsh, and so probably thought Sidney after the novelty of the change was over, for A (as A 1613), which in this sonnet agrees everywhere else with Q 2 against Q 1, here returns to the reading of the latter, 'Cald.'

Sonnet xxxix. l. 2, '*baiting :*' 2 qu. erroneously read 'bathing;'=refreshing place. See our Essay on this in particular and the whole sonnet. For 'wit,' 2 qu. read 'wits'= witty men.

Sonnet xxxix. l. 4, '*Th*'.' The variations 'Th',' 'The,' are mere variations through the carelessness of a transcriber.

Sonnet xxxix. l. 5, '*shield.*' One man, and Sleep is one, and is represented as single throughout ll. 1-4, carries one shield (A and A 1613) : hence 'shields' of 2 qu. incorrect.

Sonnet xxxix. l. 6, '*those :*' 2 qu. 'these :' the former more agrees with the sense, and is required by 'those civil wars,' l. 7.

Sonnet xxxix. l. 10, '*of.*' I take 'of,' as more Sidneian, from Q 1 and Q 2, and think 'to ... to' the Countess's or Editor's improvement. So too 'in' (l. 12) for 'by.'

Sonnet xxxix. l. 11, '*rosie garland,*' as the garland of silence (*sub rosa*)—a pun that would have delighted Thomas Fuller, and Charles Lamb if he had noticed it. For a curious instance of the same use of 'rose' for 'silence,' see H. S.'s address prefixed to the Arcadia, given in its place in the second portion of the present Volume.

Sonnet xxxix. l. 14, '*Stella's image.*' Q 1 has 'rare Stella's' —an early reading, altered probably because it required an awkward elision, Stella's' image.

Sonnet xl. l. 3, '*That :*' so our text (A 1613), in agreement with 2 qu. A has 'Thou.' I accept 'That.'

Sonnet xl. l. 3, '*nowe ;*' 'none' in our text (A 1613), in agreement with A; but in 2 qu. there is the very remarkable reading of 'nowe,' which I adopt. Granted that 'w' is a com-

mon error for ' n ;' granted also that a mind may be wrecked
while becoming base is quite a different thing. But is not this
' different thing' just what we long for a recognition of by Sidney in the conditions under which these Sonnets were composed? Is ' nowe' not that sharp cry of mingled penitence and
fascination one would wish to hear? See more of this in our
Essay.

Sonnet xl. l. 11, ' *noble*.' I accept this from A in preference
to ' noblest' of 2 qu. and A 1613 : =conquerors at all entitled
to the epithet noble.

Sonnet xl. l. 11, ' *wreckes*.' Q 1, ' wreakes :' Q 2, ' wreake :'
' wrecks,' A : ' wreckes,' A 1613. Q 1 and A and A 1613 agree
in *s*. There is in this sonnet no question of Stella revenging
herself or having cause for revenge ; but he speaks in previous
lines of the ' wreck' he is becoming, and (in l. 14) asks her not
to destroy that which is her temple, viz. himself. Perhaps one
of the most noticeable of these sonnets autobiographically.

Sonnet xli. l. 9, ' *of*' (A and A 1613) implies, and in that day
still more implied, relationship, as in offspring ; besides, the
double ' from' (Q 1 and Q 2) is awkward ; ' *from* both sides he
took his blood *from* them.'

Sonnet xli. l. 11, ' *at* :' I take ' at' (Q 1 and Q 2) rather than
' of' (A and A 1613), because ' at' is our present form, and both
were then used.

Sonnet xli. l. 14, ' *my*' (A and A 1613)—superior to ' a' (Q 1
and Q 2).

Sonnet xlii. l. 2, ' *be* :' Q 1 and Q 2 ' all'—at first an attrac-
tive reading ; but if the beams be ' all' joys, then the joys cannot be all virtues, or virtuous.

Sonnet xlii. l. 6, ' *tyrans*.' So in A, and accepted. It is to
be noted that in A, where the spelling, on the whole, has been
carefully attended to, ' tyrant' is invariably, as in Ben Jonson,
and in agreement with its derivation, ' tyran,' and plural ' tyrans.' We may take this therefore to have been Sidney's own
spelling.

Sonnet xlii. l. 7, ' *O* :' 2 qu. delete ' O,' and insert ' one'
before ' remove.'

Sonnet xlii. l. 14, ' *be* :' 2 qu. read stupidly ' best.'

   ,,   xliii. l. 4, ' *choise* :' 2 qu. ' chief'—a third instance
of this change, showing it to be intentional. See note on Sonnet ix. l. 2.

Sonnet xliii. l. 10, ' *doth* :' 2 qu. ' doe.' As in Donne and other transcripts, a constant yet inconstant interchange of 'doth' and 'doe.' A and A 1613 almost always correct in this.

Sonnet xliv. l. 5, '*And yet . . . . and yet.*' The repetition of 'and yet' is in the true mannerism of the time, and hence is preferable to 'And yet . . . . and,' it being understood that there is an elision at 'pitie' I'. Cf. Sonnet lvii. l. 5, &c. The 'yet' is used in double sense; the first 'yet' being as often= 'still' or continually, the second='still' or up to this time.

Sonnet xliv. l. 7, '*overthwart*'=opposite, cross.

„ l. 10, '*complaints :*' better than 'complaint' of 2 qu. Cf. ll. 6, 13-14.

Sonnet xlv. In this sonnet Q 1 is clearly the earlier, and A and A 1613 change in l. 8 'That from that sea deriv'd tears spring did flow,' compared with the reading in the text (A and A 1613), decisively shows the latter to be the later, the new image being according to the then philosophy of the rise of springs by 'privie ways in the earth from the ocean.' See note in our SOUTHWELL, *s.v.*, and cf. DONNE, *s.v.*; also Browne's Brit. Pastorals, Mariner's Song (i. 2).

Sonnet xlv. l. 1, '*woe :*' better than 'woes' (2 qu.), as in a 'man of woe.'

Sonnet xlv. l. 4, '*know :*' again better than 'knows,' as being more grammatically correct. Besides, the 's' form does not rhyme, as it must do, with ll. 5-8, seeing there is no instance throughout these sonnets of there being more than two rhymes in the first eight lines. The 'No' of 2 qu. for 'not' is a mistake, due to the 't' of the next word, and A and A 1613 return to Q 1, reading 'Not.'

Sonnet xlv. l. 12, '*you in me*' (A and A 1613), not 'in me you' (2 qu.), is the later text and better, because an emphasis is thrown on the 'me,' which points out that he would be considered as the sad tragedy.

Sonnet xlv. l. 13, '*thrise-sad.*' I could not resist the temptation of the epithet here 'thrise' from Q 2. Against it is the earlier Q 1, and A and A 1613 return to the earlier. Still the very inevitable elongation in reading seems the more to tell of the 'sad tragedy.'

Sonnet xlvi. l. 12, '*his pardon . . . . so long.*' He asks for Cupid's pardon until &c. There is no kind of pardon mentioned, and therefore 2 qu. are wrong in reading 'this pardon.'

Sonnet xlvi. l. 13, '*myche*'=to play truant : ''to miche' is a modern error not in A texts.

Sonnet xlvi. l. 14, '*you :*' 'thou' of 2 qu. disagrees with
'you' of l. 12, and requires 'canst.'

Sonnet xlvii. l. 7, '*tho :*' misprinted 'the' in 2 qu.

,,   l. 12, '*goe.*' A and A 1613 misread 'do,' probably from the previous 'do' and 'to.' I adopt 2 qu. 'Here'
in Q 1 and A and A 1613, 'there' in Q 2—the latter a repetition
of the 't' of 'but.'

Sonnet xlvii. l. 14, '*to give.*' So Q 1 and A 1613: 'give to,'
Q 2, A, and A 1605: former preferable. 'The lie :' 2 qu. has
badly 'a lie.'

Sonnet xlviii. l. 3, '*Paine doth learn.*' Q 1 has the variant
'scorning youthe's.'

Sonnet xlviii. l. 7, '*hel-driu'n.*' Q 1 has 'blinded'—inferior.

,,   xlix. l. 1, '*doth :*' agreeing with the nearer nominative, as in Latin.

Sonnet xlix. l. 4=the wrongs done by man I descrie in me
=myself.

Sonnet xlix. l. 6, '*humbled :*' better than 'reverent' of 2 qu.

,,   l. l. 8, '*that which in,*' A and A 1613 : 'what within,'
2 qu.: indifferent, but A perhaps stronger.

Sonnet l. l. 11, '*these :*' 2 qu. 'those'=sonnets of ll. 9-10:
hence 'these,' as in A and A 1613.

Sonnet l. ll. 13-14, '*stopt . . . bare :*' 2 qu. 'stop . . . beares;'
but 'had dashed' requires the former.

Sonnet li. l. 2, '*flauntingly,*' 2 qu.: 'fluently,' A and A
1613—the former preferable, as it introduces something different from the 'new' of l. 4.

Sonnet li. l. 5, '*the :*' 2 qu. 'your,' wrongly.

,,   li. l. 10, '*cunningst,*' 2 qu.: a better reading decidedly than 'cunning,' and later than A and A 1613.

Sonnet li. l. 11, '*waies :*' 2 qu. misread 'waues'—a transcriber's 'improvement,' to be in (supposed) harmony with
Fishers, &c.

Sonnet li. l. 13, '*een woe,*' 2 qu. : A and A 1613, inferiorly;
'euen irkt.'

Sonnet lii. l. 3, '*saith Loue :*' 2 qu. 'Loue saith that he
owes'=owns, but Q 2 and A and A 1613 preferable.

Sonnet lii. l. 11, '*manner place :*' an archaism very common in Batman on Bartholomew: 'There is a manner running
water' (l. 13, c. 21): 'And they [fishes] haue a manner lyke-
nesse and kind [nature] of creeping' (c. 29): 'And of adders
is many manner kind; and how many kind, so many manner

venim; and how many speces [species] so many manner ma-
lice, and so manner sores and aches, as there are colours, as
Isid saith' (l. 18, c. 9).

Sonnet liii. l. 3, '*people's shouts :*' Q 1 has ' people shoutes,'
and Q 2 'while that the peopl's showtes'—both erroneous. A
and A 1613 adopted.

Sonnet liii. l. 6, ' *Marses :*' so in Sonnet xvii. The 2 qu.
' Mars his'—a transcriber's variant spelling. Sidney in Astrophel and Stella nowhere uses, if I err not, the falsely-sup-
posed primitive form '—his.'

Sonnet liii. l. 7, '*I would no lesse*'=I wanted nothing less
than that epithet, I being filled with pride would have had it
least of all things. The phrase is analogous to ''tis nothing
less'=it is anything rather than (Richard II. act ii. sc. 2).

Sonnet liii. l. 9, ' *made :*' 2 qu. 'through.' The former preferable, because it does not so carry the mind to a candle behind a window, which is the light one generally sees ' through'
a window, as to the sun's dazzling light that one so often sees
(reflected but seemingly) in it. Stella, it must be remembered,
is constantly ' his sun.'

Sonnet liii. l. 13, ' *beat the air*'=beat space instead of me
in his prancing and feats of the manége. Shakespeare adapts
and revises the phrase when Angelo (Measure for Measure,
act ii. sc. 4) would rather be

' an idle plume
Which the air beats for vain.'

=which the air sways first one way and then another, as
though it were an empty thing, lighter and more variable than
itself.

Sonnet liv. l. 3, ' *of :*' 2 qu. ' with,' in error.

    „   l. 10, ' *Profess :*' ' protest,' 2 qu.

    „ lv. l. 1, ' *holy :*' Q 1 misprints ' whole,' and reads
' haue crau'd.'

Sonnet lv. l. 3, ' *despisde :*' 2 qu. badly ' disguisde.'

    „   l. 4, ' *grace :*' for the second ' grace,' 2 qu. read
' skill ;' but as ' grace' is such a sought mannerism of the time,
and agrees so much better with ' engarland,' I believe it a later
change, as in A and A 1613.

Sonnet lv. l. 10, ' *sugring.*' Cf. Sonnet xxv. l. 2 ; Sonnet
lix. l. 11 ; Sonnet lxxiii. l. 5. Here is explained the origin,
apparently hitherto overlooked, of the after well-known ' love-
locks,' though this at first love-Nazarite vow seems to have

become a mere fashion. With, I presume, interruptions—for later writers seem to call it, or some variation of it, a newly-imported French custom — it lasted through several generations, preserved by the opposition it met with and by its having become a party badge. Every one will remember one 'Deformed,' who, as Dogberry says, they say 'wears a key in his ear and a lock hanging by it.' Here the 'key' was probably an earring, or it may have been a jewel attached to the 'lock;' for in early times at least the 'lock' was worn with a silk twist or ribbon in it, often probably the colour or gift of the lady-mistress.

Sonnet lvi. l. 11, 'stuffe :' Q 1 badly misprints 'strife.'

,,   lvii. l. 1, 'fights :' Q 2, 'sighs.' The latter looks a tempting reading, but it is an error probably caused by influence of 'woe.' The context, especially l. 3, favours 'fights,' and Woe fighting by means of sighs is an image incongruous with that of slaves finding words fit for Woe's self to groan (l. 4).

Sonnet lvii. l. 2, 'growne'=[being] growne.

,,   l. 5, 'Stella 'alone.' Cf. note on Sonnet xliv. l. 5.

,,   l. 7, 'but :' wrongly omitted in Q 1.

,,   l. 8, 'pierc'd :' better than 'hurt' (2 qu.), because, as evidenced by 'thorowest' and 'sharpnesse,' the words were to pierce like a lance or to winged arrows (ἔπεα πτερόεντα). See l. 9 of next sonnet.

Sonnet lviii. l. 4, 'he :' 2 qu. 'in.' One cannot rein horses 'in' slack, and if one could, Sidney would have written 'them in.' Moreover with 'in' the expression is bad and obscure.

Sonnet lviii. l. 6, 'with :' 2 qu. 'as his'—the latter a blunder caused by sight of 'this' above.

Sonnet lviii. l. 7, 'Or else pronouncing grace,' i. e. [with] pronouncing grace. It may, however, be doubted whether Sidney intended the 'with' of 'with words' to be understood here, or whether it is to be taken out of 'wherewith.' This latter, though strange to us, can be exemplified by passages in our elder writers, who disliked such reduplications. See our DONNE; and there are these two from Henry Constable:

'An angell's face had angell's puritye,
And thou an angell's tongue didst speke withall.'
2d Sonnet to St. Katharyne.

'Yett, if those graces God to me impart
Which He inspyr'd thy blessèd brest withall'
8d Sonnet to St. M. Magd.

where we should require [with] an angel's tongue, and [with]
which—
Sonnet lviii. ll. 13-14. The construction is — Maugre the
might of my sad speeches which wooed woe (ll. 5-6 and 9-10),
even those sad words bred even in sad me ravishing delight
when breathed by Stella's pronouncing grace (l. 7). The 2 qu.
readings,

> 'With wooed words' most rauishing delight
> Eucn in bad mec a ioy to me did breede,'

do nothing with 'ravishing delight.' Hence 'with' is probably the frequent mistake for 'which,' due to the wth and w^{ch}
of mss. The rest is puzzling; perhaps the conjectural change
of some one who saw the sense intended, but could not construe the passage.

Sonnet lix. l. 2, 2 qu. 'alas' for first 'burne.'

„ l. 4, supply [he] can be but a dog.

„ ll. 13-14: alluding, as does Donne, to the saying
that a lover cannot be wise.

Sonnet lx. l. 2, 'Where :' Q 1, 'where's :' Q 2, 'where :' a
mistake, the 's' of Q 1 was struck out, and the faithful printer
kept the (').

Sonnet lx. l. 1, 'Thundring,' A : 'Thundred,' 2 qu. : and A
1613 seems to me to give, without intent, an unpleasant reference to her voice, whereas the allusion is to the black and thun-
der-bearing clouds of her disdainful looks. 'Lightnings' in
plural rather than singular of 2 qu. agrees best with sense and
with 'disdains' and 'glances.'

Sonnet lx. l. 11, 'lovely :' 2 qu. misprint 'louing.'

„ l. 12, 'I' is preferable to 'to' of 2 qu.

„ lxi. l. 1, 'uncallèd'=called forth on slight and insufficient provocation.

Sonnet lxi. l. 3, 'assaid :' same sense as 'assaild' of 2 qu.;
but shows (what he supposed was the fact) less power in the
attacking and less result on the attacked party.

Sonnet lxi. l. 5, 'in-felt :' really felt in the soul, in the
better self, not seated merely in the liver and flesh. This,
therefore, is a better reading than 'sound,' 2 qu.

Sonnet lxi. l. 7, 'selfenesse.' Query, a coinage by Sidney?

„ l. 8. His desires are already existent, and she
says 'then' he learns how evil those are, and 'then' learns
what they should be. There is also a greater fulness of
thought in 'then' and 'thence' than in 'thence' only, 2 qu.

Sonnet lxi. 1. 9. As yet in the progress of his sonnets and of his love she has confessed no 'love' (2 qu.), but is a 'saint.' Cf. Sonnets lxii. lxvi. lxvii. lxix. Besides, she says, since her 'chaste mind' hates this love in Sidney, so he, if with in-felt affection he is captived to her with 'chast'ned mind,' then she can remove him from such love. And against 'this' (2 qu.) there are two arguments : (a) that there is no love of hers previously spoken of in the sonnet ; (b) that the sentence is a continuation of her words repeated in the third person. In all these cases A and A 1613 give the better readings, and hence and from the same ' desires' is preferable to ' desire' (2 qu.).

Sonnet lxii. 1. 3, ' loue though :' Q 1, ' loue's fyres'—the latter inappropriate to her described state, and hence altered.

Sonnet lxii. 1. 4, ' sweet said that:' rhythm of A and A 1613 seems preferable to ' Sweetely said I,' especially as ' I' commences a new clause.

Sonnet lxii. 1. 6, ' loued a loue,' as in A and A 1613, gives the sense intended, and such as is given by 2 qu. ; but probably Sidney, who was fond of such repetitions, meant to alter ' with a loue' of 2 qu. to ' loued with loue,' and having left the words below, the editor struck out ' with' below ' loued,' instead of ' a.'

Sonnet lxii. 1. 10, ' these :' i.e. such as he mentions 1. 2, and which caused her to speak, hence better than ' those' (2 qu.).

Sonnet lxiii. 1. 2, ' still read'=so [may] children still read you.

Sonnet lxiii. 1. 4, ' by her owne vertue,' technical legal=by virtue of her own act.

Sonnet lxiii. 1. 8, ' once :' contrasts better with ' twise' than ' one' of 2 qu.

Sonnet lxiii. 1. 9, ' Io Pæan :' so Q 1 and A and A 1613. ' I do,' Q 2.

Sonnet lxiii. 1. 11, ' success'=result, as frequently in those days.

Sonnet lxiii. 1. 12, ' O :' 2 qu. ' ah,' not Sidneian.

,,   lxiv. 1. 6, ' trace :' 2 qu. ' try'—the latter an error caught from the rhyme ' eye' above. So too in l. 7 ' rase' is an error in 2 qu., for ' case' or ' race' has already occurred in l. 2. Hence too I accept ' with' for ' in' in l. 7 ; but in l. 2 ' with' of A and A 1613 is a misprint for ' wish' of 2 qu. In l. 5, Q 1 reads badly ' bereaues mine eyes.'

Sonnet lxv. l. 2, '*That giu'st :*' 2 qu. 'That giues.' Old writers were not very accurate in this; but we adopt A and A 1613, especially as they are in other points more correct, as l. 2, 'eare,' not 'eares' (which is not idiomatic English) : l. 3, 'should' for 'shouldst' (2 qu.), where the transcriber has been misled by 'Thou,' the true nominative being 'good turns.'

Sonnet lxv. l. 6, '*too-too :*' far more in manner of the day than 'to be' (Q 2).

Sonnet lxv. l. 10. If one looks at 'eyes . . . . light,' it will be seen that 'heart . . . . life' (A and A 1613) is the better sequence, and more regular than 'life . . . . heart' (2 qu.).

Sonnet lxv. l. 11, '*passe*' = over-pass, and therefore dominate.

Sonnet lxv. l. 13, '*hate :*' modern texts erroneously 'had.'

„   l. 14. Cf. on Sonnet lxxii. l. 8.

„ lxvi. l. 3, '*apprehending :*' the act of the faculty of apprehension seems better than 'apprehension' (2 qu.) : and l. 12, 'looke' (2 qu.), is proved to be a mistake for 'look'd' by 'sent' (l. 11) and 'did' (l. 13), *e* having in several instances in these sonnets been read for *d*. But the rhythm of l. 8 leads me to adopt the reading of the 2 qu. with 'desier' as a trisyllable and 'the' omitted, and to think 'the' an editorial amendment.

Sonnet lxvi. l. 6, '*Fortune wheels.*' If we adopt 'Fortunes =Fortune's wheels,' 'slowe' must be taken as a verb=go slow; but the 's' of wheels in Q 2 and A and A 1613, and in 'windes' of Q 1, leads me to imagine that 'Fortune wheels' (Q 2), where 'wheels' is a verb, is correct; for Fortune is only represented with one wheel. There is doubtless in this sonnet (ll. 6-7) a reminiscence of Sidney's loss of prospects by Leicester's; a loss which made him, in her friends' eyes, no longer a fit match for Stella; but it is here applied, as shown by the context, metaphorically, to his having received as yet nothing from her whence he could say he was enriched with her love.

Sonnet lxvi. l. 9, '*a hope :*' modern editions 'as,' an error.

„ lxvii. l. 3. Stella had known well for days and months that she reigned over Sidney, her conquest; and 'pitious' (l. 2) and 'take time' (on which see onward), and 'wrackèd' (l. 4), all show the thought to be, Will she relent before her conquest be an utter ruin and waste? The 'this' (2 qu.) seems an error, for 'The ruins of this' &c. is bad rhythm, nor is there any antecedent to 'this.' It was probably a conjectural insertion and an attempt to amend the ms. here 'the raigne of her.'

Sonnet lxvii. 1. 4, '*take time*.' In our day this means delay, make no undue haste, but only good speed; but besides this meaning, it also, and apparently more generally, meant, in Elizabethan phraseology, take time as it passes, take opportunity now. Cf. Tempest, act ii. sc. 1, song.

Sonnet lxvii. 1. 5, '*eye speech*' (2 qu.) = eye-speech : eyes' speech (A and A 1613, ' eyes-speech'), indifferent—for forms analogous to both are to be found. The 2 qu. reading 'fine,' 1. 7, which is better than ' true' (A and A 1613), is balanced by their errors.

Sonnet lxviii. 1. 5, '*treasures :*' better than 'treasure' (2 qu.).

„   1. 8, '*Fed . . . worth :*' 2 qu. ' Set . . . wrath.' The latter mere errors. He has called her ' wrath' still lovely, but throughout it is her ' worth' as well as beauty that makes him love ; her beauty inflames, and her worth keeps up the flame. ' Kindled' (2 qu.) corrects a very noticeable error of A and A 1613 of ' blinded.' But Q 1 makes a worse mistake in 1. 14, by reading ' annoy' for ' enioy :' also in 1. 11 the 2 qu. badly misprint ' are' for ' on.' In 1. 6 we have ˉAmphĭŏn : in 3d Song, i. 4, ˉAmphĭŏn—noted as a caution to those who find so many proofs of Shakespeare's lack of learning in such things.

Sonnet lxix. 1. 1, '*stile :*' 2 qu. misprint 'loue still.' His love has not ' still' or continually shown joy, but only ' woe.' This sonnet marks his first certainty of being loved (cf. Sonnet lxx. 1. 2). The word ' high' shows the antithetical ' low style' to be the true reading. He has several times spoken of his ' stile' as uninfluenced by the beauties with which others adorn their songs : and cf. next line also.

Sonnet lxix. 1. 2, '*state*.' This constantly so-used Elizabethan word is better than ' seat' of 2 qu.

Sonnet lxix. 1. 4, '*do :*' 2 qu. ' doth'—usual error through influence of ' delight.'

Sonnet lxix. 1. 13, '*vertuous :*' better than ' vertue's' (2 qu.) —each of which would produce the other, because it is ' virtuous' course in especial reference to this love.

Sonnet lxx. 1. 4, '*Ioue's :*' modern editions ' Loue's,' without authority.

Sonnet lxx. 11. 6-8, '*so*,' 2 qu. : ' as,' A and A 1613 : former more archaic.

Sonnet lxx. l. 9. Sidney never could write 'shew the height of delight' (2 qu.). The corrector probably altered ' force' (Q 1) to ' height,' but omitted to change ' the' (Q 1) to ' thou.'

Sonnet lxxi. l. 5, ' *vices*'.' As shown by ' night-birds, and vices,' the better reading is ' those' not ' these' (2 qu.) ; for night-birds and owls, or the like, do not fly Stella, but those owl-vices do.

Sonnet lxxi. l. 11, ' *in thee*,' A and A 1613—the usual mannerism repetition, and though Q 2 may be a variant (' in deede'), it is open to the suspicion that part only of Q 1 was corrected. It is also in favour of ' in thee' being a later change, that all the readings of A and A 1613 in this sonnet are better than those of 2 qu.

Sonnet lxxi. l. 12, ' *draws*,' A and A 1613, agrees better with ' bends' than ' driues' (2 qu.). And ' the heart'=the hearts of all minds which all strive, the word being used generally, better than ' my.' He does not now speak of his heart only : his particular addition comes in l. 14.

Sonnet lxxii. l. 4, ' *While*'=And both of you blowe.

,, l. 8. A reference to the arms assigned by fanciful heralds to Cupid, the Love spoken of.

Sonnet lxxii. l. 10, ' *will :*' 2 qu. and modern editions ' well :' but the latter makes nonsense. The true reading (A and A 1613) is undoubtedly ' will :' (*a*) because ' will,' generally used in a bad sense=sensual will (as in Shakespeare's Sonnets), is here spoken of as a purified will worthy to appear : (*b*) because each of the three lines, ll. 9-11, is made up of two clauses.

Sonnet lxxii. l. 14, ' *how shall ?*' either for shalt, metri gr. or=how shall I banish thee?

Sonnet lxxiii. l. 6, ' *suckt :*' 2 qu. misread ' sucke.'

,, l. 8. Q 1 has ' that prest so nye'—an early variant, but not só good as A and A 1613, because it does not clearly disjoin Love from Sidney's self.

Sonnet lxxiii. l. 14, ' *Anger's :*' A 1613 ' Anger selfe.'

,, lxxiv. l. 2, ' *euer*.' This recurrence from Q 2 to Q 1 and Sonnet lxiii. make me discard ' neuer' (Q 2) as a transcriber's variant.

Sonnet lxxiv. l. 7, ' *blackest brooke*'=Styx :

'Umbrarum hic locus est, Somni Noctisque soporae.'   Æn. vi. 390.

and he swears by it the strictest oath of the gods :

' Dii cujus jurare timent et fallere numen.'   Ib. 324.

Sonnet lxxiv. l. 14, 'sweet:' 2 qu. 'sure.' The latter jars so much with 'sure' (l. 13), that I regard it as a memory error: the pause too after 'sweet' gives a better closing rhythm.

Sonnet lxxv. l. 7, 'mad:' Q 1, 'make.'

  ,,   l. 13, 'knight:' 2 qu. 'king.' He has already called him 'king,' and now speaks not of his kingly acts, but of his chivalrous devotion as a true 'knight.' Line 6 refers to his reconquest of the crown; l. 8 to his attempts to reform abuses in the law-courts, so that justice might weigh with equal scales; l. 11 to his after-war with France, though the hedging of the fleur-de-lys with lions' paws is somewhat of an anachronism if it refer to the Lancastrian English, for they as a party had been broken some time previously; l. 14 refers to his marriage with Lady Elizabeth Grey, whence, as is well known, the defection of the King-maker took its rise.

Sonnet lxxvi. l. 3, 'Benighted . . . . . shining:' Q 1 has 'Bathde:' Q 2 'benighted:' 2 qu. 'shining.' With 'benighted' in 'shining' there is a foot too much. I apprehend Sidney's earlier words may have been, 'Bathde . . . . shining;' but as they made Stella, his sun, too decidedly masculine and himself feminine, he altered as in text.

Sonnet lxxvi. l. 6, 'force:' which in l. 5 refers to light and warmth. Therefore 'force,' A and A 1613, not 'face' (Q 1). We should say Aurora's. 'Mine' is better here than 'my' (2 qu.).

Sonnet lxxvi. l. 10, 'glistring:' 2 qu. 'glittering.'

  ,,   l. 11, 'ah' (A and A 1613): 'oh,' Q 2: 'O,' Q 1.

  ,,   l. 13, 'aching,' in A and A 1613 and Q 2 'walking:' in Q 1 'waking.' I read (meo periculo) 'aching,' knowing how spread-out and difficult Sidney's handwriting was. Nothing is more common than headache from an over-fierce sun. It might be 'watching,' but 'aching' might easily be misread 'wa.'

Sonnet lxxvi. l. 14, 'meeker' (Q 1), to which A and A 1613 return; 'mee her' (Q 2) being stark naught, though an easy error. Sidney going to bed with her hot beams would have been a male Semele.

Sonnet lxxvii. l. 2, 'lecture shews.' Cf. Donne's 'Love-Lecture' (vol. ii. pp. 440-1).

Sonnet lxxvii. l. 7, 'passe-praise,' A and A 1613: 'past-praise,' Q 2: 'passing,' Q 1.

Sonnet lxxvii. l. 12, 'quietst,' A and A 1613: stronger than 'quiet' (2 qu.), and better agreeing with 'best :' 'judgments' (2 qu.) agrees with 'thoughts,' and both allow of the thought of what was the fact, that he now has best thoughts and quietest judgments, now worse thoughts and unquiet judgments, troubled by the influence of desire—that he is, in fact, swayed to and fro.

Sonnet lxxviii. This sonnet is wretchedly given in both quartos, e.g. they misprint in l. 5 'harms' for 'harme :' l. 7, 'heart' for 'hurt :' l. 8, 'injuries' for 'injurie :' l. 11, 'though still' for 'stirre still'=continually.

Sonnet lxxviii. l. 13. A very curious double instance in Q 1 (partly uncorrected in Q 2) of taking a word from line below. Q 1 has, l. 12, 'as' for 'aye,' taking it from 'as' of l. 13, and for 'as' of l. 13 is taken 'that' from l. 14. Q 2 corrects l. 12 to 'aye,' but did not correct l. 13.

aye	as	aye
as	that	that
that	that	that
A and A 1613.	Q 1.	Q 2.

Sonnet lxxviii. l. 14, 'euill :' 2 qu. 'ill.' Sidney, like Southwell, used 'euill' as a monosyllable.

Sonnet lxxix. l. 2, 'sweetner :' 2 qu. 'sweeter'—the latter inferior. See also on next Sonnet, l. 6.

Sonnet lxxix. ll. 3-4, 'consort'=a tune in parts. A consort of music cannot have anything to do with 'coupling doves,' and this shows our punctuation 'part ;' is correct, and that l. 4 is a new clause and thought. 'Which,' therefore (not 'With,' Q 2) is the analogue of 'Which,' l. 2, and the sense is 'Which being coupling doues,' or 'Which coupling doves together thus guides.' The allusion is to the representations of Venus's chariot drawn by billing doves.

Sonnet lxxix. l. 5, 'fight :' 'sight,' Q 2, a printer's error.

     ,,   l. 6, 'opens :' 'openeth,' 2 qu. Indifferent, but it seems to me that 'opens' is, so to speak, more transitive. A door 'openeth' or 'opens' to, a key opens to, i.e. opens the door to.

Sonnet lxxix. l. 10, 'both :' 'do,' Q 2 : former more expressive.

Sonnet lxxix. l. 12, 'ostage'=hostage=pledge ; but 'ostage' is clearly the later revisal of 'pledge' (Q 1). Moreover 'pledge,' if taken in sense of 'oath,' is, and especially in Sidney's case was, too strong.

Sonnet lxxx. l. 1.   Cf. Song 2, vi. 1.

,,   l. 2, '*wit :*' 'best' (Q 1) probably original reading, but 'wit' (Q 2, and A and A 1613) later and better.

Sonnet lxxx. l. 5, ' *Muses :*' 'graces,' Q 1, caught from line above.

Sonnet lxxx. l. 6, '*sweetner :*' 'sweetness,' 2 qu. The latter an error. Her lips are not represented so much as the 'sweetness' of music in what they utter, but as ' sweetness' of what was already music, whether the music were *ab intra* or *ab extra*, and it agrees with the next -er forms, including 'fastner.' 'Fastness'=fortress would, in the language of that day, be a very equivocal compliment, as may be judged from the account of the tilt before Queen Elizabeth in 1581, when Sidney was a Knight of Desire.   Besides, a person, or part of a person, may be said to be dyed in grain, but a fortress so dyed is absurd; and that 'fastner' was the original word is shown because it suggested the remembrance of the 'mordants' used to fasten colours in dyeing, and so suggested the pretty thought of the dyeing Beauty's blush in Honour's grain.

Sonnet lxxx. l. 8, '*grain.*' As there has been a good deal of confusion, from which Richardson is by no means free, as to the two words 'grain,' it may not be amiss to say here that there is, 1. Grain, a scarlet, and not a gray or other coloured dye, and which is so called, according to Du Cange, *s.v.* Grana, because there is ' Italis Bacca cujusdam arboris similis hederae, cujus usus est ad tincturam ejus panni quem vocant *Scarlatum.*' Whether Du Cange be right in his natural history, and whether it be a berry or the insect cochineal, or both, does not just now matter.   What does matter is that it was a scarlet dye. 2. Grain, the word which, whatever may be its root, signifies the fabric-arrangement or the fabric itself.   Thus it is the grain of wood, that peculiarity of structure which goes through and through it, and is its characteristic and make, and of which graining in wood-painting is an imitation (of the surface).   So a rogue in grain is a rogue in every fibre ; and though a robe of grain would be (1) a scarlet robe, and though (2) dyed in grain might in a particular case mean dyed in scarlet, the phrase in its idiomatic signification is a thing not superficially or partially dyed, but dyed through and through—a dye that, as Shakespeare says, will endure wind and weather (Twelfth Night, act i. sc. 5).   In the present passage, though Sidney may have had a conceit, and made use of the double word to convey a fullest sense, it is obvious that the primary sense is the second, ' Beautie's blush dyed in Honour's web and woof.'

Sonnet lxxx. l. 10, '*mouth :*' better than 'tongue' (2 qu.), because the line runs parallel with the previous one, and because the subject of the sonnet is not the 'tongue' as a speaker, but the 'lip,' and also because there is a reference to St. Matthew xii. 34.

Sonnet lxxx. l. 11, '*doubting*' = suspecting: its frequent meaning at that time.

Sonnet lxxx. l. 12, '*his resty*,' *i.e.* his, the mouth's, race now resty: ' this,' 2 qu.—often miswritten for ' his'—rather includes the whole that race, ll. 1-8, where out of the abundance of the heart the mouth spoke — a race anything but 'resty.' 'Resty'=restive, staying or stopping, and therefore stubborn. It is so used in a translation of Calvin, and so Chapman, &c. (Il. b. 5): Richardson *s.v.* The variations of Q 1 are all early: l. 3, 'stall' is used, it must be remembered, for a cathedral or church stall, as well as for an ox-stall. Query—any inner reference to the 'stable' and 'manger' of Bethlehem?

Sonnet lxxx. ll. 13-14. Construction is, Without, sweet lip, you teach with a kiss, how far, &c.

Sonnet lxxxi. l. 2, '*gemmes :*' Q 1, 'ioyes.'

„ l. 3, '*sweetning :*' 'sweetness,' 2 qu. The meaning of this is evident, but 'sweetning' divides the thought, and makes two of it. The kiss breathes all bliss, and is also 'sweetning' to the heart. Hence 'sweetning' the later elaboration.

Sonnet lxxxi. l. 14. In a note on the following lines of his Ivy Church:

> ' Eccho could not now to the last woord yeild any eccho,
> All opprest with loue, for her ould loue stil she remembred,
> And she remembred stil that sweete Narcissus her ould loue,'

Fraunce gets quaintly irate with those who had objected that 'stil' had been repeated for the sake of the metre, and tells them that one is an adverb and one an adjective, and to express his meaning and his sarcasm in one, he says, ' and they might as well be *stil* and not speake any thing, as *stil* talk and yet say nothing.' Perhaps Sidney, in saying ' she would have him be silent' (l. 12), intended the like conceit in ' still, still kissing' =be continually silent-kissing me—kissing, not with an ordinary kiss, but with the silent-pressing kiss of passionate love.

Sonnet lxxxii. l. 3, '*lookt :*' 'lock't,' error of Q 1, Q 2, for 'lookt.'

Sonnet lxxxii. l. 6, ' *Esperian*'=Hesperian.

„   l. 8, ' *those :*' better than ' these' (2 qu), because he wishes to approach those cherries from which he is
kept. In a very unlikely place, viz. in Hausted's Rivall Friends
(1632), we have a vivid ' cherry' metaphor worthy of note here
for the student-reader.

Sonnet lxxxii. l. 11, ' *and.*' I have ventured on but one
conjectural emendation thus far. Here the last line seems to
demand that the ' an' of 2 qu. or ' a,' should be ' and.' Without this, the promise not to bite loses its force, and comes upon
one unintelligibly. It is evident too that he calls her lips
cherries to enable him to speak of the bite-kiss that he gave.

Sonnet lxxxiii. l. 1 and l. 14: A and A 1613 read ' Philip' as
a dissyllable in l. 1, and ' Phip' a monosyllable in l. 14. The
2 qu. reverse this, and hence the other changes, ' forborne,'
l. 1, and the omission of ' off,' l. 14. Philip in full seems more
correct with brother, and Sir Phip when he addresses him
finely as a sparrow and sharply—Phillip, Phip.

> ' *Gurney.* Good leave, good Philip.
> *Bastard.*   Phillip!—sparrow!—James,
> There's toys abroad.'   King John, act i. sc. 1.

He being now Sir Richard. See also Skelton's Phyllyp spa-
rowe, and Lyly's Mother Bombie, a sparrow being so called on
account of his ' peep, peep' (l. 6), when, as Catullus says,
pipilabit.

Sonnet lxxxiii. l. 3, ' *cut.*' To ' cut,' in the Caveat for Cur-
sitors, is cant for ' to speak,' and ' cutted' is given by Kersey
as scolding, brawling, quarrelsome, and is so used in Middle-
ton's Women beware Women, act iii. sc. 1. The same author,
also uses ' cut' as a noun or adjective in the same sense in the
punning phrase, ' You'd both need wear *cut* [paned or slashed]
clothes, you are so choleric' (The Mayor of Queensborough,
act v. sc. 1). Hence, in all probability, the term ' cutter' for a
swaggerer or swashbuckler, rather than for the cutting with
their weapons. At least this reconciles all the meanings of
cut, cutted, and cutter, and agrees best with its usages. See
Greene's Friar Bacon and Friar Bungay, *ad init.;* Beaumont
and Fletcher, The Scornful Lady, act v. sc. 4; and in especial,
Wit at several Weapons, act iii. sc. 1 (vol. iv. p. 54, ed. Dyce),
although the sameness of the sound would lead to the stronger
use of the word, and the adoption of the etymology given by
Baily and Nares. Cowley re-christened his surreptitiously

published comedy of 'The Guardian' as 'The *Cutter* of Coleman Street.' Here ' cut'—the only substantival use of the word known to me—means quarrelling, swaggering, or rather discontented or quarrelsome, huffing (huff=to swell out one's feathers, &c.).

Sonnet lxxxiii. l. 5, '*bare.*' Looking to 'bare' and 'borne' (l. i.), ' beare' is a careless error for ' bare' (2 qu.).

Sonnet lxxxiv. l. 1, ' *Pernassus.*' So in the ' Return from Pernassus,' 1606, Ascham in Toxophilus, &c.

Sonnet lxxxiv. l. 2, ' *vnsweet :*' 2 qu. 'unmeet.' As he is speaking of his Muse, and as we have the rhyme 'meet' (l. 6), I think ' vnsweet' the right word (A and A 1613), or at all events the later and better one.

Sonnet lxxxiv. l. 4, ' *oft :*' 'often,' 2 qu. — a syllable too much. Sidney rarely, if ever, elides the -en, except in ' heaven' and ' even,' which are constantly, if not always, monosyllabic.

Sonnet lxxxiv. l. 6, ' *safe-left*' (A and A 1613) is prettier than ' safebest' (2 qu.)=with Stella.

Sonnet lxxxiv. l. 9. From the better rhythm and the other changes, ' faire, honour'd' (A and A 1613) is later, but I am not sure that ' carefull kept' (2 qu.) does not give a better sense.

Sonnet lxxxv. ll. 1, 4-5 and 7, Q 1 gives these early readings : ' Behold my heart the house that thee contains :' ' shames:' ' braines :' ' Striue in themselues each office to.'

Sonnet lxxxv. l. 10, ' *her :*' 2 qu. misprint ' their.'

,, ll. 9-11, ' *eyes* . . . . *ties.*' This recurrence of A and A 1613 to Q 1 alone proves ' eye . . . . tie' (Q 2) to be wrong; but there are other two proofs : ' Eares, arms, and lips' are all in the plural, and ' speech' which requires ' ties.' The change is one of those quasi-grammatical alterations by a transcriber, founded here on the mistake that ' eares' is the nominative to ' ties.'

Sonnet lxxxv. l. 11, ' *wit :*' ' Let eares hear that speech which ties wit to wonder'—unites wisdom or knowledge to wonder, while ' unites will' (2 qu.) is meaningless.

Sonnet lxxxvi. l. 1, ' *came :*' ' comes,' 2 qu.—indifferent.

,, l. 14, ' *should :*' ' shall,' 2 qu.—latter wrong.

,, l. 14, ' *one's*' (2 qu.) better than ' once' (A and A 1613), albeit ' once' is defensible.

Sonnet lxxxvii. At first sight it would seem that Sidney, either from other duty or from the sense of honour spoken of

in Sonnet xci. l. 1, had forced himself away from Stella, and
the latter of these views has been adopted by Bourne in his
Life of Sidney (see our Essay, as before). It is, however, to
Stella's honour that she forced herself to leave him. The
words, ' From Stella . . . . to depart,' seem to contradict this;
but they do not necessarily do so, for ' depart,' in those days,
was often a mere equivalent of ' part,' and to ' depart from' is
merely a Latinate construction. For an example of ' depart' in
this sense, see Song x. vii. 5, a song written about the same
time with this sonnet. That it was she who left, and that the
above phrase must be construed in agreement thereto, is shown,
(a) by the Q 1 reading of l. 4, ' By Stellae's lawes of duetie to
impart' (but ' impart' a misprint for ' depart'), which shows that
the parting was by Stella's will; (b) by Sonnet lxxxix. l. 4,
where it is said, not that he left Stella, but that Stella had left
his hemisphere; (c) by Sonnet xci. ll. 3-5, where he says, ' if
this place in thy absence *yet* shew like candle-light;' (d) by
Song x. st. i. where he makes her wished sight depend on her
will; and (e) by the 2 qu. readings of st. ii. l. 2 of the same
song, ' By thine absence,' for had these words not been dic-
tated by remembrance of the fact that she had left him, and not
he her, he would have written, in natural accord with the question he asks, ' By mine absence.' Hence I intended to have
adopted in our text the reading of ' By thine absence,' as I
do the Q 1 reading of l. 4 of this sonnet. To us who can only
learn the circumstances from Sidney's verse, his poetical changes
must be less considered than a fair lady's fame—on all which
see our Essay for much more. In some of the ' Certain Sonnets' which follow ' Astrophel and Stella' in the present volume,
there is (as pointed out in its place) a notice of Sidney's own
absence in the country; and from the later sonnets of ' Astrophel and Stella,' perhaps from Sonnet xciii. onwards, Stella,
though in London with him, seems to have desired that they
should not meet. See note on Sonnet civ.

    Sonnet lxxxvii. l. 3, ' *tempests:*' 2 qu. perversely misprint
' temples.'

    Sonnet lxxxvii. l. 8, ' *sadded* ' (2 qu.) : more vivid than
' saddest' (A and A 1613).

    Sonnet lxxxvii. l. 9, ' *wept:*' 2 qu. ' weep'—the frequent
error of *d* or *t* final being omitted.

    Sonnet lxxxviii. There are variations in the 2 qu., but all
earlier readings than A and A 1613. We obey a captain wholly

and from the heart, but obedience to a 'conqueror' is different. Hence 'captainesse' is better than 'conqueror.' I would have preferred the reading of l. 4 in Q 1 :

'That to entice mee proffers present paye,'

but that I respect the thought or feeling which made Sidney soften down the words 'entice' and 'proffer' to 'win' and 'show.' In l. 13 the variations are probably author's, and I prefer A and A 1613 because, as in this and previous line, the heart and eyes are evidently his, 'my' (for 'both') is not required, and its absence agrees better with its absence throughout. 2 qu. have 'my,' and 'now' is again 'both' in Q 1. In l. 9 Q 1 reads 'When absence with her mistes obscures her light :' Q 2 as A and A 1613. In some editions of Arcadia, &c. 'mistes' is misprinted 'mistresse.' For note on this sonnet see on Sonnet xci.

Sonnet lxxxix. l. 2, '*my day* :' as he is speaking metaphorically, and of his own day or state, 'my day' is much preferable to 'the' (2 qu.).

Sonnet lxxxix. l. 3, Q 1 inadvertently inserts 'that' before 'wont'—non-metrical.

Sonnet lxxxix. l. 4, Q 1 reads 'o'recast with :' Q 2 'reaues me :' 'eyes' of l. 3 demands 'leaue,' not 'leaues.'

Sonnet lxxxix. l. 7, '*toyled*' for 'tird.'

„   l. 14, Q 1 'gleames'—all these earlier. In ll. 7-14 Sidney at the close of this sentence seems to have forgotten how he began to construct it. At least I cannot construe it satisfactorily to myself.

Sonnet xc. l. 2, '*liue but thee* :' this is strange, but not stranger than 'hope but thee,' and as prepositions 'to,' 'for,' &c. were often omitted in Elizabethan English, so is it more allowable here to omit 'for' or 'in' where the other conjoined verbs do not require either. 'Like' (2 qu.) is an anti-climax and worse after 'loue.' In l. 9 'Ne' (A and A 1613) agrees better than 'Nor' of 2 qu. with the somewhat archaic sentence in which it is placed: but 'could I' (2 qu.) is better than 'I could' of A and A 1613 : and so, l. 10, the transposition of 2 qu. better than 'to me thereof.'

Sonnet xci. l. 2, '*light of light*' (2 qu.) — error of repetition for 'light of life' (A and A 1613).

Sonnet xc. l. 3, '*whiles*' (Q 1), as beginning a parallel clause with l. 1, is preferable to 'that' of Q 2, A and A 1613.

Sonnet xci. l. 5, ' *like :*' 2 qu. 'by.' Stella, his sun, is
absent, and he left in night. ' If, therefore,' he continues,
' meaner beauties having some or some one of thy attributes—
amber hair, milk hands, black eyes, and the like—show " like"
candle-light to me and attract me, understand that they please
me as models of thee.' As Stella is his sun, so are they candle-light to him in his darkness. Thence ' like,' not ' by,' is
the right word.

Sonnet xci. l. 8, ' *seeing gets :*' ' seeming jet.' If 2 qu. be
correct (' seeming jet'), as Mr. Collier (Bibl. Catal. *s.n.*) supposes, then we have two beauties spoken of—the first a blonde,
the second a brunette. But if these particulars be compared
with Sidney's other descriptions of Stella, it will be seen that
in their totality they describe her, and that what he says is ' if
some beauty's piece' have amber hair, another milk hands,
another rose cheeks, and so on, I like them because each is a
poor model of some piece of your perfections. But ' seeming
jet' was no part of Stella's general appearance ; and on the
first supposition that some different and dark Beauty is spoken
of, who can conceive a brunette praised as ' seeming jet black'?
Part, however, of Stella's strange beauty consisted in her amber
hair, fair complexion, and black eyes (see former Note on Sonnet ix.), and I make no doubt but that this, after lips, was the
other piece of beauty that he particularised. If so, both readings are wrong and both partly right, and we should read ' Or
seeing' or ' Or seeings' (=eyes) jet black. I say ' seeing' or
' seeing*s*,' because the latter might account for the ' s' of ' gets,'
and because the plural more definitely substantizes the word,
and because, the first excepted, all the other nouns are plurals
—hands, cheeks, and lips. The use of the participial form as
=the organ of seeing or the seeing parts, is so intelligible and
so idiomatic (cf. for instance ' understanding'), that no other
alteration seems needed or called for. I therefore read ' seeings jet-blacke.'

Sonnet xci. l. 14, ' *O no :*' more expressive than ' No, no,'
2 qu.

It may be remarked here of Sonnets lxxxix. to xci., that
their tone and their subject lead one to imagine, either that
Sidney was endeavouring to rouse Stella's jealousy and so
induce her to return, or that his sonnets were becoming more
of a poetical exercise, and that in the decay of his passion—if
it ever decayed—he could console himself otherwise than by

solitude and melancholy. Those accustomed to the analysis of actions and motives may be inclined to believe both these suppositions. See more on this and the whole subject of Stella (Lady Rich) and Sidney in our Essay, as before.

Sonnet xcii. l. 2, '*mee them*' (A and A 1613) runs better than 'them mee' (2 qu.).

Sonnet xcii. l. 3, '*curted:*' ' cutted' (Q 2, A and A 1613). The latter does not agree with the sense of the passage nor with Spartan character. But Spartan brevity does : hence, irregular as the word is, I accept ' curted' from A 1605 and later. Q 1 has 'do you the Caconians imitate?'—unintelligible to me.

Sonnet xcii. l. 9, '*did*' (2 qu.), omitted, by error, in A and A 1613 : ' do' seems a modern interpolation from ignorance of 2 qu. Similarly, in l. 13, ' daine' of 2 qu. is the several times repeated error of omitting final *d* or *t*, or mistaking it for *e*. Cf. how often did she talk, &c.

Sonnet xcii. l. 12, '*pastimes*' (2 qu.) is probably correct, and seems better than ' pastime :' ' journeys' for ' journey' is more doubtful, unless he took it according to its etymology as=daily courses. I adopt the former, refuse the latter. ' Totall' (of l. 5) is a rather curious use=you tote or sum up my questions in one general and therefore short and single answer.

Sonnet xciii. l. 1, '*fate:*' A 1605 and later editions read ' faire,' and a pathetic passionate meaning might underlie the word in relation to the abrupt ' fault,' ' curse,' &c.

Sonnet xciii. l. 5, '*may :*' 2 qu. ' might'—not so good.

        ,,   l. 10, '*I haue—liue I and know this!—harmèd thee*' (A and A 1613): infinitely superior to 2 qu., ' I do sweete Loue' (=give myself this excuse), a repetition from l. 9, ' and [yet] know that this harmèd thee.'

Sonnet xciii. l. 11, ' *Tho' :*' 2 qu. ' the,' which is not sense : but ' worlds' (A 1613) is deeper and stronger than ' words' (A), and than ' world' (2 qu.).=This alone is his comfort, that his own woes are eased by his adopting and bearing her griefs; his feeling for her griefs deadens his own : ' quite'=acquit.

Sonnet xciv. The readings of Q 1, as shown in l. 1 (' vaine' for ' braine'); l. 3 (' euen mine' for ' inherit'); l. 8 (' and of' for ' lodge there'); l. 9 (' The execution of my fate' for our text), and l. 10 (' not vouchsaft' for ' worthy so'), as taken with l. 11, are clearly earlier; but ' wit' (l. 6) must be an error, and probably also in l. 1 ' vaine,' and not a variant; for the sick-

ness that now tries his is, as described in ll. 7-8, paralysis, a
disease of the brain and spinal cord.

Sonnet xciv. l. 8, '*harbengers*' (2 qu.): I prefer this to 'har-
benger :' 'his' is=death. He is addressing 'grief,' and therefore it must be 'thy loue,' not 'the'—just as we have 'wail
thyself'=wail thine own case, and 'shewe.'

Sonnet xciv. l. 9, '*mine :*' 2 qu. 'mind,' error as in MS. Sonnets ii., iii., and A in Sonnets ix. l. 13, for 'mine' (Q 1, A and
A 1613)=my plaint or pains. The thought is very forced, and
in none of the variations has he succeeded in making ll. 9-10
agree with context.

Sonnet xciv. l. 11, '*wail :*' 2 qu. grossly misprint 'waye.'

„   xcv. l. 2, '*left :*' 'best,' Q 1, is a good reading, but
'least' (Q 2), which in itself is nonsense, shows that the original
from which it was taken had, like it, 'left,' *i.e.* left by every one
else, or desolate: or query—deeper still, a sub-allusion to Stella's
having 'left' him (as in Sonnet lxxxvii.). As Q 2 original was
different from that of A and A 1613 (see ll. 7-8), the coincidence
proves 'left' to be correct, and an author's variant.

Sonnet xcv. l. 7. Our text (from 2 qu.) is far better than A
and A 1613—

   'Delight protests he is not for the[_e] accurst ;'

for the essence of the accusation, he sware himself my mate
in arms, lies in the defection of this mate, not in his being
also 'curst,' a thing that would rather make him a partner of
Sidney's fortunes than otherwise. Besides, when Delight is
cursed, he is no longer Delight. Of course in favour of A and
A 1613 is the consequent that 'curst' he must still be Sidney's
mate at arms, and therefore not forsworne, but *sans reproche.*
Yet is Q 1 deeper and fuller.

Sonnet xcv. l. 8. The 'oft' swearing makes the abandon-
ment the greater and more shameful. 2 qu. transpose 'himself' before 'he sware.'

Sonnet xcvi. l. 1, '*Thought :*' usually misprinted 'Though.'

„   l. 2, '*liverte :*' 2 qu. misprint 'libertie :' and
'kin' for 'kind' is Gray's and modern editors' error.

Sonnet xcvi. l. 6, '*Slow heauinesse :*' 'Low,' Gray's and
modern editors' error, and 'heauens' (2 qu.) a misreading for
'heauinesse.' Cf. silence, heaviness, and solitariness, in which
they agree. Besides, his 'thought' could not be said to have
'slow heavens,' and there is no reason why 'slow heavens'

should be full of doubt; there is no agreement between 'slow' as applied to the progress of the Night, and 'full of doubt.'

Sonnet xcvi. l. 10, ' *Sprites :*' modern error of punctuation. The construction is, In night stir the ghastly powers of sprites, In thee, &c.

Sonnet xcvi. ll. 8-10. Taking the punctuation 'solitariness' (2 qu. and A and A 1613), we must change ' to' (A and A 1613) into ' do,' thus making it agree with ' stur' (Q 2) and ' slurr,' Q 1 (a misprint for 'sturr'), except that A and A 1613 scan ' powers,' and 2 qu. 'pŏwĕrs.' If we read ' solitariness,' then ' to' can stand; but this seems forbidden by 'amazeful' or ' woeful' (2 qu.), which makes l. 9 a separate clause, describing the effect of solitariness on us. I look, however, on A and A 1613 thus altered (viz. ' to' to ' do') as later than 2 qu.; because 'thought' being the thing addressed, the change to ' In our sprites' (2 qu.) alters the name, and in some degree the personality, while the idea in A and A 1613, that 'thought' at one time raises up grisly phantoms, and at another is pale with a ghostly ghastliness, is fuller and better than 2 qu.

Sonnet xcvi. l. 9, ' *amazeful :*' far better than ' woefull,' because we have just had tears in the preceding line, and because it had a much stronger sense then than now, agreeing more with its primitive 'maze.' Thus Shakespeare speaks of ' mated and amazed' (Macbeth, act v. sc. 1).

Sonnet xcvii. l. 2, ' *Shewes her :*' 2 qu. 'Doth shew'—indifferent.

Sonnet xcvii. ll. 3-4, '*chace*' is here used generally for ' hunt,' and he is speaking of that kind of hunting affected by ladies, when the hunters do not follow their game, but move to what is technically called ' their standings,' whence they shot at the passing game (as in Love's Labour's Lost).

Sonnet xcvii. l. 4, ' *hits :*' 2 qu. ' hurts,'—the latter does not express the sense, as does the vaguer ' hits' (A and A 1613), because the allusion is to the effect of the stars on men's destinies. It was only at the close of his life that the stars in their courses fought against Sisera.

Sonnet xcvii. l. 10, ' *delights*'=varied delights, not ' delight' (2 qu.), which is hardly English, except in the sense of delight to her.

Sonnet xcvii. l. 14, ' *sight :*' 2 qu. ' light,'—indifferent.

   „   xcviii. l. 4, ' *lee-shores :*' 2 qu. ' low shroudes :'—the latter is a certain error. The shrouds of a vessel are those

stays to the mast that are formed into a ladder, and have no
analogue in a bed, and neither in a ship nor in the high-cano-
pied beds of those days could any such be called 'low.' Pos-
sibly the original 'low or lee stronds;' the sighs storm the
bed, to others a refuge, as the winds and waves beat on a rest-
less lee-shore, that is no comfort, but danger, to the tossed
mariner.

Sonnet xcviii. l. 7, 'though gald' (A 1613), badly; 'though
gold' (A and A 1605): 2 qu. also misread the passage.

Sonnet xcviii. l. 10, 'to:' 2 qu. 'in:' the former preferable,
because he looks on Woe's face, and marks each wrinkled line.
A 1613 has, badly, 'makes.'

Sonnet xcix. Several of these later Sonnets are very incorrect in the 2 qu.; the next especially, and the present has some
errors.

Sonnet xcix. l. 2, 'graunteth:' 2 qu. 'granted.' Night per-
suades to sleep those eyes which at that time may have neither material nor artificial light; therefore 'graunteth' (A and
A 1613), 'granted' without 'hath,' not only means they were
without it at some other time, but were always without light.

Sonnet xcix. l. 5, 'mind' (A and A 1613), as preferable to
'heart' (2 qu.). There is no reason why his heart should be
viewing the darkness, and the complaint is he lies broad awake.
And yet, as Sidney's whole passion was of the 'heart' rather
than of the 'mind,' there seems little doubt 'heart' is an Author's variant.

Sonnet xcix. ll. 7-8. This thought of harmony has been
elaborated in Sonnet xcvi., and he says that his wakeful mind
looking on the darkness takes in that sad, that visible darkness,
with which the inward night of his mazed powers is in perfect
harmony. This at once shows 'might' (2 qu.) to be a misreading: Q 2, again, rightly seeing there was no sense in Q 1, when
the inward might of his mazed powers kept harmony with the
surrounding darkness, made apparently an attempt at sense,
by interpolating 'he,'—an attempt which makes the outward
sad hue one and the same with the inward might! Lastly, if
the inward might of his mind be in harmony with the outer
darkness, it cannot take its hue from it. And if it could, and
did, it would have done exactly the reverse of what Sidney
would express, and has expressed in Sonnets lxxxix. xci. xcvi.
and xcvii.; because saying the mind gets dark at dark, involves
the idea that during the day it was lightsome. Therefore 'And

takes that' must be rejected for 'Takes in' (A and A 1613);
though the marked want of 'and' or a personal pronoun makes
it very unpleasant to our ears. One would like to think that
the 'And' had dropped down from the line above. ' Powres' in
Q 1 is dissyllabic, in Q 2 and A and A 1613 monosyllabic.

Sonnet xcix. l. 9, '*charme* :' 2 qu. 'chirpe.' One cannot
accept ' aires ;' for the expression is uncouth, and it would seem
to be an accidental repetition of ' aire,' of ' sweet aire.' The
old word 'charme' still used in Devon, is far more expressive
of the pleasant soundings of their united voices. So too in
Scotland still, ' chirm.'

Sonnet xcix. l. 11, '*floure* :' 2 qu. ' heauen :' the latter seems
an over-strong term for either the morning or the morning
skies ; and ' floure' seems an equally over-strong reference to
the rose that enamels the skies. We can only remember that
Sidney was a Poet and—a Lover.

Sonnet xcix. l. 12, '*In tombe*' (A and A 1613) is more like
Sidney's style, and that of his day, than 'intomb'd,' and more
accurate grammatically.

Sonnet c. l. 1, '*raine* :' 2 qu. ' showres'—the latter softer,
but ' raine' simpler and preferable.

Sonnet c. l. 3. 2 qu. read ' Which are most faire, now fairer
needs must show.'

Sonnet c. l. 5, ' Oh, minded' (2 qu.), ' sighted' (Q 1), are
errors—the latter for ' sigh'd,' as changed in A and A 1613 to
' sobbed'—deeper and better : and while we can in l. 4 understand how ' graceful Pity beautifies Beauty' (A and A 1613),
it is impossible to understand why Pity should be ' grateful'
(2 qu.).

Sonnet c. l. 7. 2 qu. 'Winged with woe's breath, so doth
Zephire blow.' This does not scan ; or else makes with ' wingèd'
an unrhythmical length of ten syllables. Again, while ' Woe's
breath' (2 qu.) is a strange refresher in Hell, Sidney's after-use
of ' pleasing' (A and A 1613) shows that the transcriber's mind
—thinking of ' plaints' and ' sighs'—confusedly transformed
' whose' into ' woe's.'

Sonnet c. l. 8, ' *might*' (2 qu.) : better and deeper than ' can'
(A and A 1613), with a touch of pathos in it.

Sonnet ci. l. 4, ' *brags* :' 2 qu. 'brings,' badly. A, but not
A 1613, has ' grace :' 2 qu. and A 1613 ' graced.'

Sonnet ci. l. 5, ' *so* :' Sidney's usual word : better than
' such' (2 qu.).

Sonnet ci. l. 8. The thought is very forced, but joy being inseparable from Stella's eyes, she could weep 'in it' (A and A 1613), but not 'with it' (2 qu.); for that involves joy weeping for grief. Hence the reading cannot be 'with thee.' 'With me' (2 qu.) gives a sort of sense, but probably a transcriber's rather than the Author's. We must then read joy as = O Joy, —an apostrophe to joy, and 'which .... eyes' as an interjectional clause. This introduces a thought wholly foreign to the rest of the Sonnet, which shows how Stella's sweetness, grace, beauty, and joy—all inherent in her—behaved during her sickness. Her eyes, says Sidney, were always a bright joy to others, and still are a joy, though they weep. 2 qu. 'vnseuered' for 'inseparate' (A and A 1613).

Sonnet ci. l. 10, '*runs*' (2 qu.) seems better than 'comes' (A and A 1613), and so, l. 11, 'swage' than 'asswage :' but l. 12, 'seeks' (2 qu.), has nothing that she seeks for, and 'sweates' (A and A 1613) not unlikely refers to the perspirations which relieved the febrile state.

Sonnet ci. l. 9, '*Loue moues thy paine :*' so all editions, and were there not other examples to prove such persistence in error in these Sonnets, one would be unable to understand how so palpable a blunder for 'mone' (= moan) escaped correction. Besides these errors, the very same occurs in the last of the four Sonnets on his Lady's sickness, as printed with Constable's Diana in 1594. There, by a curious error, some transcriber wrote 'mone' for 'plaine,' and an after error-maker changed it to 'moue.' These four Sonnets, it may be remarked, cannot, as witnessed in especial by this fourth, refer to Sidney's wife, and must therefore, according to Spenser's account of his constancy, refer to Stella. If so, then there seems every probability that they refer to the illness spoken of in this and the next Sonnet; for this Astrophel and Stella series, which is the diary of his love, makes mention of no other sickness. Other arguments are, that the Sonnets are the same in substance and tone. In the most plaining of all there is no fear expressed, not even such fear as an anxious lover finds in ailments which may or may not be serious. In agreement with this, the four Sonnets dwell on pain and pain only, and so this speaks of weakness—a probably febrile breathing and perspiration, and pain that causes weeping—but of nothing that interferes with her sweetness, grace, or beauty, or with the brightness of her eyes, or with the willingness of all to tend her. Should this view be accepted—and surely it must be? and *en passant* I remark that cii. speaks only of her pallor during convalescence, and says nothing of her escape from danger, or even disfigurement, and thus sets aside the A 1613 and Bodleian MS. statement that she had small-pox—it is inconceivable that Sidney should write in such a strain, and dwell on pain only, and not at all on his own fears, when Stella or any one he cared for was attacked with so loathsome a disease—one which especially attacks the face and destroys its beauty, and which is often virulent and dangerous, and at that time disfiguring in its results, if not fatal.

Sonnet cii. l. 1, in 2 qu. reads inferiorly ' Where be those roses, which so sweetned our eyes?'—unrhythmical, and less expressive than our text (A and A 1613).

Sonnet cii. l. 2, in 2 qu. reads ' Where be those red cheekes, which faire increase did frame?' won't scan or make sense: ' with' was probably omitted; but as the talk is of blushing, and as Stella was not always blushing, ' oft' (A and A 1613) is far better than 'be' (2 qu.): 'did' (2 qu., A and A 1613): 'doth,' a mistake of A 1605.

Sonnet cii. l. 3, ' *The* :' 2 qu. ' No'—a ludicrous mistake, completely reversing the sense, which is, that in the kindly (or natural) badge of shame, *i.e.* the blush, she shows honour's height; in other words, her blushes are chaste blushes, the tokens of a chaste love.

Sonnet cii. l. 4, ' *my*.' The crimson weeds had been stolen from his morning skies, from Stella's face now pale: ' the' (2 qu.) would imply the reverse, that Stella had stolen crimson from the skies.

Sonnet cii. l. 5, '*vade*' (A and A 1613) is here the right word, not 'fade' (2 qu.). See note in SOUTHWELL, *s. v.*: ' eies' (2 qu.), the most preposterous error in the book, Nature making Stella ferret-eyed, and being praised for it; and more, the loss of their vermilion-hue gravely asserted and plaintively lamented. Further to increase these absurdities, Nature, in l. 9, ' engraued' this redness. See note on ' grain,' in Sonnet lxxx.

Sonnet cii. l. 8, ' *still unto;*' *i.e.* though absent, it yet has force—far preferable, therefore, to ' in so great' (2 qu.).

Sonnet cii. l. 9, ' *adoptiue*'—better than ' adopted' (2 qu.), which seems to say that Galen, dead for centuries, had adopted them.

Sonnet cii. l. 10, '*of.*' The fault is paleness and absence of red, so that ' as' (A and A 1613) seems better; but ' of' (2 qu.) is undoubtedly the favourite particle with Sidney: accepted.

Sonnet cii. l. 11, '*proofe*' (2 qu. and A 1613): 'pulse' (A), Author's variants : feeling=sympathising. 'Feeling the pulse' is used in ' Certain Sonnets,' as see in the place noted : 'furre' stronger and better than ' sure' (2 qu.). Sidney uses this rhyme ' fur' and ' stur' in Sonnet xcvi. A and A 1613 make the blunder of putting ' say they' in ( ), thus reversing the sense.

Sonnet ciii. l. 3, '*Ioye's livery*' (A and A 1613), better, as proved by ll. 1, 2, 3 and 5, than ' Loue's.'

Sonnet ciii. l. 6, '*beauties*' = all her several beauties : he has just spoken of her eyes : better than ' beauty' (2 qu.).

Sonnet ciii. l. 8, ' O' is dropped by error in 2 qu.—required by metre.

Sonnet ciii. l. 9, '*And :*' 2 qu. 'But :' out of place, and ' but' is in next line : ' friendly words' (2 qu.), poor, when he has just said ' wanton winds.'

Sonnet ciii. l. 12, '*disheueld :*' 2 qu. ' discouered'—perhaps indifferent, but the former the later, as shown by l. 9.

Sonnet ciii. l. 13, ' O,' more appropriate than ' ah' (2 qu.).

,,   civ. l. 2, '*poysonous*' (A 1613)=malevolent, empoisoned, hence ' poisoned' of 2 qu. : ' wits' (2 qu.) probably an error by repetition for ' lookes.'

Sonnet civ. l. 11. The meaning is, If I am sick, &c. Though the gladness be but the result of wine.

Sonnet civ. l. 12, '*morall*' (A and A 1605) : ' mortall,' error of A 1613, &c.

Sonnet civ. ll. 12-13.   There has been an attempt to make sense of the error of 2 qu. in l. 12 by putting (,) after there, and it succeeds in giving some sense, though strange English, to that line.   Line 13, however, becomes nonsensical, and remains nonsense, if we take away (,), and this makes nonsense also of l. 12 : for who ever heard of noting a man's meaning out of his ribs, especially when it was the joy in his face and the stars on his armour that they saw?   2 qu. read for ' and, puffing'—' a whirlwind.'   On l. 8 be it remarked, that Sidney does not mean that he had left, or that Stella had, but merely that he was debarred her presence.   The presence of the wits, and the mention of tilting-armour, shows he was in some populous place, and it can hardly be doubted, especially if one has regard to the previous sonnets, that he was at Court.   It is also clear that Stella was there, by the mention of the happy window. The ensuing song, or serenade, confirms this, that she was present, and yet—by a rule she had laid down both for herself and him—absent. See next sonnet and notes.

Sonnet cv. This sonnet recounts his endeavour to see Stella as she passed on a dark night, and confirms the view taken of the preceding sonnet. The 'dead glasse' is a telescope, and it is obvious the words must be 'thy dazling race' (A and A 1613), not 'my' (2 qu.), and 1. 8, '*the* way'=the telescope's line of sight, not 'her' (2 qu.), Stella's way. In l. 6 'who' (A and A 1613) better than 'that' (2 qu.), and l. 8 'what' (ib.) than 'that' (2 qu.). Line 6, 'I loue and lacke' is, under the circumstances, the better oath. In all these later sonnets it is his love that he speaks of, not hers ; and this is very notice-able after Song x. and its preceding sonnets, and from Sonnet xciii. inclusive ; so that it may be judged that she had chidden him for speaking of her love, or refused to see him, or done both. More of all this in our Essay, as before.

Sonnet ov. l. 10, '*thereof*' (A and A 1613): 'therefore' (2 qu.)—either, according to the old use of therefore, will suit. 'Nectar' (A and A 1613): 'necklace' (2 qu.)—the latter may be an early variant and refer to some gift of his ; but it is lack of seeing her that he bemoans, and hence is hardly likely to have mentioned a mere necklace, even if he had given Stella one ; and if he did, he wisely altered it. If the conjectures in the note on the sonnet are correct (l. 6), he could not antici-pate that she would necessarily wear a gift of his.

Sonnet cv. l. 12, '*your strife*' (A and A 1613): 'your will' (2 qu.). Both refer to her eyes using the telescope rather than, perhaps, the telescope itself. The word 'strife' [with dark-ness] is much more expressive.

Sonnet cv. l. 13, '*that*' (2 qu.) reads better than 'which' (A and A 1613).

Sonnet cv. l. 14, '*Which*' is error of later A for 'With' (2 qu., A and A 1605 and 1613) : and these later also have 'whence' for 'whane,' l. 11: 'lesse' (2 qu.), 'worse' (A and A 1613). Though by adopting a subtlety of thought=my curse in not seeing her is so great that I can wish him no worse in kind—this latter gives a similar sense with 'lesse,' it is not so good as it.

Sonnet cvi. l. 4, '*say :*' 2 qu. 'saw,'—an error ; as 'cleare' (ib.) for 'cheare' (l. 5).

Sonnet cvi. l. 6, '*toldst*' (A and A 1613), 2 qu. 'would'st :' the former demanded by 'false-flattering' (l. 2) and 'rest.'

Sonnet cvi. l. 7, '*But how art thou*' (2 qu.): probably in transcript 'But thou art now' ('now' for 'gone'), and transposed in the endeavour to make sense of the phrase itself, though nonsense as regards the rest.

Sonnet cvi. l. 14. With all their blunders in this sonnet, the reading of 'and so forget his' (2 qu.), which in reality is that also of Q 1, seems better, and is perhaps later, than A and A 1613, 'and not thinke of.'

Sonnet cvii. l. 5, '*while :*' 'time' (2 qu.)—indifferent.

    ,,   l. 7, '*thoughts :*' 'thought' (2 qu.): a lieutenant (*i.e.* one in place of the general-in-chief, as Cassio was Othello's lieutenant) commands more than one, and we have 'powers' (l. 2); therefore 'thoughts,' not 'thought.'

Sonnet cvii. l. 8, '*use :*' 'wit' (2 qu.) was probably the original word (see l. 10); but it is the lieutenant who should 'use' wit; and besides, 'wit' seems to deprive Stella's 'art' of wisdom : hence 'use,' his thoughts being the soldiers practised in work and trained to obey.

Sonnet cvii. l. 11. Error of 'still' (2 qu.) for 'Till' (A and A 1613) seems to have led to further error of 'to' for 'it,' as in Sonnet cvi. l. 7 : 'haue' (2 qu., A and A 1613) : 'hath,' modern reading.

Sonnet cvii. l. 12. From what precedes, the thought evidently is [Do this, for] servants' shame doth bring masters' blame, *i.e.* is often cause of blame to the masters; the masters are often blamed for the servants' errors, and so might you be for mine. This is only given by 'On . . , . sit' (A and A 1613), not 'For.' The next clause is a different thought, My works are all done under your influence, and if you take not this order, my unregulated doings will be a scorn.

Sonnet cvii. l. 13, '*reproue :*' 2 qu. 'approve'—error which reverses the real meaning.

Sonnet cviii. l. 3, '*to*' (A and A 1613) : 'of' (2 qu.). Both seem at first sight admissible; but looking to the phrase ' sorrow weighs down the heart,' and to its being Sorrow's lead that is here spoken of, I take it that the dark furnace is his boiling breast, and that the lead is poured into the heart opprest. If the 'heart' be the 'furnace,' as it must be with 'of,' then are the 'fires' in the heart; and besides that such an idea is rather incongruous with the intended thought, Sidney has markedly divided the one from the other. The 'dark furnace' was so called, perhaps, with reference to the dark flames of Hell—a philosophy then common, and afterwards adopted by Milton.

Sonnet cviii. l. 6, '*flutters to thee*' (A and A 1613) explains what is not otherwise explained, who or what is the 'nest.' 'His' (ib.) is also more appropriate than 'her' (2 qu.), as the love of a male for a female is in question.

Sonnet cviii. l. 7, '*rude*' (A and A 1613): 2 qu. 'dead.' The former preferable, as shown by 'daily 'vnbidden.'

Sonnet cviii. l. 11, '*doores :*' 2 qu. 'darts'—error.

,, l. 12, '*in*' (A and A 1613): 2 qu. 'on'—error.

,, l. 14, '*onely*' (A and A 1613), and punctuated 'onely', which is clearly what is meant by 'onel 'anoy,' 2 qu.

Sonnets cix. and cx. I refer to our Essay, as before, for reasons that constrained me to place these two Sonnets, cix. and cx., as the fitting, and by the Author the intended, close of Astrophel and Stella. They are interpenetrated with passion, but a passion that recognises how idle and misdirected such love as he has been dallying with is—and so he closes his Sonnets. 'Grow *rich*,' of cx. l. 3, is not an accidental use of the word 'rich.' Usually at the end of this last sonnet there is added the Latin motto, 'Splendidis longum valedico nugis,' which gathers into itself fresh significance as belonging to the close of Astrophel and Stella; otherwise is meaningless.

SONGS.

THE whole of these are verses which by their construction, even if there were no proofs such as may be found in the first and last stanzas of the first song, and the closing stanza of the eleventh, were clearly set to music and sung. Hence they are more properly Songs, and are so called in A and A 1613, though headed 'Sonets' in 2 qu. I have brought them together here rather than interspersed them among the Sonnets, as in A and A 1613, but not originally (*e.g.* 2 qu.), because they interrupt the thought and study of the sonnets, and because they form an entirely different type of poetry. But see our Essay, for a critical examination of the inter-relations of Sonnets and Songs.

Song I.

There is a mistake running through all A and the greater part of 2 qu. The first two lines of each stanza are questions or questioning exclamations, and require (?) or (!). I have placed (!). In line 3 the 2 qu. often substitute 'be' for 'is,' but there are no changes in sense or construction which require this change, and 'is' is the stronger word.

i. l. 2, '*surcharg'd*.' Sidney did not certainly affect French words, and in the last stanza, which is a repetition of this, 2 qu. and A and A 1613 have 'orecharged.' Still I accept the singularly passionate and expressively full word '*surcharg'd*' of 2 qu. here. 2 qu. badly misprint 'with' music, which makes Sidney guilty unnecessarily of self-laudation. A=he lends (or in other phrase marries) to music the words of his surcharg'd breast.

ii. l. 4, '*forgate*,' *i.e.* in past tense=when they made her. Better than 2 qu. 'forget.'

iii. l. 2, '*stayneth*'=stains other womankind by comparison. Her 'passing ['surpassing'] fairenesse' makes that of others ugliness.

iv. l. 1, '*all*.' Nothing is planted, and hence I read with 2 qu. 'all' for 'of,' A and A 1613. But as 'planteth' is singular, with A and A 1613 retain 'step' (=steps collectively), not 'steps.'

v. l. 1, '*patience*. A and A 1613 read 'passions.' The thought seems obscure, but 'patience,' 2 qu., is clearer than 'passions:' adopted,

vi. l. 2, '*long-dead*:' stronger than 'long-hid' of 2 qu., and agrees better with 'renew.'

vi. l. 4, '*rueth*:' 2 qu. badly 'endeth,' which does not rhyme.

vii. l. 1, '*loosest* . . . . *fastest*' read better than ' -eth,' 2 qu.

viii. l. 2, '*bolts*.' Both sense and our English idiom require 'bolts' rather than 'bolt,' 2 qu.--the latter probably a conjectural or accidental change, due to 'thunders' in singular.

viii. l. 4, '*not*:' better than 'no' (2 qu.)=wonders are not miracles.

Song II.

i. l. 1. Falstaff adopts this in his feigned ecstasy at meeting Mistress Ford: ' Have I caught thee, my heavenly jewel?' My good friend Mr. Staunton strangely suggests that Falstaff sang this, as an explanation of 'thee' interpolated, *i.e.* by the players.

their singing would be rather a reason against the interpolation surely.

viii. 1. 4, '*Fool! more fool'*=Fool for running away, more fool for not taking more, *i.e.* not a single kiss, but kisses.   Cf. Sonnet lxxiii. &c.

Song III.

i. 1. 4.   See note on relative Sonnet.

ii. 1. 1, '*shepheard :*' better and more usual than ' 's,' 2 qu.

ii. 1. 2, '*dainty :*' 2 qu. badly drop this word.   The construction is—to make a dull lizard taste, &c.   ' This story, and suchlike, give great colour of truth to that which Democritus reporteth, namely, Thoas in Arcadia saued his life by means of a dragon.   This Thoas being but a very childe, had loued this dragon when he was but young, very well, and nourished him ; but at last, being somewhat fearfull of his nature, and not well knowing his qualities, and fearing withal the bignes that now he was growne vnto, had carried him into the mountains and deserts ; wherein it fortuned that he was afterward set vpon and invironed by theeves, whereupon he cried out, and the dragon knowing his voice, came forth and rescued him.'   Holland's Pliny, N. H. l. viii. c. 17: cf. Ælian. l. vi. c. 63.

ii. 1. 4, '*As her eyes were his light,*' 2 qu. : better than ' As his light was her eyes.'   ' There hapned a marvellous example about the city Sestos of an Egle ; for which in those parts there goes a great name of an egle, and highly is she honored there.   A yong maid had brought vp a yong egle by hand : the egle again to requite her kindnes would first, when she was but little, flie abroad a birding, and euer bring part of that shee had gotten vnto her said nurse.   In processe of time being grown bigger and stronger, would set vpon wild beasts also in the forrest, and furnish her yong mistresse continually with store of venison.   At length it fortuned that the damosell died ; and when her funerall fire was set a burning, the egle flew into the mids of it, and there was consumed into ashes with the corps of the said virgin.   For which cause, and in memoriall thereof, the inhabitants of Sestos and the parts there adjoyning, erected in that very place a stately monument, such as they call Heroum, dedicated in the name of Jupiter and the virgin, for that the egle is a bird consecrated vnto that god.'   Pliny, N. H. l. x. c. 5.

ii. 1. 6, ' *lo :*' preferable to 'for,' 2 qu.

iii. l. 1, ' *beasts, birds,*' 2 qu.—this keeps the sequence given in the previous lines : A and A 1613 ' Birds, beasts.'

Song IV.

i. l. 4, '*pain*' countenances 'reward,' A and A 1613, rather than ' rewards,' 2 qu.

ii. l. 4, ' *himself,*' 2 qu. : better than ' itselfe,' A and A 1616, albeit Jealousy is not=Lord Rich, for stanza vii. shows Stella was away from home, *i.e.* from Lord Rich.

iii. l. 2, ' *knot,*' 2 qu. : better than ' yoke,' A and A 1613, which is not appropriate.

iii. l. 3, ' *our,*' 2 qu. : better than ' on,' A and A 1613.

iv. l. 2, ' *but,*' A and A 1613 : ' for,' 2 qu., badly.

iv. l 3, ' *hap*'=good luck : ' heart,' 2 qu., gives a doubtful sense.

v. l. 4, '*fooles,*' 2 qu.—gayer and yet deeper than 'folks' of A and A 1613, which is commonplace.

vi. l. 3, ' *he :*' 2 qu. 'she;' but Time is never feminine.

vi. l. 4, '*frame*'=design or build up [it, the time or opportunity].

viii. l. 5. I adopt the transposition of ' thee' and ' me,' made by A and A 1613 against 2 qu. in this stanza only. ' Take me' is contradictory to the previous four lines; so he says, Do nothing, agree; take thee to me.

Song V.

i. l. 3, '*grew :*' 2 qu. ' drew'—the former stronger, being ⇄tongue and pen became, not merely drew, records.

ii. l. 1, ' *wert,*' 2 qu. : better than ' art,' which seems an error of A and A 1613.

ii. l. 3, ' *that :*' 2 qu. ' would'—former more alliterative and probably later.

ii. l. 6, ' *I . . . . as :*' 2 qu. ' is . . . . that'—former better, because it is all ' I said,' and because 'is' is a wrong tense. The error from reduplication of 's' of ' said.' 'As' more alliterative than ' that.'

iii. l. 2, ' *though :*' 2 qu. misprint ' thought ;' for not thought only, but thought and speech both live and were metamorphosed.

iii. l. 4, ' *thought :*' 2 qu. ' wrote'—former better, because he is here writing of thinking, and in l. 5 of speaking: cf. l. 2 and ll. 4-5 : and because one may think one way, and write another.

iv. l. 1, ' *Then thou,*' 2 qu. :. 'Thou then,' A and A 1613— former accepted.

iv. l. 2, '*worth :*' 2 qu. 'worke ;' error, as in DONNE. So ' inheritance' for ' inheritrix.'

iv. l. 3, ' *state,*' 2 qu. : A and A 1613 ' seat'—former accepted.

iv. l. 6. 2 qu. read 'Whom fault once casteth downe'—is ambiguous, for it might mean the fault of some one else cast the sufferer down.

v. l. 3, ' *kindest,*' better than ' highest,' 2 qu.—the Muse being the person and nurse.

v. l. 5, ' *while,*' far better than ' and' of 2 qu.

vi. l. 2. I follow the 2 qu. construction, making ' Defiance' a genitive : not ' Revenge . . . Muse. Defiance trumpet.' ' Revenge, revenge !' and ' Vindicta, vindicta !' were known phrases. But for (, ,) I substitute (! !).

vi. l. 3. There has been a great alteration here, and probably by the Author. The playful mock rage seems to prove A and A 1613 (our text) to be the later. ' Threaten, and do more than you threaten,' agrees better with ' Defiance' trumpet blow.' Cf. also beaten, l. 6. ' Threate, threat' of 2 qu. is better with its own readings, and ' Threaten' with its context.

vii. l. 1, ' *snow*'=skin : therefore ' odour'd' is better than ' shining' of 2 qu.

vii. l. 4, ' *so*' 2 qu. drop out in error.

vii. l. 5. Our text more expressive than 2 qu., ' there thou dost'=thou dost most oppress my most faith that is greater than that of any other.

vii. l. 6, ' *euils*'—as usual=' ills.' So xii. l. 6 and xiv. l. 2.

viii. l. 1, ' *worst :*' 2 qu. misprint ' worse.'

viii. l. 2, ' *chief :*' 2 qu. misprint ' a thief.'

viii. l. 3, ' *but :*' 2 qu. misprint ' for.'

viii. l. 4, ' *ioyes :*' 2 qu. misprint ' goods'—for the strength of the accusation is that thieves steal ' goods' that can be recovered, but that she, rich in ' ioyes,' steals his ' ioyes.'

viii. l. 6, ' *spoyle,*' Q 1 and A and A 1613 : ' spoyles' of Q 2 takes its ' s ' from ' is,' and that verb shows the plural is wrong. ' Worse' is stronger, and agrees better with ' evil' than ' more,' 2 qu.

x. l. 1, '*murder*' (collectively used) is proved to be right both by 'fault' and 'seemes:' 2 qu. have 'murthers.'

x. l. 2, '*unjustest :*' 2 qu. misprint 'injustice.'

x. l. 4, '*dost lord my heart*' is much more expressive of usurped tyranny than 'for thou art my heart's lord.'

x. l. 6, '*unright :*' 2 qu. 'unrightful'—former sharper, more cutting, and fuller.

xi. l. 2, '*vagabonding :*' 2 qu. 'blackest blot of'—the latter tempting; but it is too strong, seeing that he blackens her more and more in each succeeding stanza. Here he merely blots any white she might have as a valiant rebel by proving her a vagabond also.

xiii. l. 3, '*my sight . . . face :*' 2 qu. 'mine eyes . . . sight,' was probably altered, as in A and A 1613, because 'eyes' are plural, and the rhyming 'enjoyeth' singular.

xiv. l. 6. The construction is [those] who . . . are : therefore 'tempt' and 'plague' (A and A 1613), not 'tempts . . . . plagues :' l. 6, 2 qu. 'by' for 'all.'

Song VI.

i. l. 3. Cf. stanza ix. l. 5, in both 'whether'=which of the two.

i. l. 5, '*bate*'=contention. See Glossarial Index, *s.v.* Query =our 'de-*bate*'?

ii. l. 1. All the editions have 'doth' with a nominative which being double is plural, but where there is only one on each side, and the action of each separate.

ii. l. 5, '*their :*' not 'the,' as in 2 qu. Both could not plead '*the* right.' The construction is, Only-true delight is the bar at which they plead, or rather where each pleads his right.

iv. l. 2, '*hew :*' 2 qu. misprint 'view.'

v. l. 1, '*loftly :*' 2 qu. 'lustie'—a misplaced epithet, albeit its meaning has much changed since.

v. l. 4, '*action :*' more idiomatic and technical than 'actions.' Hence in i. l. 4, 'former' (A and A 1613)=the first of two, is probably the later, as it is superior to 'better' of 2 qu.

vii. l. 6, '*Eye-iudgement*' (A and A 1613)=the special or 'expert' judgment of that organ: far more vivid than 'The judgement' of 2 qu.

Song VII.

i. l. 1, '*consort*,' A and A 1613, as against 'comfort' (2 qu.)

is proved by 'tunes' and l. 2 generally, and by the accentuation.

i. l. 2, '*do*,' A and A 1613, not ' doth' (2 qu.). The nominative is 'tunes,' and 'delight' is the accusative.

i. l. 3, '*closde*,' A and A 1613: the 2 qu. have 'cloi'd.' The former is preferable, for he does not mean to represent them as having a superabundance of wit, but only as 'closed up' in their own appreciation of their wit, and closed up against the delight they would otherwise welcome and enjoy. This is borne out by l. 4. Here 'it' might, at first sight, be supposed to refer to 'wit;' but 'a title vain' is the epithet they give, expressive of their view of its foolishness, that is, of the foolishness of the delight, or of the music that caused the delight. I say 'music,' because the intermediate 'therein' seems to have led Sidney to refer to sweet tunes, or rather to the main thought—the music contained in them—by a pronoun in the singular. Such ideal, rather than grammatical, concord was not uncommon in Elizabethan writings, and is not uncommon in conversation at the present day.

i. l. 4, '*title :*' 2 qu. stupidly misprint 'little.'

ii. l. 2, '*wooden*'=foolish.

ii. l. 4, '*thoughts*,' A and A 1613 : 2 qu. 'hearts.' The latter seems to agree better with 'loving,' but 'thoughts' agrees better with 'frothy,' and this was a phrase frequently used a little later, as in Marston's Satires, &c. It will also be noted, that in the three lines all is referred to the intellect—' wooden wits' —'muddie minds'—'frothie thoughts.' In 'eas'ly,' A and A 1613, and ' easie' (2 qu.), the reading is indifferent.

iii. l. 1, '*adoring*,' A and A 1613, is stronger, and agrees better with following lines, than 'admiring' (2 qu.) ; l. 4, 'life-giuing,' A and A 1613. The 2 qu., in error, read 'life-given' =the sun and moon, whose beams were life-giving in old philosophy.

iii. l. 2, '*descended*,' A and A 1613 : 'discerned' (2 qu.). Each may be a mistake for the other ; but as both give sense, probably they are Author's variants. No gifts such as are given to mere mortals, no merely earthly fruits, are to be viewed here or 'discerned,' or have here 'descended' from the heavens.

Song VIII.

It may be that the additional verses in A and A 1613 editions (stanzas xviii. to xxvi.) of the present and Song x. were, from

motives of delicacy, not included in the copies (MS.) given by
Sidney to others than his intimates; and this is supported by
the absence previous to A of Sonnet xxxvii., the plainest of those
in which the name of Rich is introduced. While therefore, as
against this must be set the strangeness that these additional
stanzas must have been first ' divulged' in an edition published
and edited, so far at least as the Arcadia is concerned, by the
Countess of Pembroke, I do not insist on the argument that
these additions betoken later versions. As in the others, however, the internal evidence in Song viii. proves this. The 2 qu.
give one correction, ' woe' for ' woes' (v. l. 2).

i. l. 4. May is not so much growing new perfumes, since
they were the same year by year, as he is newly perfumed
with the newly-opened flowers. Nor is he intended to be represented as a perfume-plant grower for Rimmel, as a youth gar-
landed with flowers, and newly perfumed thereby. Hence A
and A 1613 is the better, new-perfumed, and (,) removed, as in
A 1613.

ii. l. 4. The metre being—◡ ' in the' (A and A 1613) is more
rhythmical than ' in each' (2 qu.), besides being rather more
correct.

v. l. 2, ' Woes,' A and A 1613, is probably an error for ' woe'
(2 qu.) through influence of ' sighs.' But in v. l. 1, ' sigh
they did' is a subtle after-change from ' sigh'd they had' (2 qu.),
and far more descriptive. As they ' had wept' (stanza iv.), they
had of course sighed; now still he says they sighed, even in the
joy of their meetings, but their sighs of grief at Fortune, their
foe, were mingled with sighs of gladness.

viii. l. 2, ' Triumphres' (2 qu.) has an uncouth sound, and if
invented by Sidney, was probably on after-thought discarded:
' in' (2 qu.) cannot be right; the ' annoy' is his ' annoy.'   ' Of'
=off or from, is, on the other hand, admissible.

ix. l. 3, ' ‾Once āre,' A and A 1613, better than ' āre ōnce'
(2 qu.).

xi. l. 2, ' each character,' A and A 1613, more expressive
than ' the characters' (2 qu.).

xi. l. 3, ' sweete,' 2 qu.: an insufficient and poor epithet,
when one speaks of all-surpassing loveliness.

xi. l. 4, ' thy . . . it,' A and A 1613: ' the' (2 qu.) is almost
without doubt an error for ' thy;' and though ' yet' (2 qu.) gives
sense, our text is by each of the changes made the clearer.

xii. l. 3, ' grant—O me,' A and A 1613. This third repetition of 'grant,' without ability to proceed, is far more expressive than 'to me' (2 qu.): 'fault' (ib.) is more fitting than 'sin' (2 qu.).

xiii. l. 3, '*proue*,' 2 qu. : no sense with ' and.'

„ l. 4, ' *nere*,' 2 qu. : reverses Sidney's meaning.

xvii. l. 3, ' *repelling*,'. A and A 1613 : 2 qu. ' compelling'— bad.

xvii. l. 4. Her after-words do not admit of ' expelling' (2 qu.): and ' excelling,' A and A 1613, is the far better description, and one which agrees with other sayings of Sidney regarding her. Her refusal was a grace, her repulse a movement excelling all grace in its very denial.

xviii. l. 2, ' *so*,' A and A 1613 : evidently a change from ' with' (2 qu.), and for the better.

Song IX.

i. l. 4, ' *Fro*,' A and A 1613 : ' For' a modern error.

ii. l. 4, '*measures*,' 2 qu. : error for ' mischief's,' A and A 1613 : probably through influence of rhyme.

ii. l. 5, '*mischief's :*' 2 qu. ' measure's'—error.

iv. ll. 1-2. In 2 qu. l. 1, ' fairest' for ' fiercest ;' l. 2, ' fairest' for ' fiercest,' and ' cruelst' for ' fairest' of A and A 1613. The changes in A and A 1613 accord better with l. 3, as well as his supposed thoughts. So l. 3, ' O' (A and A 1613) for ' the' (2 qu.) ; but though ' do' is shown by these changes to be later, it may be questioned whether, to our ears, it sounds as well as ' still,' 2 qu.

v. l. 4, '*to us*,' 2 qu.: a strange meaningless error for ' ewes' (A and A 1613).

vi. l. 3. To make sense out of Muse, 2 qu., a (.) has been placed after ' served,' but he is talking to his flock—not to his Muse, who has no business there. I read ' must,' A and A 1613, and re-punctuate.

vii. l. 1. I prefer rhythm of A and A 1613, and in l. 4 ' helpless' for ' hopeless' (2 qu.). He could not be said to be ' hopeless:' cf. ll. 1-2,—but he says, if she love as she says, why does she leave me without relief ? These are sufficient to prove A and A 1613 later and better ; and hence I adopt their readings in stanzas ix. and x. against 2 qu.—viz. ix. l. 3, ' Knowing if she should display ;' x. l. 1, ' my dear flocke now.' In ix. l. 4, ' her' (A and A 1613) is required by the metre, and is erroneously omitted in 2 qu.

Song X.

i. l. 2. I prefer 'shall' (A), both because of 'shall' above, and because it is more expressive of present deprivation than 'may.'

ii. l. 2, '*aught*,' A and A 1613 : 'oft' (2 qu.) — former far better. As to the rest, 'after parting' (A and A 1613) is clearer, though not so expressive of her having left him, as 'By thine absence oft forgot :' but I adopt the former. See note on Sonnet lxxxvii.

v. l. 2, '*my*,' A 1613 : 2 qu. and all seemingly, oddly mis-print 'thy.'

vii. l. 3, '*moaning, passèd*,' the sense being anguish [being] passèd; l. 5, 'depart'=part with. See note on Sonnet lxxxvii.

viii. l. 1, '*thought*,' A and A 1613, as a being that has thoughts—his intellectual part. Cf. stanzas ii. l. 5, iii. l. 1, iv. l. 1, and v. l. 1, vi. l. 1. vii. l. 1.

x. l. 3, '*melts* :' 2 qu. 'fleetes.'

Song XI.

This first appeared in A 1598 : A 1613 has two gross errors, viz. stanza viii. l. 5, 'thee' for 'there,' as in A 1598 and 1605. In the Bright MS. 'there' correctly.

ix. l. 3, '*uniust*,' A and A 1605 and 1613 : 'unjust is,' later A : 'unjustest,' Bright MS.

ix. l. 5, '*lowts*'=obeisances. See Glossarial-Index. G.

THE EPISTLE

To the worshipfull and his very good Freende, MA. FRAUNCIS FLOWER *Esquire, increase of all content.*

IT was my fortune, right worshipfull, not many daies since, to light vpon the famous deuice of *Astrophel and Stella*, which carrying the generall commendation of all men of iudgment, and being reported to be one of the rarest things that euer any Englishman set abroach, I haue thought good to publish it vnder your name, both for I know the excellencie of your worships conceipt, aboue all other to be such as is onely fit to discerne of all matters of wit, as also for the credite and countenaunce your patronage may giue to such a worke. Accept of it, I be-

seech you, as the first fruites of my affection, which ,desires to
approoue it selfe in all dutie vnto you : and though the Argument perhaps may seeme too light for your graue viewe, yet
considering the worthines of the Author, I hope you will entertaine it accordingly. For my part, I haue beene very carefull
in the Printing of it, and where as being spred abroade in written Coppies, it had gathered much corruption by ill Writers : I
haue vsed their helpe and aduice in correcting and restoring it
to his first dignitie, that I knowe were of skill and experience
in those matters. And the rather was I moued to sette it forth,
because I thought it pittie anie thing proceeding from so rare a
man shoulde bee obscured, or that his fame should not still be
nourisht in his works, whom the works [qy. world?] with one
vnited griefe bewailed. Thus crauing pardon for my bold attempt,
and desiring the continuance of your worshippes fauour vnto mee,
I ende. Yours alwaies to be commaunded,   THO. NEWMAN.

SOMEWHAT TO READE FOR THEM THAT LIST.

Tempus adus [sic] *plausus aurea pompa venit,* so endes the
Sceane of Idiots, and enter *Astrophel* in pompe. Gentlemen that
haue seene a thousand lines of folly, drawn forth *ex vno puncto
impudentiæ,* and two famous mountains to goe to the conception
of one Mouse, that haue had your eares defned with the eccho
of Fame's brasen towrps, when only they haue been toucht with
a leaden pen, that haue seene *Pan* sitting in his bower of delights, and a number of *Midasses* to admire his miserable horne-
pipes, let not your surfeted sight, new come frō such puppet
play, think scorne to turn aside into this Theater of pleasure,
for here you shal find a paper stage streud with pearle, an artificial heau'n to ouershadow the fair frame, and christal wals to
encounter your curious eyes, while the tragicommody of loue is
performed by starlight. The chiefe Actor here is *Melpomene,*
whose dusky robes dipt in the ynke of teares, as yet seeme to
drop when I view them neere. The Argument cruell chastitie,
the Prologue hope, the Epilogue dispaire, *videte quæso, et lin-
guis animisque favete.* And here peraduenture, my witles
youth may be taxt with a margent note of presumption, for
offering to put vp any motion of applause in the behalfe of so
excellent a Poet (the least sillable of whose name sounded in
the eares of iudgement, is able to giue the meanest line he

writes a dowry of immortality), yet those that obserne how
iewels ofte̅times com to their hands that know not their value,
and that the cockscombes of our days, like *Esop's* Cock, had
rather haue a Barly kernell wrapt vp in a Ballet, then they wil
dig for the welth of wit in any ground that they know not, I
hope wil also hold me excused though I open the gate to his
glory and inuite idle eares to the admiration of his melancholy.

     ' Quid petitur sacris nisi tantum fama poetis ?'

Which although it be oftentimes imprisoned in Ladyes casks,
and the president bookes of such as cannot see without another
man's spectacles, yet at length it breakes foorth in spight of his
keepers, and vseth some priuate penne (in steed of a picklock)
to procure his violent enlargement. The Sunne, for a time,
may maske his golden head in a cloud; yet in the end the thicke
vaile doth vanish, and his embellished blandishment appeares.
Long hath *Astrophel* (England's Sunne) withheld the beames of
his spirite from the common veiw of our darke sence, and night
hath houered oure the gardens of the nine Sisters, while *ignis
fatuus* and grosse fatty flames (such as commonly arise out of
dunghilles) haue tooke occasion, in the middest eclipse of his
shining perfections, to wander a broade with a wispe of paper
at their tailes like Hobgoblins, and leade men vp and downe in
a circle of absurditie a whole weeke, and neuer know where
they are. But now that cloude of sorrow is dissolued, which
fierie Loue exhaled from his dewie haire, and affection hath
vnburthened the labouring streames of her wombe, in the lowe
cesterne of his Graue: the night hath resigned her iettie throne
vnto *Lucifer*, and cleere daylight possesseth the skie that was
dimmed; wherfore breake of your daunce, you Fayries and
Elues, and from the fieldes with the torne carcases of your
Timbrils, for your kingdome is expired. Put out your rush
candles, you Poets and Rimers, and bequeath your crazed qua-
terzayns to the Chaundlers; for loe, here he cometh that hath
broek your legs. *Apollo* hath resigned his Iuory Harp vnto
Astrophel, and he, like *Mercury*, must lull you a sleep with his
musicke. Sleepe *Argus*, sleep Ignorance, sleep Impudence, for
Mercury hath *Io*, and onely *Io Pæan* belongeth to *Astrophel.*
Deare *Astrophel*, that in the ashes of thy Loue, liuest againe
like the *Phœnix ;* O might thy bodie (as thy name) liue againe
likewise here amongst vs : but the earth, the mother of mortali-
tie, hath snacht thee too soone into her chilled colde armes, and

will not let thee by any meanes be drawne from her deadly imbrace; and thy diuine Soule, carried on an Angel's wings to
heauen, is installed in *Hermes'* place, sole *prolocutor* to the
Gods. Therefore mayest thou neuer returne from the Elisian
fieldes like *Orpheus;* therefore must we euer mourne for our
Orpheus.

Fayne would a seconde spring of passion heere spend it
selfe on his sweet remembrance : but Religion, that rebuketh
prophane lamentation, drinkes in the riuers of those dispaireful
teares, which languorous ruth hath outwelled, and bids me looke
back to the house of honor, where frō one and the selfe same
root of renowne, I shal find many goodly branches deriued,
and such as, with the spreading increase of their vertues, may
somewhat ouershadow the Griefe of his los. Amongst the which
fayre sister of *Phœbus*, and eloquent secretary to the Muses,
most rare Countesse of *Pembroke*, thou art not to be omitted,
whom Artes doe adore as a second *Minerua*, and our Poets
extoll as the Patronesse of their inuention ; for in thee the
Lesbian Sappho with her lirick Harpe is disgraced, and the
Laurel Garlande which thy Brother so brauely aduaunst on his
Launce, is still kept greene in the Temple of *Pallas.* Thou
only sacrificest thy soule to contemplation, thou only enter-
tainest emptie-handed *Homer*, and keepest the springs of *Cas-
talia* from being dryed vp. Learning, wisedom, beautie, and
all other ornaments of Nobilitie whatsoeuer, seeke to approue
themselues in thy sight, and get a further seale of felicity from
the smiles of thy fauour :

> ' O Joue digna viro ni Joue nata fores.' [sic]

I feare I shall be counted a mercenary flatterer, for mixing
my thoughts with such figuratiue admiration, but generall report that surpasseth my praise, condemneth my rhetoricke of
dulnesse for so colde a commendation. Indeede, to say the
truth, my stile is somewhat heauie-gated, and cannot daunce,
trip, and goe so liuely, with oh my loue, ah my loue, all my
loues gone, as other Sheepheards that haue beene fooles in the
Morris time out of minde ; nor hath my prose any skill to imitate the Almond leape verse, or sit tabring flue yeres together
nothing but to bee, to hee,. on a paper drum. Onely I can
keepe pace with Grauesend barge, and care not if I haue water
enough, to lande my ship of fooles with the Tearme (the tyde
I shoulde say). Now euery man is not of that minde ; for

some, to goe the lighter away, will take in their fraught of span-
gled feathers, golden Peebles, Straw, Reedes, Bulrushes, or any
thing, and then they beare out their sayles as proudly, as if
they were balisted with Bulbiefe. Others are so hardly bested
for loading that they are faine to retaile the cinders of *Troy*,
and the shiuers of broken trunchions, to fill vp their boate that
else should goe empty : and if they haue but a pound weight of
good Merchandise, it shall be placed at the poope, or pluckt in a
thousand peeces to credit their carriage. For my part, euery
man as he likes, *meus cuiusque is est quisque*. 'Tis as good to
goe in cut-fingred pumps as corke shooes, if one wore Cornish
diamonds on his toes. To explain it by a more familiar example, an Asse is no great statesman in the beastes commonwealth, though he weare his eares *vpseuant muffe*, after the
Muscouy fashion, and hange the lip like a Capcase halfe open,
or looke as demurely as a sixpenny browne loafe, for he hath
some imperfections that do keepe him frō the cōmon Councel :
yet of many he is deemed a very vertuous mēber, and one of
the honestest sort of men that are ; So that our opinion (as
Sextus Empedocus affirmeth) giues the name of good or ill to
euery thing. Out of whose works (latelie translated into English, for the benefit of vnlearned writers) a man might collect
a whole booke of this argument, which no doubt woulde proue a
worthy commonwealth matter, and far better than wit's waxe
karnell : much good worship haue the Author.

Such is this golden age wherein we liue, and so replenisht
with golden asses of all sortes, that if learning had lost it selfe
in a Groue of Genealogies, wee neede doe no more but sette an
olde Goose ouer halfe a dozen pottle pots (which are as it were
the eggs of inuention), and wee shall haue such a breede of
bookes within a little while after, as will fill all the world with
the wilde fowle of good wits ; I can tell you this is a harder
thing then making golde of quick siluer, and will trouble you
more then the morrall of *Æsop's* Glow-worme hath troubled our
English Apes, who striuing to warme themselues with the flame
of the philosopher's stone, haue spent all their wealth in buy-
ing bellowes to blowe this false fyre. Gentlemen, I feare I
haue too much presumed on your idle leysure, and beene too
bold, to stand talking all this while in an other man's doore ;
but now I will leaue you to suruey the pleasures of *Paphos*, and
offer your smiles on the Aulters of *Venus*.

Yours in all desire to please,   THO. NASHE.

* [EPISTLE]

To the Reader. [*Arcadia*, 1593.]

The disfigured face, gentle Reader, wherewith this Worke not long since appeared to the common view, moued that noble Lady, to whose Honour consecrated, to whose protection it was committed, to take in hand the wiping away those spottes wherewith the beauties thereof were unworthely blemished. But as often in repairing a ruinous house, the mending of some olde part occasioneth the making of some new: so here her honourable labour, begonne in correcting the faults, ended in supplying the defectes; by the view of what was ill done guided to the consideration of what was not done. Which part, with what aduise entred into, with what successe it hath beene passed through, most by her doing, all by her directing, if they may be entreated not to define, which are unfurnisht of meanes to discerne, the rest (it is hoped) will fanourably censure. But this they shall, for theyr better satisfaction, vnderstand, that though they finde not here what might be expected, they may finde neuerthelesse as much as was intended, the conclusion, not the perfection of Arcadia: and that no further then the Authour's own writings, or knowen determinations could direct. Whereof who sees not the reason, must consider there may be reason which hee sees not. Albeit I dare affirme hee either sees, or from wiser iudgements then his owne may heare, that Sir Philip Sidneie's writings can no more be perfected without Sir Philip Sidney, then Apelles' pictures without Apelles. There are that thinke the contrary: and no wonder. Neuer was Arcadia free from the comber of such Cattell. To vs, say they, the pastures are not pleasaunt: and as for the flowers, such as we light on we take no delight in, but the greater part growe not within our reach. Poore soules! what talke they of flowers? They are Roses, not flowers, must doe them good, which if they finde not here, they shall doe well to go feed elswhere: any place will better like them. For without Arcadia nothing growes in more plenty then Lettuce, sutable to their Lippes. If it be true that likenes is a great cause of liking, and that contraries inferre contrary consequences, then is it true that the wortheles Reader can neuer worthely esteeme of so worthye a writing: and as true that the noble, the wise, the vertuous, the curteous, as many as haue had any acquaint-

ance with true learning and knowledge, will with all loue and
dearenesse entertaine it, as well for affinity with themselves, as
being child to such a father; whom albeit they do not exactly and
in euery lineament represent, yet considering the father's un-
timely death preuented the timely birth of the childe, it may
happily seeme a thanke-worthy labour, that the defects being
so few, so small, and in no principall part, yet the greatest vn-
likenes is rather in defect then in deformity.   But howsoeuer
it is, it is now, by more then one interest, the Countesse of
Pembroke's Arcadia : done, as it was, for her ; as it is, by her.
Neither shall these pains be the last (if no vnexpected accident
cut off her determination) which the euerlasting loue of her excellent brother will make her consecrate to his memory.

H. S.

On Newman and Nash's edition of Astrophel and Stella, see
our Essay. Of Francis Flower, to whom it was dedicated, I have
only been able to recover these slight details from my friend
Colonel Chester's MSS., viz. that he was of Gray's Inn, and as-
sisted Bacon, Hughes, and others, in the production, before
Queen Elizabeth, at Greenwich, in 1587, of the tragedy of The
Misfortunes of Arthur.   Further, on 30th December 1591, he
occurs in an entry in the Stationers Company's Books as having
some privilege concerning licensing ; and Mr. Collier says in a
note: ' We have already met with Flower's name in connection
with the licensing of books for the press, but what was his particular office, and what the privilege he at this time enjoyed, we
are without information' (Notes and Queries, 3d Series, i. 143).

G.

II.

SIDERA.

WERE it not that the following Sonnets and Songs have some-
how been always left out of the Astrophel and Stella series,
most unquestionably we should have given them in their places
therein. As it is, we assign probable reasons for their exclu-
sion and confused printing hitherto (in our Essay, as before),
and arrange them immediately after Astrophel and Stella. We
have not hesitated to add as Sonnets cix. and cx. of Astrophel
and Stella sonnets proper, two of these fugitive sonnets, because
they must be recognised by every critical reader, who has stu-
died the whole and the whole story, to be their inevitable close.
But inasmuch as the others, though self-revealingly belonging
to Stella, are of various dates and occasions—fitting-in indeed
with others of Astrophel and Stella—we have collected them
together here in close relation to, but distinct from, Astrophel
and Stella. The opening four of this division are shown, by
the last of the four, not to have been 'made' of Sidney's wife,
and seem to us to belong to the same subject and circumstances
with ci. of Astrophel and Stella. The fifth, 'A Farewell,' bears
on the face of it to have been a ' farewell' when he left (as he
thought) Stella, and the sixth seems to have been written on
his return ' Finding those beams :' while the seventh and eighth,
' In wonted walks' and ' If I could think,' were clearly composed at Wilton between the preceding two. The ninth, ' The
seven wonders of England,' by its close again brings us to
Stella in Sidney's constant theme of his love and desire, and
her chasteness; and so too the song to the tune of a Neapolitan Villanel, ' All my sense,' pp. 217-18. The tenth, ' Since

shunning paine,' does not refer to any known part of Sidney's history, and may have been intended for the Arcadia. The eleventh, 'When Loue puft vp,' may or may not have been a Stella sonnet. Both these are more obscure than Sidney's other sonnets, alike in thought and expression. They seem of a lower rank. The twelfth, 'The Nightingale,' is certainly a song of the Stella series. The heading in Arcadia folios of 'To the same tune,' arises from the insertion in the Arcadia of 'The fire,' &c., of a poem to this tune that belongs to the Arcadia itself, and hence was withdrawn from the 'Certain Sonnets,' but without correction of the heading, which ought thereupon to have been made. The withdrawn poem is given in its place in vol. ii. The thirteenth, 'Ring out your bells,' I make the close of this division, because (*meo periculo*) I assign it to the marriage of Stella, and st. iii. as expressing Sidney's repentance of his rage —if rage it were that was so sad—on learning that she was an unwilling sacrifice. These are all taken from a division of the folio Arcadia, &c., headed since 1598 as 'Certaine Sonets written by Sir Philip Sidney: Neuer before printed.' So slavishly and ill-informedly is this heading adhered to, that even the words 'Neuer before printed' are invariably added, as also the, original 'some new additions' of the general title-page. The first use of 'Neuer before printed' was itself an error, seeing that 'Since shunning paine,' 'When Loue puft vp,' the 'Four Sonnets made when his Ladie had paine in her face,' 'In wonted walks,' and 'Oft haue I mus'd,' were printed (and for the first time) as Sonnets 2-8 of Decade iii., and Sonnet 9 of Decade iv. in Henry Constable's Diana, 'with divers quatorzains of honorable and learned personages,' 1584 [1594]. As with all the sonnets in this little pocket volume, no name was given, and some of the transcripts from which those of Sidney were printed were incorrect and from earlier originals. Two of these sonnets, 'Thou Pain,' and 'And have I heard' (iii. and iv. of the four sonnets on Pain), have also been published by Dr. Bliss from a ms. in the Bodleian (Rawlinson Poet. 85). Mr. Collier not having observed that the others of Sidney named (*supra*)

had appeared in Constable's 'Diana,' rebukes and corrects
the imagined error of Dr. Bliss in giving these two to Sidney
(Poet. Decameron, vol. i. addl. notes). Our heading of this
division is intended to express the relation of the whole to
Astrophel and Stella. See Notes and Illustrations added as
usual at its close.   G.

SIDERA.

I. 'PAINE.'

THAT scourge of life, and death's extreame disgrace,
  The smoke of hell,—that monster callèd Paine :
Long sham'd to be accurst in euery place
  By them who of his rude resort complaine ;
Like crafty wretch, by time and trauell tought,
  His vgly euill in others' good to hide,
Late harbours in her face, whom Nature wrought
  As treasure-house where her best gifts do bide,
And so by priuiledge of sacred seate
  (A seate where beauty shines and vertue raignes),
He hopes for some small praise, since she hath great,
  Within her beames wrapping his cruell staines.
Ah, saucy Paine, let not thy errour last ;
More louing eyes she draws, more hate thou hast.

II. 'WO, WO !'

Wo, wo to me ! on me returne the smart :
  My burning tongue hath bred my mistresse paine ;
For oft in paine to paine, my painefull heart
  With her due praise did of my state complaine.

I praisde her eyes, whom neuer chance doth moue ;
    Her breath, which makes a sower answer sweete ;
Her milken breasts, the nurse of child-like loue;
    Her legges (O legges !); her ay well-stepping feete.
Paine heard her praise, and full of inward fire
    (First sealing vp my heart as pray of his),   prey
He flies to her, and, boldned with desire,
    Her face (this age's praise) the thiefe doth kisse.
O Paine, I now recant the praise I gaue,
And sweare she is not worthy thee to haue.

III. 'LOTHED PAINE.'

Thou Paine, the onely guest of loath'd Constraint,
    The child of Curse, man's weaknesse' foster-child,
Brother to Woe, and father of Complaint;
    Thou Paine, thou lothèd Paine, from heau'n exilde,
How holdst thou her whose eyes Constraint doth feare,
    Whom curst do blesse, whose weaknesse vertues
        arme,
Who others' woes and plaints can chastly beare,
    In whose sweet heau'n angels of high thoughts
        swarm ?
What courage strange hath caught thy caitife hart?
    Fear'st not a face that oft whole harts devowres ?
Or art thou from aboue bid play this part,
    And so no helpe 'gainst enuy of those powers?
If thus, alas, yet while those parts haue wo,
So stay her toung that she no more say 'O.'

IV. 'O CRUELL PAINE.'

And haue I heard her say, 'O cruell Paine !'
And doth she know what mould her beautie beares?
Mournes she in truth, and thinkes that others faine?
Feares she to feel, an l feeles not others' feares?
Or doth she thinke all paine the minde forbeares?
That heauie earth, not fierie sprites, may plaine?
That eyes weepe worse then hart in bloodie teares?
That sense feeles more then what doth sense con-
taine?
No, no, she is too wise, she knowes her face
Hath not such paine as it makes others haue;
She knows the sicknesse of that perfect place
Hath yet such health as it my life can saue.
But this, she thinkes, our paine high cause excuseth,
Where her, who should rule Paine, false Paine abus-
eth.

V. A FAREWELL.

Oft haue I musde, but now at length I finde
Why those that die, men say they do depart :
Depart ! a word so gentle to my minde,
Weakely did seeme to paint Death's ougly dart.
But now the starres, with their strange course, do
binde
Me one to leaue, with whom I leaue my heart :

I heare a crye of spirits fainte and blinde,
 That parting thus, my chiefest part I part.
Part of my life, the loathèd part to me,
 Liues to impart my wearie clay some breath ;
But that good part wherein all comforts be,
 Now dead, doth shew departure is a death;
Yea, worse then death ; death parts both woe and ioy
From ioy I part, still liuing in annoy.

VI. 'ABSENCE FOR TO PROUE.'

Finding those beames which I must euer loue,
 To marre my minde, and with my hurt to please,
I deemd it best, some absence for to proue,
 If farther place might further me to ease.
My eyes thence drawne where liuèd all their light,
 Blinded forthwith in darke despaire did lye ;
Like to the moule, with want of guiding sight,
 Deep plung'd in earth, depriuèd of the skie.
In absence blind, and wearied with that woe,
 To greater woes, by presence, I returne :
Euen as the flye which to the flame doth go,
 Pleased with the light that his small corse doth
  burne.
Faire choice I haue, either to liue or dye :
A blinded moule, or else a burnèd flye.

VII. 'WONTED WALKS.'

In wonted walkes, since wonted fancies change,
    Some cause there is, which of strange cause doth
        rise ;
For in each thing whereto mine eye doth range
    Part of my paine me-seemes.engrauèd lyes.
The rockes, which were of constant mind the marke,
In clyming steepe now hard refusall show;
    The shading woods seeme now my sunne to darke ;
And stately hilles disdaine to looke so low ;
    The restfull caues now restlesse visions giue ;
In dales I see each way a hard ascent ;
    Like late-mowne meades, late cut from ioy I liue ;
Alas, sweete brookes do in my teares augment.
Rockes, woods, hilles, caues, dales, meads, brookes an-
        swer me:
Infected mindes infect each thing they see.

VIII. 'REBELL SENCE.'

If I could thinke how these my thoughts to leaue,
    Or thinking still, my thoughts might haue good
        end ;
If rebell sence would reason's law receaue,
    Or reason foyld would not in vaine contend ;
Then might I thinke what thoughts were best to
        thinke ;
Then might I wisely swimme, or gladly sinke.

If either you would change your cruell heart,
　　Or, cruell still, time did your beautie staine;
If from my soule this loue would once depart,
　　Or for my loue some loue I might obtaine;
Then might I hope a change, or ease of minde,
By your good helpe or in myselfe to finde ;
　　But since my thoughts in thinking still are spent,
With reason's strife by sences ouerthrowne;
　　You fairer still and still more cruell bent,
I louing still a loue that loueth none ;
　　I yeeld and striue, I kisse and curse the paine—
　　Thought, reason, sense, time, you, and I main-
　　　　taine.

IX. THE SEVEN WONDERS OF ENGLAND.

　I. Neere Wilton sweete huge heapes of stones are
　　　found,
　　　But so confusde that neither any eye
　　　Can count them iust, nor Reason reason trye,
What force brought them to so vnlikely ground.
To stranger weights my minde's waste soile is
　　　bound,
　　　Of passion-hilles, reaching to Reason's skie
From Fancie's earth; passing all numbers' bound,
　　　Passing all ghesse whence into me should fly
So mazde a masse, or, if in me it growes,
A simple soule should breed so mixèd woes.

ii. The Bruertons haue a lake, which, when the sunne
     Approching warmes, not else, dead loges vp
        sends
     From hideous depth; which tribute, when it
        ends,
Sore signe it is the lord's last thred is spun.
My lake is Sense, where still streames neuer runne
     But when my sunne her shining twinnes there
        bends ;
Then from his depth with force in her begunne,
     Long-drownèd hopes to watrie eyes it lends ;
But when that failes my dead hopes vp to take,
Their master is faire warn'd his will to make.

iii. We haue a fish, by strangers much admirde,
       Which caught, to cruell search yeelds his chiefe
          part ;
       (With gall cut out) closde vp againe by art,
Yet liues untill his life be new requirde.
A stranger fish myselfe, not yet expirde,
       Though rapt with Beautie's hooke, I did impart
Myselfe vnto th' anatomy desirde,
       Instead of gall, leauing to her my hart :
Yet liue with thoughts closde vp, till that she will,
By conquest's right, instead of searching, kill.

iv. Peake hath a caue, whose narrow entries finde
      Large roomes within, whose droppes distill a-
         maine,

Till knit with cold, though there vnknowne re-
maine,
Decke that poor place with alabaster linde.
Mine eyes the streight, the roomie caue my minde,
   Whose cloudie thoughts let fall an inward
   raine
Of sorrowe's droppes, till colder reason binde
   Their running fall into a constant vaine   vein
Of trueth, farre more then alabaster pure,
Which though despisde, yet still doth truth en-
dure.

v. A field there is, where, if a stake be prest
   Deep in the earth, what hath in earth receipt
   Is chang'd to stone in hardnesse, cold, and
   weight,
The wood aboue doth soone consuming rest.
The earth her eares, the stake is my request,
   Of which, how much may pierce to that sweet
   seate,
To honor turnd, doth dwell in honor's nest,
   Keeping that forme, though void of wonted
   heate;
But all the rest, which feare durst not applie,
Failing themselues, with witherèd conscience dyé.

vi. Of ships by shipwrack cast on Albion coast,
   Which rotting on the rockes their death do
   dye:

From wooden bones and bloud of pitch doth
    flie
A bird, which gets more life then ship had lost.
My ship, Desire, with winde of Lust long tost,
    Brake on faire cleeves of constant Chastitie; cliffs
Where, plagu'd for rash attempt, giues vp his
    ghost;
    So deepe in seas of vertue, beauties ly :
But of this death flies vp the purest loue,
Which seeming lesse, yet nobler life doth moue.

VII. These wonders England breedes; the last remaines;
    A ladie, in despite of Nature, chaste ;
    On whom all loue, in whom no loue is plaste,
Where Fairenesse yeelds to Wisdome's shortest
    raines.
An humble pride, a skorne that fauour staines;
    A woman's mould, but like an angell graste ;
An angell's mind, but in a woman caste;
    A heauen on earth, or earth that heauen con-
    taines :
Now thus, this wonder to myselfe I frame,—
She is the cause that all the rest I am.

X. 'I EASE CAN NEUER FIND.'

Since shunning paine I ease can neuer find ;
    Since bashfull dread seekes where he knowes me
    harmed;

Since will is won, and stoppèd eares are charmed ;
Since force doth faint, and sight doth make me blind;
Since loosing long, the faster still I bind ;
    Since naked sence can conquer reason armed ;
    Since heart in chilling feare with yce is warmed ;'
In fine, since strife of thought but marres the mind ;
    I yeeld, O Loue, vnto thy loathèd yoke ;
But crauing law of armes, whose rule doth teach,
    That hardly vsde, whoeuer prison broke,
In justice quit, of honour made no breach :
    Whereas if I a gratefull gardien haue,
    Thou art my lord, and I thy vowèd slaue.

XI. 'ONLY BONDAGE GAINE.'

When Loue, puft vp with rage of hy disdaine,
    Resolu'd to make me patterne of his might,
    Like foe, whose wits inclin'd to deadly spite,
Would often kill, to breed more feeling paine ;
He would not, arm'd with beautie, only raigne
    On those affectes which easily yeeld to sight ;
    But vertue sets so high, that reason's light,
For all his strife can onlie bondage gaine :
    . So that I liue to pay a mortall fee,
Dead-palsie-sicke of all my chiefest parts ;
    Like those whom dreames make vglie monsters see,
And can crie helpe with nought but grones and starts :
    Longing to haue, hauing no wit to wish,—
    To staruing minds such is god Cupid's dish.

XII. SONG : 'THE NIGHTINGALE.'

To the tune of 'Non credo già che più infelice amante.'

The nightingale, as soon as Aprill bringeth
Vnto her rested sense a perfect waking,
While late bare earth, proud of new clothing, springeth,
Sings out her woes, a thorne her song-booke making,
And mournfully bewaling,
Her throate in tunes expresseth
What grief her breast oppresseth
For Tereus' force on her chaste will preuailing.
O Philomela faire, O take some gladnesse,
That here is iuster cause of plaintfull sadnesse :
Thine earth now springs, mine fadeth ;
Thy thorne without, my thorne my heart inuadeth.

II.

Alas, she hath no other cause of anguish
But Tereus' loue, on her by strong hand wrokne,
Wherein she suffring, all her spirits languish,
Full womanlike complaines her will was brokne.
But I, who, dayly crauing,
Cannot haue to content me,
Haue more cause to lament me,
Since wanting is more woe then too much hauing.
O Philomela faire, O take some gladnesse,
That here is iuster cause of plaintfull sadnesse :
Thinc earth now springs, mine fadeth ;
Thy thorne without, my thorne my heart inuadeth.

XIII. 'LOUE IS DEAD.'

Ring out your belles, let mourning shewes be spread ;
For Loue is dead :
    All Loue is dead, infected
With plague of deep disdaine :
    Worth, as nought worth, reiected,
And Faith faire scorne doth gaine.
        From so vngrateful fancie,
        From such a femall franzie,
        From them that vse men thus,
        Good Lord, deliuer us !

Weepe, neighbours, weepe ; do you not heare it said
That Loue is dead ? `
    His death-bed, peacock's follie ;
His winding-sheete is shame ;
    His will, false-seeming holie ;
His sole exec'tour, blame.
        From so vngrateful fancie,
        From such a femall franzie,
        From them that vse men thus,
        Good Lord, deliuer us !

Let dirge be sung, and trentals rightly read,
For Loue is dead ;
    Sir Wrong his tombe ordaineth
My mistress' marble heart ;

Which epitaph containeth,
' Her eyes were once his dart.'
From so vngratefull fancie,
From such a femall franzie,
From them that vse men thus,
Good Lord, deliuer us !

Alas, I lie : rage hath this errour bred ;
Loue is not dead ;
Loue is not dead, but sleepeth
In his vnmatchèd mind,
Where she his counsell keepeth,
Till due deserts she find.
Therefore from so vile fancie,
To call such wit a franzie,
Who Loue can temper thus,
Good Lord, deliuer us !

NOTES AND ILLUSTRATIONS.

Sonnet i. See notes on Sonnet ci. in Astrophel and Stella.

„ l. 2, '*that*' ('Diana' 1594) better than 'the' as usual.

Sonnet i. l. 5, '*crafty catif*' (ibid.).

„ l. 6, '*ills*' for 'euills' (ibid.)—the latter so pronounced. See note in our SOUTHWELL.

Sonnet i. l. 8, '*do bide :*' 'abide' (ibid.).

„ l. 10. This line (ibid.) properly enclosed in ( ).

„ l. 13, '*thine*' for 'thy' (ibid.).

„ „ '*errour :*' so too in 'Diana' 1594—Arcadia, &c. 1598 and 1613. Arcadia, &c. 1605, erroneously prints 'terrour'—drawn from the 't' of 'thy,' probably; and Gray and modern editors follow suit.

Sonnet i. In l. 3, '*long sham'd*' is= [being or having been] long ashamed.

Sonnet ii. l. 4, '*did :*' 'Diana' 1594 erroneously 'didst.'

„ l. 8, ibid. 'day' by mistake for 'ay,' but rightly 'well-stepping.'

Sonnet ii. l. 10, '*sealing :*' ibid. 'sayling,' and begins parenthesis at ('as,' &c.

Sonnet iii. l. 4, '*lothed*' ('Diana' 1594)—better than the usual 'hated.'

Sonnet iii. l. 6, ibid. very absurdly reads 'Who . . . . who weakneth.'

Sonnet iii. l. 7, '*beare :*' ibid. 'heare'—the latter a good reading, but not so good as 'beare,' if, as we are satisfied it was, the date be that of Sonnet ci. in Astrophel and Stella ; for then (and this agrees with 'whose weakness vertues arm') she had acknowledged her love for Sidney, yet resisted temptation.

Sonnet iii. l. 13, '*while :*' ibid. 'whilst.'

„ l. 14, '*No :*' Gray and modern editors absurdly misprint 'O'—whence derived I have not been able to find.

Sonnet iv. l. 3. It shows how readily such mistakes are made in transcription, when later Arcadias, &c. read 'what' for 'that :' 1613 'that.'

Sonnet iv. l, 5, ' Or :' 'Diana' 1594, ' O.'

,, l. 6, ibid. reads ' Or on the earth no,' and at end it has ' mone,' a mistake for ' mone,' and that a curious error for 'plaine.'

Sonnet iv. l. 10, ' others :' ibid. 'Lovers'—probably an author's variant.

Sonnet iv. l. 13, ' thus :' ibid. 'thus,' and 'paines' for ' paine.'

It may be noted that these four Sonnets do not rhyme as Petrarchian sonnets do—do not, that is, in the first eight lines have two sets of rhymes of four lines each. Perhaps this merely superficial reason excluded them from Astrophel and Stella.

Sonnet v. l. 10, ' clay-some :' 'Diana' 1594, ' day-some.'

Sonnets vi. vii. viii. In the former, ' Oft haue I mus'd,' Sidney tells of his departure from Stella ; ' In wonted walks' and ' If I could think' he describes his state in absence ; and in 'Finding those beams' his return after his vain attempt at self-cure. These also have the superficial difference noted above. In vii. l. 5, ' Diana' 1594 reads ' minds' for ' mind ;' l. 7, 'shadie' or ' shading.' In viii. l. 6, the closing conceit is obscure. It seems forced to interpret it as=I myself thought, reason, &c. fail, but you and I at one [could] maintain them in me. Might ' and' be a misreading for 'not' ?

Sonnet ix. In st. iii. l. 6, ' rapt' is a noticeable use of the parciple of ' rape' in its primary sense of seized and carried away by violence. In st. iv. ll. 3-4, the construction is [They] though [they] there, &c. Line 10=yet, being truth, doth endure as truth doth, namely, for aye. In st. v. l. 2, ' receipt'=receiving place, as ' receipt of custom' (St. Matthew ix. 9, &c.). In st. vi. l. 1, the construction ' From wooden bones of ships,' &c. Line : in so forced a simile it is perhaps hardly worth while noting at this line seems introduced merely to fill up the measure, and introduces the incongruous metaphor of Desire, a ship, owning like a living being in the over-deep sea, and of this over-deep sea of virtues, though he had just spoken of the rock-reefs of chastity. The reference in the ' bird' is of course to one of the strangest of old fictions—the myth of the barnacle goose ; one reported as occurring on the Scottish coast, and so amusingly, if wickedly, introduced by Marvell in his ' Loyal Scot'

—and Sidney, it will be observed, says not Englănd, but Albion—by grave geographers, such as Münster, and one which was as gravely extracted and related in English books published about the date at which these verses were written. In st. vii. l. 2=Not in despite of her own particular nature, but of the nature of womankind—a thought the result of Italian and continental influence. Cf. the thoughts on this subject of Iago and Iachimo in Othello and Cymbeline. Line 4, ' shortest' —and therefore most restraining or curbing.

Sonnet x. l. 8, ' bind'—apparently used in reflective sense —' I bind myself.'

Sonnet xi. l. 1, ' rage'=apparently with rage of my high disdain of him : in Dublin A, ' hope.'

Sonnet xi. l. 6, ' which :' ' Diana' 1524, ' that.'

„ l. 10, ibid. ' Dead-palsy'—accepted.

„ l. 12, ibid. 'And ory, O helpe' — an inferior, though it may be an earlier, reading.

Sonnet xi. l. 14, ibid. erroneously ' stammering . . . . good.' In l. 4, ' would often kill'—either wishes to kill one often, or who often goes to the verge of killing by tortures and the like, in which latter case ' killing' would have the sense in which it is still used in Ireland and among ourselves. In l. 6, ' affects' =affections, feelings.

Sonnet xii. See on this our preliminary note to this division. In Sonnet i. l. 8 and Sonnet ii. l. 2, Tereus is misspelled ' Thereus,' which is continued even in 1613 Arcadia, &c.

Sonnet xiii. See on this our preliminary note to this division, and our Essay for Tennyson's catching-up of the 'ringing of these bells, across the centuries. G.

III.

PANSIES
FROM PENSHURST AND WILTON.

I give the heading of ' Pansies from Penshurst and Wilton'
(' pansies for thoughts:' Hamlet, iv. 5) to such of the Verse
of Sidney as has not been hitherto brought together, and which
does not find a fitting place under the other divisions. The first,
' Two Pastoralls,' and the second, 'Disprayse of a Courtly
Life,' are from Davison's Poetical Rhapsody (1602); the third is
from Dr. Bliss's Bibliographical Miscellanies (Oxford, 1813, 4to,
p. 63), taken from Bodleian Rawlinson ms., Poet 85; the fourth
from England's Helicon; the fifth from Dr. Bliss's edition of
Wood's Athenæ (vol. i. p. 525); the sixth from Cottoni Posthuma,
p. 327; seventh to twentieth are from 'Certaine Sonetts,' as before—being the remainder of those not given in our preceding
division; twenty-first to twenty-fifth are from ' The Lady of
May—a Masque;' twenty-sixth from the autograph at Wilton;
and twenty-seventh, translations, are from Mornay's Trewnesse
of the Christian Religion, 1592. G.

PANSIES FROM PENSHURST AND WILTON.

I. TWO PASTORALLS.

Made by Sir Philip Sidney, vpon his meeting with his two
worthy Friends and fellow-Poets, Sir Edward Dyer and
Maister Fulke Greuill.[1]

> Ioyne, mates, in mirth to me,
> Graunt pleasure to our meeting;
> Let Pan, our good God, see
> How gratefull is our greeting.
>> Ioyne hearts and hands, so let it be;
>> Make but one minde in bodies three.
>
> Ye hymnes and singing skill,
> Of God Apolloe's giuing,
> Be prest our reedes to fill   =ready
> With sound of musicke liuing.
>> Ioyne hearts and hands, so let it be;
>> Make but one minde in bodies three.
>
> . Sweete Orpheus' harpe, whose sound
> The stedfast mountaynes moued,
> Let heere thy skill abound,   hear
> To ioyne sweet friends beloued.

[1] From Davison's Poetical Rhapsody, 1602 (Collier's reprint,
pp. 7-9).

Ioyne hearts and hands, so let it be ;
Make but one minde in bodies three.

My two and I be met,
A happy blessed trinitie,
    As three most ioyntly set
In firmest band of vnitie.
    Ioyne hearts and hands, so let it be ;
    Make but one minde in bodies three.

Welcome my two to me,   E.D. F.G. P.S.
The number best beloued ;
    Within my heart you be
In friendship vnremoued.
    Ioyne hearts and hands, so let it be ;
    Make but one minde in bodies three.

Giue leave your flockes to range,
Let vs the while be playing ;
    Within the elmy grange
Your flockes will not be straying.
    Ioyne hearts and hands, so let it be ;
    Make but one minde in bodies three.

Cause all the mirth you can,
Since I am now come hether,   hither
    Who neuer ioy but when
I am with you together.
    Ioyne hearts and hands, so let it be ;
    Make but one minde in bodies three.

Like Louers do their loue,
So ioy I in you seeing,
Let nothing mee remoue
From alwayes with you beeing.
    Ioyne hearts and hands, so let it be ;
    Make but one minde in bodies three.

And as the turtle-doue
To mate with whom he liueth,
Such comfort fervent loue
Of you to my heart giueth.
    Ioyne hearts and hands, so let it be ;
    Make but one minde in bodies three.

Now ioynèd be our hands,
Let them be ne'r a sunder,
But linkt in binding bands   bonds
By metamorphoz'd wonder.
    So should our seuer'd bodies three‑
    As one for euer ioynèd be.

II. DISPRAYSE OF A COURTLY LIFE.[1]

Walking in bright Phœbus' blaze,
Where with heat oppresst I was,   .
I got to a shady wood,
Where greene leaues did newly bud,
And of grass was plenty dwelling,
Deckt with pyde flowers sweetely smelling.

---

[1] From Davison's Poetical Miscellany, as in preceding, pp.
9-12. G.

In this wood a man I met,
On lamenting wholly set ;
Rewing change of wonted state,
Whence he was transformèd late ;
Once to shepheards' God retayning,
Now in servile Court remayning.
There he wandring, malecontent,
Vp and down perplexèd went,
Daring not to tell to mee,
Spake vnto a senceless tree,
One among the rest electing,
These same words, or this effecting:
' My old mates I grieue to see
Voyde of me in field to bee,
Where we once our louely sheepe
Louingly like friends did keepe ;
Oft each other's friendship prouing,
Neuer striuing but in louing.
But may loue abiding bee
In poore shepheards' base degree ?
It belongs to such alone
To whom arte of loue is knowne:
Seely shepheards are not witting
What in art of loue is fitting.
Nay, what neede the arte to those
To whom we our loue disclose ?
It is to be vsèd then
When we doe but flatter men:

Friendship true, in hart assurèd,   heart
Is by Nature's giftes procurèd.
Therefore shepheardes, wanting skill,
Can loue's duties best fulfill ;
Since they know not how to faine,
Nor with loue to cloake disdaine,
Like the wiser sort, whose learning
Hides their inward will of harming.
Well was I, while vnder shade
Oten reedes me musicke made ;   oaten
Striuing with my mates in song,
Mixing mirth our songs among :
Greater was the shepheard's treasure
Then this false, fine, courtly pleasure ;   than
Where, how many creatures be,
So many pufft in minde I see ;
Like to Junoe's birdes of pride,
Scarce each other can abide :
Friends like to blacke swannes appearing,
Sooner these than those in hearing.
Therefore, Pan, if thou mayst be
Made to listen vnto me,
Grant, I say (if seely man
May make treaty to god Pan),
That I, without thy denying,
May be still to thee relying.
Only for my two loues' sake,   Sir Ed. D. and M. F. G.
In whose loue I pleasure take ;

Only two do me delight
With their euer-pleasing sight;
Of all men to thee retaining,
Grant me with those two remaining.
So shall I to thee alwayes
With my reedes sound mighty praise;
And first lambe that shall befall,
Yearely deck thine altar shall;
If it please thee be reflected,
And I from thee not reiected.'
So I left him in that place,
Taking pity on his case;
Learning this among the rest,
That the meane estate is best;
Better fillèd with contenting,
Voyde of wishing and repenting.

III. ' AFFECTION'S SNARE.'

The darte, the beames, the stringe so stronge I proue,
    Whiche my chefe parte dothe passe throughe,
        parche, and tye,
That of the stroke, the heat, and knott of loue,
    Wounded, inflamde, knitt to the deathe, I dye.
Hardned and coulde, farr from affectione's snare
    Was once my mynde, my temper, and my lyfe;
While I that syghte, desyre, and vowe forbare,

Whiche to auoide, quenche, loose, noughte booted
    stryfe. .
Yet will not I greife, ashes, thralldom change
For others' ease, their frutte or free estate, .
So braue a shott, deere syre, and bewtye strange,
    Bid me pearce, burne, and bynde longe time and
    late,
And in my woundes, my flames, and bondes, I fynd
A salue, freshe ayre, and bryghte contented mynde.

IV. 'AN EXCELLENT SONNET OF A NIMPH.'

Vertue, beautie, and speeche did strike, wound, charme
My heart, eyes, eares with wonder, loue, delight;
First, second, last did binde, enforce, and arme
His works, showes, sutes with wit, grace, and vowes'
    might.
Thus honour, liking, trust, much, farre, and deepe,
Held, pearst, possesst my iudgment, sence, and will;
Till wrongs, contempt, deceite did grow, steale, creepe,
Bands, fauour, faith to breake, defile, and kill;
Then griefe, vnkindnes, proofe, tooke, kindled, taught,
Well-grounded, noble, due, spite, rage, disdaine.
But ah, alas, in vaine, my minde, sight, thought
Doth him, his face, his words leaue, shunne, refraine:
    For nothing, time nor place, can loose, quench, ease
    Mine owne, embracèd, sought, knot, fire, disease.

V. 'LOVE.'

Ah, poore Loue, whi dost thou liue,
    Thus to se thy seruice lost?
Ife she will no comforte geue,
    Make an end, yeald vp tho goaste;
That she may at lengthe aproue
    That she hardlye long beleued,
That the harte will dye for loue
    That is not in tyme relieued.
Ohe that euer I was borne,
    Seruice so to be refused,
Faythfull loue to be foreborne!
    Neuer loue was so abused.
But, swet Loue, be still a whylle;
    She that hurte thee, Loue, maye healle thee;
Sweet, I see within her smylle
    More than reason can reueale thee.
For, thoughe she be riche and fayre,
    Yet she is bothe wise and kynde,
And therefore do thou not despayre,
    But thy faythe may fancy fynde.
Yet, allthoughe she be a quene,
    That maye suche a snake despyse,
Yet, withe sylence all vnseene,
    Runn and hide thee in her eyes:
Where if she will let thee dye,
    Yet at latest gaspe of brcathe,
Saye that in a ladye's eye
    Loue both tooke his lyfe and deathe.

VI. WOOING-STUFFE.

Faint Amorist, what! do'st thou think
    To tast Loue's honey, and not drink
One dram of gall? or to devour
    A world of sweet, and tast no sour?
Do'st thou ever think to enter
    Th' Elisian fields, that dar'st not venture
In Charon's barge? a lover's mind
    Must use to sayle with every wind.
He that loves, and fears to try,
    Learns his mistris to deny.
Doth she chide thee? 'tis to shew it,
    That thy coldness makes her do it;
Is she silent? is she mute?
    Silence fully grants thy sute;
Doth she pout, and leave the room?
    Then she goes to bid thee come;
Is she sick? why then be sure
    She invites thee to the cure;
Doth she cross thy sute with No?
    Tush, she loves to hear thee woo;
Doth she call the faith of man
    In question? nay, 'uds-foot, she loves thee than;
And if ere she makes a blot,
    She's lost if that thou hit'st her not.
He that after ten denialls
    Dares attempt no farther tryals,

Hath no warrant to acquire
The dainties of his chaste desire.

VII. CHILD-SONG.

To the tune of ' Basciami vita mia.'

Sleepe, babie mine, Desire's nurse, Beautie, singeth ;
Thy cries, O babie, set mine head on aking.
The babe cries, ''Way, thy loue doth keepe me
waking.'   away
Lully, lully, my babe, Hope cradle bringeth
Vnto my children alway good rest taking.
The babe cries, ''Way, thy loue doth keepe me
waking.'
Since, babie mine, from me thy watching springeth,
Sleepe then a little, pap Content is making.
The babe cries, ' Nay, for that abide I waking.'

VIII. VERSES.

To the tune of the Spanish song, ' Se tu señora no dueles
de mi.'

O faire ! O sweete ! when I do looke on thee,
In whome all ioyes so well agree,
Heart and soul do sing in me.
This you heare is not my tongue,
Which once said what I conceauèd,
For it was of vse bereauèd,
With a cruell answer stoug.
No ; though tongue to roofe be cleauèd,

Fearing least hé chastisde be,
Heart and soule do singe in me.

O faire ! O sweete ! when I do looke on thee,
    In whome all ioyes so well agree,
Heart and soul do sing in me.
    Iust accord all musicke makes ;
In thee iust accord excelleth,
Where each part in such peace dwelleth,
    One of other, beautie takes.
Since, then, truth to all mindes telleth
    That in thee liues harmonie,
    Heart and soule do sing in me.

O faire! O sweete ! when I do looke on thee,
    In whome all ioyes so well agree,
Heart and soul do sing in me.
    They that heauen haue knowne do say,
That whoso that grace obtaineth,
To see what faire sight there raigneth,
    Forcèd are to sing alway :
So, then, since that heauen remaineth
    In thy face, I plainly see,
    Heart and soule do singe in me.

O faire! O sweete! when I do looke on thee,
    In whome all ioyes so well agree,
Heart and soul do sing in me.
    Sweete, thinke not I am at ease,

For because my cheefe part singeth ;
This song from deathe's sorrow springeth,
    As to swanne in last disease :
For no dumbnesse nor death bringeth
    Stay to true loue's melody:
    Heart and soul do sing in me.

IX. TRANSLATED OUT OF HORACE,

[Book ii. Ode x.] which beginnes 'Rectius viues, Licini,' &c.

You better, sure, shall liue, not euermore
    Trying high seas ; nor, while sea's rage you flee,
Pressing too much upon ill-harboured shore.   to
    The golden meane who loues liues safely free
From filth of foreworne house, and quiet liues,
    Release from Court, where enuie needes must be.
The winde most oft the hugest pine-tree greeues ;
    The stately towers come downe with greater fall ;
The highest hills the bolt of thunder cleeues ;
    Euill happes do fill with hope, good happes appall
With feare of change, the courage well preparde ;
    Fowle Winters, as they come, away they shall.
Though present times and past with euils be snarde,
    They shall not last; with citherne silent Muse
Apollo wakes, and bowe hath sometime sparde.
    In hard estate, with stowt shew valor vse,
The same man still, in whom wisedome preuailes ;
In too full winde draw in thy swelling sailes.

X. OUT OF CATULLUS.

[Carm. LXX.]

I. Nulli se dicit mulier mea nubere malle,
   Quam mihi; non si se Iupiter ipse petat.
   Dicit; sed mulier cupido quae dicit amanti,
   In vento, et rapida scribere oportet aqua.

Englished.

Vnto nobody, my woman saith, she had rather a wife
   be
Then to myselfe, not though Ioue grew a suter of
   hers;
These be her words; but a woman's words to a loue that
   is eager,
In wind or water's streame do require to be writ.

[OUT OF SENECA, Œdipus, 705-6.]

II. Qui sceptra saevus duro imperio regit,
    Timet timentes; metus in authorem redit.

Faire, seek not to be feard; most louely, beloued by thy
   seruants;
For true it is, that they feare many whom many
   feare.

XI. ' THE SEELED DOUE.'

Like as the doue, which sealed vp doth flie,
   Is neither freed nor yet to seruice bound,

But hopes to gaine some helpe by mounting hie,
   Till want of force do force her fall to ground :
Right so my minde, caught by his guiding eye,
   And thence cast off, where his sweet hurt he found,
Hath neither leaue to liue, nor doome to dye,
   Nor held in euill, nor suffered to be sound ;
But with his wings of fancies vp he goes,
   To hie conceits, whose fruits are oft but small ;
Till wounded, blind, and wearied spirite lose
   Both force to flie, and knowledge where to fall.
O happy doue, if she no bondage tried !
More happie I, might I in bondage bide.

XII. 'THE SATYR.' BY E. D.

Prometheus, when first from heauen hie
   He brought downe fire, ere then on earth not seene,
Fond of Delight, a Satyre, standing by,
   Gaue it a kisse, as it like sweete had beene ;
Feeling forthwith the other burning power,
   Wood with the smart, with showts and shryking
      shrill,   maddened
He sought his ease in riuer, field, and bower ;
   But, for the time, his griefe went with him still.
So, silly I, with that vnwonted sight,
   In humane shape an angell from aboue,
Feeding mine eyes, the impression there did light,
   That, since, I runne and rest as pleaseth loue :

The difference is, the satyre's lippes, my hart;
He for a while, I euermore haue smart.

XIII. 'THE SATYR:'
Answered by Sidney.

A Satyre once did runne away for dread
   With sound of horne, which he himselfe did blow;
Fearing and feared, thus from himselfe he fled,
   Deeming strange euill in that he did not know.
Such causelesse feares when coward minds do take,
   It makes them flie that which they faine would haue;
As this poore beast, who did his rest forsake,
   Thinking not why, but how, himselfe to saue.
Euen thus might I, for doubts which I conceaue
   Of mine owne wordes, my owne good hap betray;
And thus might I, for feare of may be, leaue
   The sweete pursute of my desirèd pray.   prey
Better like I thy satyre, deerest Dyer,
Who burnt his lips to kisse faire shining fire.

XIV. 'A CONSTANT FAITH.'

My mistresse lowers, and saith I do not loue:
   I do protest, and seeke with seruice due,
In humble mind, a constant faith to proue;
   But, for all this, I cannot her remoue
   From deepe vaine thought that I may not be true.
   If othes might serue, euen by the Stygian lake,
Which, poets say, the gods themselues do feare,

I neuer did my vowèd word forsake;
For why should I, whom free choise slaue doth
    make,
Else-what in face than in my fancie bear?
My Muse, therefore, for onely thou canst tell,
Tell me the cause of this my causelesse woe;
    Tell how ill thought disgrac'd my doing well;
    Tell how my ioyes and hopes thus fowly fell
To so lowe ebbe, that wonted were to flowe.
    O, this it is,—the knotted straw is found;
In tender harts small things engender hate;
    A horse's worth laid wast the Troian ground;
    A three-foote stoole in Greece made trumpets sound;
An asse's shade e'er now hath bred debate.
    If Greekes themselues were mou'd with so small
        cause,
To twist those broyles, which hardly would vntwine;
    Should ladies faire be tyed to such hard lawes,
    As in their moodes to take a lingring pawse?
I would it not; their metall is too fine.
    My hand doth not beare witnesse with my hart,
She saith, because I make no woful laies,
    To paint my liuing death and endlesse smart;
    And so for one that felt god Cupid's dart,
She thinkes I leade and liue too merrie daies.
    Are poets, then, the onely louers true,
Whose hearts are set on measuring a verse;
    Who think themselues well blest if they renew

Some good old dumpe that Chaucer's mistresse
    knew,
And vse but you for matters to rehearse ?
    Then, good Apollo, do away thy bowe ;
Take harp, and sing in this our versing time,
    And in my braine some sacred humour flowe ;
    That all the earth my woes, sighs, teares may
        know ;
And see you not that I fall now to ryme ?
    As for my mirth, how could I but be glad,
Whilst that me-thought I iustly made my boast
    That only I the only mistresse had ?
    But now, if ere my face with ioy be clad,
Thinke Hannibal did laugh when Carthage lost.
    Sweet ladie, as for those whose sullen cheare,
Compar'd to me, made me in lightnesse sound ;
    Who, stoick-like, in clowdie hew appeare,
    Who silence force to make their words more deare ;
Whose eyes seem chaste because they looke on ground,—
    Beleeue them not ; for physick true doth finde
    Choler adust is ioyed in woman-kinde.

XV. A DIALOGUE BETWEEN TWO SHEPHERDS.
Vttered in a Pastorall Show at Wilton.

WILL. Dick, since we cannot dance, come, let a cheare-
    full voyce
    Shew that we do not grudge at all when others
      do rejoyce.

DICK. Ah Will! though I grudge not, I count it feeble
      glee,
      With sight made dymme with dayly teares, an-
      other's sport to see.
      Whoeuer lambkins saw (yet lambkins loue to
      play)
      To play when that their louèd dammes are stoln
      or gone astray?
      If this in them be true, as true in men think I,
      A lustles song, forsooth, thinks hee, that hath
      more lust to cry.   =pleasureless

WILL. A tyme there is for all, my mother often sayes,
      When she, with skirts tuckt very hy, with girles
      at football playes.
      When thou hast mynd to weepe, seeke out some
      smoky room:
      Now let those lightsomme sights we see thy
      darknes ouercome.

DICK. What ioy the ioyfull sunne giues vnto blearèd
      eyes;
      That comfort in these sports you like, my mynde
      his comfort tryes.

WILL. What! is thy bagpipe broke, or are thy lambs
      miswent;
      Thy wallet or thy tar-box lost; or thy new ray-
      ment rent?

DICK. I would it were but thus; for thus it were too
      well.

WILL. Thou see'st my eares do itch at it : good Dick,
      thy sorow tell.

DICK. Hear, then, and learne to sigh : a mistress I do
      serue,

      Whose wages makes me beg the more, who feeds
      me till I sterue ;

      Whose lyuerie's such as most I freeze apparelled
      most,

      And lookes so neere vnto my cure, that I must
      needes be lost.

WILL. What ! these are riddles, sure ; art thou, then,
      bound to her ?

DICK. Bound, as I neither power haue, nor would haue
      power, to stir.

WILL. Who bound thee ?

DICK.   Loue, my lord.

WILL.   What witnesses thereto?

DICK. Faith in myself, and worth in her, which no
      proofe can vndoe.

WILL. What seale ?

DICK.   My hart deep grauen.

WILL.   Who made the band so fast?

DICK. Wonder that, by two so black eyes, the glittring
      stars be past.

WILL. What keepeth safe thy band?

DICK.   Remembrance is the chest
      Lockte fast with knowing that she is of worldly
      things the best.

WILL. Thou late of wages playnd'st: what wages mayst
thou haue?

DICK. Her heauenly looks, which more and more do
giue me cause to craue.

WILL. If wages make you want, what food is that she
giues?

DICK. Teares' drink, sorrowe's meat, wherewith not I,
but in me my death liues.

WILL. What liuing get you, then?

DICK.   Disdayne, but iust disdayne :
So haue I cause myselfe to plaine, but no cause
to complayne.

WILL. What care takes she for thee?

DICK.   Hir care is to preuent
My freedom, with show of hir beames, with virtue, my content.

WILL. God shield vs from such dames! If so our
downes be sped,
The shepheards will grow leane, I trow; their
sheep will ill be fed.
But, Dick, my counsell marke : run from the
place of wo :
The arrow being shot from far doth giue the
smaller blowe.

DICK. Good Will, I cannot take thy good aduice : before
That foxes leaue to steale, they finde they dy
therefore.

WILL. Then, Dick, let vs go hence, lest wee great folkes
       annoy;
    For nothing can more tedious bee then plaint
       in time of ioy.
DICK. Oh hence! O cruell word! which euen doggs
       do hate:
    But hence, euen hence I must needes go; such
       is my doggèd fate.

XVI. SONG.

To the tune of 'Wilhelmus van Nassau,' &c.

Who hath his fancie pleasèd
With fruits of happie sight,
   Let here his eyes be raisèd
On Nature's sweetest light;
   A light which doth disseuer,
And yet vnite the eyes;
   A light which—dying neuer—
Is cause the looker dyes.

   She neuer dies, but lasteth
In life of louer's hart;
   He euer dies that wàsteth
In loue his chiefest part.
   Thus is her life still guarded
In neuer-dying faith;
   Thus is his death rewarded,
Since she liues in his death.

Looke then, and dye; the pleasure
Doth answere well the paine;
　Small losse of mortall treasure,
Who may immortall gaine.
　Immortall be her graces,
Immortall is her minde;
　They, fit for heauenly places,
This heauen in it doth bind.

　But eyes these beauties see not,
Nor sence that grace descryes;
　Yet eyes depriuèd be not
From sight of her faire eyes,
　Which, as of inward glorie
They are the outward seale;
　So may they liue still sorie,
Which die not in that weale.

　But who hath fancies pleasèd
With fruits of happie sight,
　Let here his eyes be raysèd
On Nature's sweetest light.

XVII. THE SMOKES OF MELANCHOLY.

1. Who hath euer felt the change of loue,
　And knowne those pangs that the loosers proue,
　May paint my face without seeing mee,
　And write the state how my fancies bee,
　The lothsome buds growne on Sorrowe's tree.

But who by hearesay speakes, and hath not fully
    felt
What kind of fires they be in which those spirits
    melt,
Shall gesse, and faile, what doth displease,
Feeling my pulse, misse my disease.

II. O no! O no! tryall onely shewes
    The bitter iuice of forsaken woes;
    Where former blisse present euils do staine;
    Nay, former blisse addes to present paine,
    While remembrance doth both states containe.
    Come, learners, then, to me, the modell of mis-
        happe,
    Engulfèd in despaire, slid downe from Fortune's
        lappe ;
    And, as you like my double lot,
    Tread in my steppes, or follow not.

III. For me, alas, I am full resolu'd
    Those bands, alas, shall not be dissolu'd;
    Nor breake my word, though reward come late;
    Nor faile my faith in my failing fate ;
    Nor change in change, though change change my
        state :
    But alwayes own myselfe·with eagle-eyde Trueth,
        to flie
    Vp to the sunne, although the sunne my wings do
        frie ; ·

For if those flames burne my desire,
Yet shall I die in Phœnix' fire.

XVIII. 'MY DEADLY PLEASURE.'

When to my deadlie pleasure,
When to my liuelie torment,
Ladie, mine eyes remainèd
Ioynèd, alas, to your beames;
With violence of heau'nly
Beautie, tïëd to vertue,
Reason abasht retyrèd;
Gladly my senses yeelded.
Gladly my senses yeelding,
Thus to betray my hart's fort,
Left me deuoid of all life.
They to the beamie sunnes went,
Where, by the death of all deaths,
Finde to what harme they hastned.
Like to the silly Syluan,
Burn'd by the light he best liked,
When with a fire he first met.
Yet, yet, a life to their death,
Lady, you have reseruèd;
Lady, the life of all loue.
For though my sense be from me,
·And I be dead, who want sense,
Yet do we both liue in you.

Turnèd anew, by your meanes,   metamorphosed
Unto the flowre that ay turnes,
As you, alas, my sunne bends.
Thus do I fall, to rise thus ;
Thus do I dye, to liue thus ;
Chang'd to a change, I change not.
Thus may I not be from you ;
Thus be my senses on you ;
Thus what I thinke is of you ;
Thus what I seeke is in you ;
All what I am, it is you.

XIX. VERSES.

To the tune of a Neapolitan song, which beginneth
'No, no, no, no.'

No, no, no, no, I cannot hate my foe,
 Although with cruell fire,
 First throwne on my desire,
She sackes my rendred sprite :
 For so faire a flame embraces
 All the places
Where that heat of all heats springeth,
That it bringeth
 To my dying heart·some pleasure,
 Since his treasure
Burneth bright in fairest light.
 No, no, no, no.

No, no, no, no, I cannot hate my foe,
 Although with cruell fire,
 First throwne on my desire,
She sackes my rendred sprite :
 Since our lives be not immortall,
 But to mortall
Fetters tyed, to waite the hower
Of deathe's power,
 They haue no cause to be sorie,
 Who with glorie
End the way, where all men stay.
 No, no, no, no.

No, no, no, no, I cannot hate my foe,
 Although with cruell fire,
 First throwne on my desire,
She sackes my rendred sprite :
 No man doubts, whom beautie killeth,
 Faire death feeleth,
And in whome faire death proceedeth,
Glorie breedeth :
 So that I, in her beames dying,
 Glorie trying,
Though in paine, cannot complaine.
 No, no, no, no.

XX. SONG.

To the tune of a Neapolitan Villanell.

All my sense thy sweetnes gainèd;
Thy faire haire my hart enchainèd;
My poore reason thy words moued,
So that thee, like heauen, I loued.
Fa, la, la, leridan, dan, dan, dan, deridan;
  Dan, dan, dan, deridan, deridan, dei:
While to my minde the outside stood
For messenger of inward good.

Now thy sweetnesse sowre is deemèd,
Thy haire not worth a haire esteemèd;
Reason hath thy words remoued,
Finding that but words they proued.
Fa, la, la, leridan, dan, dan, dan, deridan;
  Dan, dan, dan, deridan, deridan, dei:
For no faire signe can credit winne,
If that the substance faile within.

No more in thy sweetnesse glorie,
For thy knitting haire be sorie;
Vse thy words but to bewaile thee,
That no more thy beames availe thee.
    Dan, dan,
    Dan, dan,
Lay not thy colours more to view,
Without the picture be found true.

Wo to me, alas, she weepeth!
Foole, in me what follie creepeth!
Was I to blaspheme enraged,
Where my soule I haue engaged !
   Dan, dan,
   Dan, dan,
And wretched I must yeeld to this;
The fault I blame her chastness is.

Sweetnesse! sweetly pardon folly;
Ty me, haire, your captiue holly: **wholly**
Words! O words of heauenlie knowledge!
Know, my words their faults acknowledge;
   Dan, dan,
   Dan, dan,
And all my life I will confesse,
The lesse I loue, I liue the lesse.

XXI. TRANSLATED OUT OF THE DIANA OF MONTE-MAIOR,

In Spanish; where Sireno, a shepheerd, pulling out a little of
his mistresse' haire wrapt about with greene silk, who now
had vtterlie forsaken him: to the haire he thus bewaild
himselfe :

What changes here, O haire,
 I see, since I saw you!
How ill fits you this greene to weare,
 For hope the colour due!
Indeed, I well did hope,
 Though hope were mixte with feare,
No other shepheard should haue scope .
 Once to approch this heere.   **hair**

Ah, haire, how many dayes
  My Diane made me shew,
With thousand pretty childish plaies,
  If I ware you or no!
Alas, how oft with teares,—
  O teares of guilefull breast!—
She seemèd full of iealous feares,
  Whereat I did but ieast.

Tell me, O haire of gold,
  If I then faultie be,
That trust those killing eyes I would,
  Since they did warrant me?
Haue you not seene her mood,
  What streames of teares she spent,
Till that I sware my faith so stood,
  As her words had it bent?

Who hath such beautie seene
  In one that changeth so?
Or where one's loue so constant bene,
  Who euer saw such woe?
Ah, haire, are you not greiu'd
  To come from whence you be,
Seeing how once you saw I liu'd,
  To see me as you see?

On sandie bank of late
  I saw this woman sit,

Where, 'Sooner die then change my state,'
　She with her finger writ: ·
Thus my beleefe was staid.
　Behold Loue's mightie hand
On things were by a woman said,
　And written in the sand.

XXII. THE SAME SIRENO IN MONTE-MAIOR,

Holding his mistresse' glasse before her, and looking vpon h
while shee viewed herselfe, thus sang :

Of this high grace with blisse conioyn'd,
　No further debt on me is laid ;
Since that is selfe-same metall coin'd,
　Sweet ladie, you remaine well paid ;
For if my place giue me great pleasure,
Hauing before me Nature's treasure,
　In face and eyes vnmatchèd being,
　You haue the same in my hands, seeing
What in your face mine eyes do measure.
Nor thinke the match vneu'nly made,
　That of those beames in you do tarie ;
The glasse to you but giues a shade,
　To me mine eyes the true shape carie ;
·For such a thought most highlie prizèd,
Which euer hath Loue's yoke despisèd,
　Better then one captiu'd perceiueth,
　Though he the liuely forme receiueth,
The other sees it but disguisèd.

XXIII. SUPPLICATION.

To one whose state is raisèd ouer all,
  Whose face doth oft the brauest sort enchaunt,
Whose mind is such as wisest minds appall,
  Who in one selfe these diuerse giftes can plant;
How dare I, wretch, seeke there my woes to rest,
Where eares be burnt, eyes dazled, harts opprest!

Your state is great, your greatnesse is our shield;
  Your face hurts oft, but still it doth delight;
Your mind is wise, your wisedome makes you mild:
  Such planted gifts enrich euen beggers' sight.
So dare I wretch, my bashfull feare subdue,
And feede mine eares, mine eyes, my hart in you.

XXIV. SONG-CONTEST.

Therion chalenged Espilus to sing with him, speaking these
sixe verses:

THERION.

Come, Espilus, come, now declare thy skill,
  Shew how thou canst deserue so brave desire;
Warme well thy wits, if thou wilt win her will,
  For water cold did neuer promise fire:
Great, sure is she, on whom our hopes do liue,
Greater is she who must the iudgement giue.

But Espilus, as if he had bene inspired with the Muses,
began forthwith to sing; whereto his fellow-shepheards set in
with their recorders, which they bare in their bags like pipes;
and so of Therion's side did the foresters, with the cornets
they wore about their neckes, like hunting-hornes in baudrikes.

ESPILUS.

Tune vp, my voice, a higher note I yeeld,
  To high conceipts the song must needes be high:
More high then stars, more firme then flintie field,
  Are all my thoughts, in which I liue or die.
Sweete soule, to whom I vow`ed am a slaue,
Let not wild woods so great a treasure haue.

THERION.

The highest note comes oft from basest mind,
  As shallow brookes do yeeld the greatest sound;
Seeke other thoughts thy life or death to find;
  Thy stars be fal'n, plow'd is thy flintie ground.
Sweete soule, let not a wretch that serueth sheepe
Among his flocke so sweete a treasure keepe.

ESPILUS.

Two thousand sheepe I haue as white as milke,
  Though not so white as is thy louely face;
The pasture rich, the wooll as soft as silke,
  All this I giue, let me possesse thy grace.
But still take heede, lest thou thyselfe submit
To one that hath no wealth, and wants his wit.

THERION.

Two thousand deere in wildest woods I haue;
  Them can I take, but you I cannot hold:
He is not poore who can his freedome saue;
  Bound but to you, no wealth but you I would.
But take this beast, if beasts you feare to misse,
For of his beasts the greatest beast he is.

ESPILUS, kneeling to the Queen.

Iudge you, to whom all beautie's force is lent.

THERION.

Iudge you of Loue, to whom all loue is bent.

XXV. TALES IN SONG.

ESPILUS.

Syluanus, long in loue, and long in vaine,
　　At length obtain'd the point of his desire,
Who being askt, now that he did obtaine
　　His wishèd weale, what more he could require:
Nothing, sayd he, for most I ioy in this,
That Goddesse mine, my blessèd being sees.

THERION.

When wanton Pan, deceiu'd with lion's skin,
　　Came to the bed where wound for kisse he got,
To wo and shame the wretch did enter in,
　　Till this he tooke for comfort of his lot;
Poore Pan, he sayd, although thou beaten be,
　　It is no shame, since Hercules was he.

ESPILUS.

Thus ioyfull I in chosen tunes reioice
　　That such an one is witnesse of my hart,
Whose clerest eyes I blisse, and sweetest voyce,
　　That see my good, and iudgeth my desert.

THERION.

Thus wofull I in wo this salue do find,
My foule mishap came yet from fairest mind.

XXVI. TO QUEEN ELIZABETH.

Found in a folio copy of Arcadia &c. at Wilton House.

This Lock of Queen Elisabeth's owne Hair was presented to Sir Philip Sidney by Her Majesty's owne faire hands, on which He made these verses, and gaue them to the Queen, on his bended knee.   Anno Domini 1573.

Her inward worth all outward Show transcends,
Envy her Merits with Regret Commends,
Like Sparkling Gems her Vertues draw the Sight,
And in her Conduct She is alwaies Bright;
When She imparts her thoughts her words have force,
And Sence and Wisdom flow in Sweet Discourse.

XXVII. TRANSLATIONS FROM PHILIP OF MORNAY.

1. All things that are, or euer were, so shall hereafter
      bee,
   Both man and woman, beast and bird, fish, worme,
      herb, grasse, and tree,
   And euery other thing, yea, euen the auncient gods
      each one,
   Whom wee so highly honor heere, come all of one
      alone.

   Aristotle, Philosophie and of the World, p. 26.

2. The Ioue almightie is the King of Kings and God
      of Gods,
   One God, and all, the Father both and Mother of
      the Gods.

   Valerius Soranus, p. 34.

3. Looke up to that same only King, Which did the
    world create:

Who being only one, self-bred, all other things be-
    gate :

And being with them all, unseene of any mortall
    wight,

Beholdeth all things, giuing man now wealth and
    heart's delight,

Now wofull warre : for sure there is none other
    King but Hee.

I see Him not, because the clowdes a covert to Him
    bee,

And in the eye of mortall man there is but mortall
    sight,

Too weake to see the lightfull Iouve that ruleth all
    with right :

For, sitting in the brazen Heauen aloft in throne of
    golde,

Hee makes the Earth His footestoole, and with
    either hand doth holde

The outmost of the Ocean-waues; and at His pre-
    sence quake

Both mountaynes huge, and hideous seas, and eke
    the Stygian Lake :

    . . . .

The endlesse skie and stately heauens, and all things
    eke beside,

Did once within the thundering Ioue closse hoorded
   up abide :
The blessèd Gods and Goddesses, whose being is for
   aye,   ,
And all things past or yet to come, within Ioue's
   bowels lay:
From Ioue's wide wombe did all things come; Ioue
   is both first and last ;   .
Beginning, Middle, and Ende is Ioue; for Ioue are
   all things past.
Iouve laydc foundation of the Earth and of the
   starrie skie ;
Iouve reigneth King ; the selfe-same Iouve of all
   things farre and nie
The Father and the Author is: one power, one God
   is Hee.
A lonely great one, Lord of All.   This royall masse
   which wee
Beholde, and all [the] things that are conteynèd in
   the same,
As fire and water, earth and ayre, and Titan's
   golden flame
That shines by Day and drowns the Night, and
   euerie other thing,
Are placèd in the goodly House of Ioue, the heauenly King.

Hymn of Orpheus to Musæus, pp. 33-4.

4. Certesse of Goddes there is no mo but one,
   Who made the Heauens, and ecke the Earth so
       round ;   [=embraces
   The dreadfull Sea, which cleaps the same about, clips
   And blustring windes which rayze the waues aloft :
   But we fond men, through folly gon astray,
   Euen to the hurt and damning of our soules,
   Haue set up idols made of wood and stone :
   Thinking, like fooles, by meanes of honoring them
   To giue full well to God His honor due.
                             Sophocles in Cyrillus, p. 36.

5. Thou Neptune, and thou Iupiter, and all
   You other Goddes, so wicked are you all,
   That if due iustice unto you were doone,
   Both Heauen and temples should be emptie soone.
                                   Euripides, p. 36.

6. There is but onely one true God, right great and
       euerlasting,
   Almightie and inuisible, Which seeth euery thing,
   But cannot bee beheld Himselfe of any fleshly man.
                        Oracles of the Sibylles, p. 38.

7. The self-bred, bred without the helpe of Moother,
   Wife of Himselfe, Whose name no wight can tell,
   Doth dwell in fyre, beyond all reach of thought :
   Of Whome we angelles are the smallest part.
                             From Lactantius, p. 39.

8. I am but Phœbus, more of mee ye get not at my
   hand;
   It is as little in my mynd as I can understand.

Porphyrius, p. 39.

9. Apollo is not of that mynd; beware
   How thou dost deale : he is too strong for thee :
   For God it is that makes him undertake
   This enterprize, and doth the same mayntayne,—
   Euen God, I tell thee, under Whom both Heauen
   And Earth and Sea and euery thing therein,
   And Phœbus eke, and Hell itselfe, doth quake.

Ibid. p. 39.

10. Wee feends, which haunt both Sea and Land
    through all the world so wide,
    Do tremble at the whip of God, Which all the
    world doth guide.

Ibid. p. 39.

11. First God, and next the Word, and then their Sprite,
    Which three be One and ioyne in One al Three :
    Their force is endlesse : get thee hence, frail wight;
    The man of life unknowne excelleth thee.

The Oracles, p. 83.

12. Unhappie Priest, demaund not me, the last
    And meanest Feend, concerning that diuine
    Begetter, and the deere and onely Sonne
    Of that renownèd King, nor of His Spirit,

Conteining all things plenteously, throughout
Hilles, brookes, sea, land, hell, ayre, and lightsome
    fire.
Now wo is me, for from this house of mine
That Spirit will me driue within a while ;
So as this Temple, where men's destenies
Are now foretold, shall stand all desolate.

The Oracles, p. 83.

XXVIII. FROM CONSTABLE'S ' DIANA,' 1594.

Woe to mine eyes, the organs of my ill,
Hate to my heart for not concealing ioy ;
A double curse vpon my tongue be still,
Whose babling lost what els I might enioy.
When first mine eyes did with thy beauty toy,
They to my hart thy wondrous virtues told,
Who, fearing least thy beames should him destroy,
What ere he knew did to my tongue vnfold.
My teltale tongue, in talking over bold
What they in private counsell did declare,
To thee in plaine and publique tearmes vnrould,
And so by that made thee more coyer farre.
What in thy praise he spoake that didst thou trust,
And yet my sorrowes thou doost hold vniust.

NOTES AND ILLUSTRATIONS.

I. On the 'Two Pastorals' and the Friendship celebrated, see our editions of FULKE GREVILLE, LORD BROOKE and of SIR EDWARD DYER.

St. i. l. 6, '*one minde in bodies three.*' So Priamond, Diamond, Triamond:

> 'These three did love each other dearly well,
> And with so firm affection were allied,
> *As if but one soul in them all did dwell.*'

St. x. l. 4, '*metamorphoz'd wonder*'—query=by the wonder (wondrous power or virtue) of metamorphosis? This gives a true and good sense, at least.

II. st. iii. l. 6, '*or this effecting :*' in same sense, as we say, or words to this effect, *i.e.* effecting the same purpose or intent.

St. v. l. 5, '*seely :*' see note in SOUTHWELL, pp. 174-6.

St. ix. l. 1, '*where*' refers to the Court, included in the idea 'courtly pleasure.'

St. ix. l. 6. A qualification of l. 5 : '*sooner*' indeed would one see 'these' black swans than 'those' who are friends—'In hearing,' which latter qualification may from l. 4 be supposed to mean, who are friends, even as to their outward or lip words.

III. The peculiarity of this sonnet is, that verbs, or nouns referring to these three nouns, are given in ll. 2-4, 7-9, 11-13, and words referring to their opposites in ll. 10 and 14, and in this it resembles another sonnet (in Arcadia), 'Vertue, beauty, and speech,' with which it is also so closely connected, that I place it immediately after it here. If now we look to the third of these other verbs and nouns, we find tie, knot, knit, vow, thraldom (free estate, l. 10), beauty, bind, bonds (night-contented mind, l. 14). Hence as 'stinge' does not agree with these, but is a mere repetition of 'dart,' the original MS. seems to have been misread for 'stringe.' This word had not quite so weak a meaning as it now has, *c.g.* the sinews were called strings, and the word is here strengthened by the general epi-

thet 'strong.'   Similarly in l. 8 'lose' is=a variant spelling of
'loose,' as applied to 'knots' and 'vows,' as is also shown by
the 'loose' and 'knot' of ll. 13-14 in the next sonnet.   This
error in l. 8 confirms that in l. 1 'listed' (which gives no sense)
is a misprint for 'booted'=profited or advantaged, to avoid,
&c., which strife advantaged naught, or was of no avail.   But
with all elucidation, there is a shadow of obscurity over this
sonnet and the succeeding.   'Thee' throughout is spelt 'the.'

iv. See on this sonnet on above, and our Essay, as before.

v. From Dr. Bliss's 'Bibliographical Miscellanies,' as before.

vi. 'Wooing Stuff :' from 'Cottoni Posthuma :' but I think
I have met with it earlier.

vii. ll. 3-6, 'ay,' 1598 A: but 'away,' A 1613, &c. is the
word, i.e. Go away—agreeing with l. 7, and with child-lips.

viii. Modern editors, e.g. Gray, &c. have omitted third line
of refrain.

ix. Ib.

x. l. 4 is an excellent illustration of how blunders are more
blundered by attempts at correction.   In 1598 we have 'optet'
for 'oportet,' and some one with inattentive care, or knowing
just enough Latin to remember that optare was of the first con-
jugation, altered 'optet' in 1605 to 'optat.' Modern editors put
lines even, while they are hexameter and pentameter; and so
in No. ii. of these imitations; while to make the pentameter
scan as an hexameter, 'do' is unwarrantably introduced.

xi. l. 1, 'seeled'=eyelids closed by a thread passed through
them lightly.

l. 11, 'Sprite' is dissyllabic here, and the nominative to
'lose' and the article 'the'—'till' ['the' or 'his']—being, as
often, omitted.

xii.-xiii. See our collection of the writings of Sir Edward
Dyer in Fuller Worthies' Library, and the Dr. Farmer Chetham
ms. as edited by us, for Nos. xii. and xiii. In addition to our defence of 'Delight' in the former, be it noted that 'fond' is here=
foolish=foolish through delight at the new fair-shining toy. So
that more than ever must we refuse to follow Dr. Hannah in
reading 'Light.' See also st. v. of Sidney's 'When to my deadly
pleasure' (No. xvii. of this division).

xiv. In st. iv. l. 1, 'knotted straw is found'—a bit of unex-
plained Folk-lore.

St. iv. l. 4, 'three-foot stool.' What?

St. iv. 1. 5, '*Asse's shade.*' Balaam's?   ·
St. vii. 1. 3, '*dump*'=a doleful tune or song. Cf. our edition
of LOE.
St. xi. 1. 2, '*adust*' = parched or burnt up, adj. of adustion
(*adustio*). Those in whom the bile or cause of melancholy is
burnt up (by the fire of love—for the seat of bodily love was
supposed to be in the liver) are those who are joyed with
woman-kind.
    xv. 1. 10, '*stool-ball.*' Strutt, *s.v.*, says, 'stool-ball is fre-
quently mentioned by the writers of the three last centuries,
but without any proper definition of the game. I have been
informed that a pastime called stool-ball is practised to this
day in the northern parts of England, which consists in simply setting a stool upon the ground, and one of the players
takes his place before it, while his antagonist, standing at a
distance, tosses a ball with the intention of striking the stool;
and this it is the business of the former to prevent, by beating
it away with the hand, reckoning one to the game for every
ꞃoke of the ball; if, on the contrary, it should be missed by
ꞁnd and touch the stool, the players change places. I
ᵗhe same also happens if the person who threw the ball
ꞁly any player] can catch and retain it when driven
ꞏ ꞏꞃ, ꞵꞓꞁꞓꞏꞁ it reaches the ground. The conqueror at this
game is he who strikes the ball most times before it touches
the stool,' &c. The game, in fact, would seem to be a form of
the school-game 'rounders,' where the ball is struck with a
short stick instead of with the hand, and where the 'in' party
occupy a round of stations, and become in succession the
strikers, while the 'out' party comprise the thrower and
catchers of the ball. Nares, *s.v.*, gives quotations showing
that it was a favourite women's game; and from a song in
D'Urfey's play of Don Quixote, quoted by Strutt, it appears
that, like kiss-in-the-ring and other games, both sexes often
joined at rural merry-makings in playing it.
    Ibid. l. 14 = that comfort tries (vexes) my mind's comfort.
It is a curious illustration of the difference of the ages that
this real love and love for a married woman should have been
thus spoken of in a show or masque. It is to be regretted
that we cannot tell whether Sidney spoke the part he wrote, or
whether he, like Hamlet, wrote it for a player to interpolate.
In l. 39 'downes' (A 1613) is usually misprinted 'dames.'

XVI. In st. iii. ll. 7-8, They = her graces: This = her mind. In l. 21 all former editions 'liuerie is.'

XVII. On this see our Essay, as before.

XVIII. Ib.

XIX. Ib.

XX. The 'dan dan' of the later stanzas was probably a MS. abbreviation for 'Fa la la dan,' &c.; and though we have not filled it in, perhaps we ought to have done so. In st. ii. l. 1 'Now' is misprinted 'Nor' by modern editors, as Gray.

XXI.-XXII. The 'Diana' may be accounted the model of the Arcadia, and this and the next are the second and third pieces of verse in it; but the headings are not the words of the Romance, but of Sidney or some other for him. As a coinciaence, it may be noted that the English translation of the 'Diana' by Bartholomew Yong (1598)—but finished in MS. 'May 1st, 1583'—was dedicated to Lady Rich. May these have been translated by Sidney when thinking of, and about the time of, Stella's marriage?

XXIII.-XXIV. In the context-note of the closing song it is said that Espilus sings this song; but st. ii. is the consoling thought of Therion, and for Espilus to sing it, and then to continue in st. iii. 'Thus joyfully' when Pan was anything but joyful, is out of the question. Again, it is still more absurd for him to sing in one and the same stanza first, 'Thus joyfully,' ll. 1-4, as he really is, and then in l. 5 to change to 'Thus woful I,' which he is not. 'Thus woful I' could have been sung by no one but Therion. These parts being thus apportioned, the sense and the corresponding words in l. 5 'Thus woful I' require 'Thus joyfull I' instead of the misreading 'joyfully,' and so 'wofull I' for like misreading of 'wofully'—'wofull I' being A 1613 reading. Nos. xxiii.-xxv. are from the Lady of May, a Masque (A 1598).

XXVII. These Translations are taken from 'A Worke concerninge the Trewnesse of Christian Religion, written in French: Against Atheists, Epicures, Paynims, Iewes, Mahumetists, and other Infidels. By Philip of Mornay, Lord of Plessie-Marke. Begunne to be translated into English by Sir Philip Sidney, Knight, and at his request finished by Arthur Golding. At London, Printed by Robert Robinson for I. B., dwelling at the great North doore of St. Paul's Church, at the signe of the Bible.' 1592, 4to, pp. 22 and 552. I have

VOL. I.   R

not ventured to go beyond p. 83 of this 'begunne' translation; nor indeed was there any temptation to do so.

XXVIII. With reference to Constable's 'Diana' (1594), in Dec. iii. st. x. occurs the present — which is the only one, beyond the ten therein known to be his—which has a smack of Sidney. I therefore have given it place among these ' Pansies.' G.

END OF VOL. I.

LONDON :
ROBSON AND SONS, PRINTERS, PANCRAS ROAD, N.W.

O